D0011266

Making Sense of
Social Problems

Social Problems, Social Constructions

Joel Best and Scott R. Harris, series editors

Making Sense of Social Problems

New Images, New Issues

edited by
Joel Best
Scott R. Harris

LYNNE
RIENNER
PUBLISHERS

BOULDER
LONDON

Published in the United States of America in 2013 by
Lynne Rienner Publishers, Inc.
1800 30th Street, Boulder, Colorado 80301
www.rienner.com

and in the United Kingdom by
Lynne Rienner Publishers, Inc.
3 Henrietta Street, Covent Garden, London WC2E 8LU

© 2013 by Lynne Rienner Publishers, Inc. All rights reserved

Library of Congress Cataloging-in-Publication Data
Best, Joel.
  Making sense of social problems : new images, new issues /
Joel Best and Scott R. Harris.
    p. cm. — (Social problems, social constructions)
  Includes bibliographical references and index.
  ISBN 978-1-58826-855-6 (hc : alk. paper) —
  ISBN 978-1-58826-880-8 (pb : alk. paper)
    1. Social problems. 2. Social perception.
I. Harris, Scott R., 1969 Sept. 16– II. Title.
  HN18.3.B47 2012
  301—dc23

                                        2012017855

British Cataloguing in Publication Data
A Cataloguing in Publication record for this book
is available from the British Library.

Printed and bound in the United States of America

 The paper used in this publication meets the requirements
of the American National Standard for Permanence of
Paper for Printed Library Materials Z39.48-1992.

5 4 3 2 1

Contents

Preface

Making Sense of Social Problems: New Images, New Issues consists of fourteen case studies of contemporary problems, ranging from pet grief to teen suicide to natural disasters to our current financial crisis. Introductory and concluding chapters outline the constructionist perspective and explain its strengths and weaknesses.

The chapters in the book are contemporary in the sense that they deal with current claims; in most cases, they address problems that have only begun to attract public attention during the twenty-first century. In addition, the authors' approaches to their topics contribute to constructionist work by incorporating recent intellectual currents within sociology, such as globalization and the study of emotions.

We suspect that instructors will find various ways to use this collection: some may choose to adopt it as a stand-alone text for a course on social problems; others may use it to supplement another text (such as Donileen Loseke's *Thinking About Social Problems,* second edition, or Joel Best's *Social Problems,* second edition). However it is used, we hope that students and scholars alike will enjoy reading the book.

—*Joel Best*
Scott R. Harris

Making Sense of
Social Problems

1

Studying the Construction of Social Problems

Scott R. Harris

If you follow the news, or occasionally have a serious conversation with friends, you may know more about social problems than you realize. You are not starting from scratch.

Think about it. Just in the past year, has anyone complained to you about the rising cost of gasoline, college tuition, or health care? Have you heard about a new study linking cancer to something you enjoy doing, such as talking on your cell phone? Have you read or watched a news report about a major drought, flood, earthquake, or wildfire that struck somewhere in the United States or the world? Has someone warned you about a growing danger on the roadways, insisting that our bridges are crumbling or that too many drivers are drunk, sleepy, angry, or distracted? Have you been confronted with some of the consequences of a faulty economy, such as unemployment or homelessness?

In the space of even a single year, the list of issues that might be brought to your attention is long and daunting. A brief alphabetical sample could include anorexia, binge drinking, cyber-bullying, discrimination (by race, age, sex, height, etc.), election fraud, food poisoning, global warming, HIV/AIDS, incivility in politics and in everyday life, juvenile delinquency, kids growing up too soon, litter, marital rape, narcissism, oppressive government regulations, police brutality, road rage, stalking, terrorism, underfunded schools, video game addiction, white-collar crime, xenophobia, youth violence, and—who knows—maybe even zebra attacks.

It seems a safe bet that you have already heard and thought quite a bit about social problems in the past year, and even more so over your lifetime. Nevertheless, you probably have not considered the topic as carefully or systematically as you could. You probably have not tried to develop a consistent approach for making sense of problems in general, no matter what the specific issue may be. This book will help you develop a framework that you can use to analyze the arguments that people make about social problems of any sort.

It's in your interest to become a critical thinker about social problems. Otherwise, people may find it all too easy to influence or even manipulate you by playing to your fears, sympathies, and outrage. You need to evaluate the claims you encounter, to decide which issues merit your concern, and which causes deserve your support.

What Are Social Problems?

To think critically about social problems, we need a definition. What makes something a "social problem"? What kinds of issues deserve that label?

The Objectivist Answer

One way to answer this question is to focus on the "factual" or "objective" aspects of the problems themselves. For example, we might define social problems as "conditions or behaviors that have harmful effects on large numbers of people." Then, we could decide whether an issue—water pollution or child abuse, perhaps—fits the definition, by asking whether the condition causes serious harm to a significant portion of the population.

This is a tempting path to follow, to try to define social problems in *objectivist* terms. This approach is used in many textbooks and seems to fit our commonsense notion of what might be a social problem. However, there are serious drawbacks to adopting an objective definition. First, there is no easy way to decide what qualifies as a "large number of people." Is 100,000 enough? How about 10,000 or 1,000? Does the problem need to affect more than 1 percent of a nation's population—which in the United States would be at least 3 million people? Deciding whether a problem "affects enough people" to merit consideration is not an easy task; it involves subjective choices.

Similarly, the idea of "harm" is no easier to clarify. There are different kinds of harm—physical, emotional, economic, and so on. How much harm is necessary, and how does one measure it? Who gets to decide whether something is harmful? With contentious social issues, sometimes there is heated debate over whether *any* harm has occurred. For instance, some groups claim that same-sex marriage undermines the foundation of society, while others believe that it acts as a stabilizing force in the lives of individuals and their communities.

An objective answer to the question "What are social problems?" might also attempt to distinguish *social* from *nonsocial* problems. Cancer and erectile dysfunction might be classified as "physical health" issues," flooding and hurricanes might be considered "natural disasters." But here again, things are not clear-cut. If "social" refers to "things people do," then there is arguably a human element in problems that seem merely physical, natural, or nonsocial in other ways. For example, cancer might reasonably be linked to the social behavior of corporations (which sell cigarettes, unhealthy food, cell phones) and consumers (who use the products). Or, the problem of flooding could be connected to governmental decisions regarding where to build levees (which may divert excess water toward downstream communities) and where to allow homes to be built.

At first glance, an objective, fact-based definition seems to enable us to focus on real social problems. But as we have seen, dilemmas of interpretation crop up from every direction. These dilemmas point toward the utility of the approach endorsed in this book—an approach that focuses on the subjective or interpretive dimensions of social problems.

The Constructionist Answer

What makes something a social problem? From a constructionist perspective, the answer is that people decide what is and is not a social problem by the way they react to things. Human beings *create* or *construct* social problems when they give a particular meaning or "spin" to potentially troublesome conditions. To put it another way, social problems are ambiguous situations that can be viewed in different ways by different people, and that are defined as troubling by some people. Social problems are subjective interpretations rather than objective conditions. It is the process of calling attention to a troubling condition, not the condition itself, that makes something a social problem. For a social problem to exist, at least one person has to (1) notice a situation, (2) interpret it as bothersome, and (3) tell other people about it. Let's explore each of these processes.

First, it seems safe to say that people rarely—if ever—argue about things they don't notice. If I don't perceive an annoying behavior or detrimental situation, then I won't tell others what's going on, why it's happening, or what to do about it. People ignore or take for granted all sorts of things, all the time. We all have a lot to think about in any given day. We don't have time to pay close attention to everything that might bother us, whether as individuals or as groups. Even the US federal government—with its millions of employees and a budget in the trillions—must select which problems to work on and which to ignore.

Neglect is not necessarily a conscious, deliberate choice. There may be problems that go unrecognized simply because people don't have the ability to conceptualize them. If you are living in a culture where a man's wife and children are considered his property, then you probably have not been exposed to the concepts of spousal abuse and child abuse, and probably have not been socialized to notice such behavior. Or consider global warming (a.k.a. climate change). There are likely significant portions of the global population who have not heard of this problem or who haven't been encouraged to care about it at all.

Temperatures may begin to change and wounds may be inflicted regardless of whether anyone notices. But from a constructionist perspective, the existence of a problem in a society—as a matter to be argued about and acted upon—depends on its public recognition. Can you think of any potential social problems that are currently ignored or underappreciated in our society?

Once a potential problem is noticed, it must be interpreted as bothersome—and bothersome in a particular way. Consider public intoxication. In different times and places, communities may adopt a variety of attitudes toward those who drink heavily and act "out of control." Some may consider public intoxication quite normal, expected, and even healthy; but others may argue that it is a sin, a crime, an illness (physical or mental), or simply poor judgment. Each of these definitions creates—constructs—a different type of problem out of this ambiguous situation, and each tends to be accompanied by corresponding claims regarding causes and solutions. If public intoxication is considered a sin, then the cause might be portrayed as temptation or a lack of moral fortitude, and the suggested solution might be prayer, divine intervention, or spiritual counseling. On the other hand, if public intoxication is argued to be a crime or a disease, then other causes and remedies might be proposed (e.g., the solutions of prison or treatment or both). Of course, in a given society, people may disagree about which interpretation is correct; rather than settling on a single interpretation, they may combine or alternate between a variety of distinct viewpoints.

As people tell others about the problems they see, a number of reactions are possible. Clearly, we don't always fully listen to, or believe, or act upon all the claims we hear. In the twenty-first century, stories about the problem of witchcraft are not likely to receive the grave response they did in late-seventeenth-century Salem, Massachusetts. Today, few journalists, politicians, and police officers would take witchcraft seriously in their work. Activists and the general public would not demonstrate in the streets, or even start e-mail chains, in order to generate concern over the dangers posed by witches casting magical spells. To become a "real" social problem, an issue needs to be legitimated by enough people. And it's not just the number of people: some individuals and groups (i.e., those with resources or power) can validate an issue more effectively than others can. Prominent politicians, religious leaders, journalists, or celebrities are among those who can generate concern and legitimacy. You might recall that, in recent years, superstar George Clooney has helped sound the alarm in the United States over the problem of rape and genocide in Darfur, while actress Pamela Anderson has drawn attention to the plight of animals in this country.

Even when an issue is deemed real enough to merit attention and action, the exact nature of the problem may continue to be a matter of debate. As articles are written, hearings held, laws and policies formulated, government agencies created, and so on, different groups tend to make competing arguments about the extent, causes, and solutions to the problem. In some years, "immigration" may become a prominent concern and widely recognized as a social problem. However, consensus may never be reached on the degree to which immigrants are beneficial or harmful to a country, the factors that encourage or discourage immigration, or what new policies (if any) should be adopted to deal with it. Interpretations of all these matters will vary greatly. Just as there is no objective definition of "social problems" in general, there is no objective depiction of any single social problem in particular.

This discussion hints at one reason is why you should be highly motivated to read this book—or why it is important to develop a framework for understanding and evaluating the claims you hear about social problems: Given the prevalence of competing claims about problems, it would be foolish of us to quickly or haphazardly agree (or disagree) with any particular assertion or story about a problem. We need to think carefully. We need to compare a range of interpretations before we form a confident opinion or pursue a course of action. By approaching social problems as interpretations rather than as objective conditions, you can become a more effective consumer of the many claims you are likely to encounter in your daily life.

How to Think Like a Constructionist

This book can guide you toward a more consistent and sophisticated way of thinking about problems. It offers a coherent approach for making sense out of the diverse problems you hear about, rather than seeing each issue as a new and unique phenomenon. You don't always have to think like a constructionist, but you can cultivate the ability to do so when you choose.

When a constructionist hears people talking about social problems, he or she has a large collection of conceptual tools to use to make sense of what people are doing. Let's look at just a few of the more important concepts, and discuss them briefly. Additional concepts are discussed in the chapters that follow and in other constructionist books and articles (e.g., see Best 2008; Holstein and Miller 2003; Loseke 2003).

Claims and Claimsmakers

When thinking objectively, you might be inclined to treat people's statements as "information" or as "reports," especially when the source is an authoritative government official, scientist, journalist, or similar figure. If the source seems less authoritative, or if the speaker is saying something that you disagree with, you might be inclined to invoke the terms "wrong," "mistake," or "lie." A liberal might be inclined to treat a statement by a Democratic official as conveying information, while a Republican might be inclined to treat it as wrongheaded, even foolish.

In contrast, a constructionist prefers to use the term *claim*. From the constructionist point of view, *all* assertions about social problems are claims, regardless of the source. A constructionist does not want to decide (or at least, not until later on in the analysis) whether a statement is true or false. The first task of a constructionist is to begin to gather competing claims about social problems, and to study them. A constructionist wants to know:

- How many different types of claims are being made about this problem? What is the full range of interpretations?
- Who are the people making the claims? What groups tend to be associated with the different types of claims?
- How do the different claimsmakers give different meanings to the problem at hand? Do they categorize the problem in different ways? Suggest various causes and solutions to the problem? Propose different kinds of victims or villains? Invoke contradictory evidence to support their points of view?

Referring to a statement as a *claim* does not imply that you disbelieve it—or even believe it, for that matter. Rather, the intention behind the word *claim* is to treat every assertion as just one of many possible interpretations. Later on, you may want to decide that one claim makes more sense or that a particular claimsmaker is more reliable, but then you'll be stepping outside of the constructionist framework, or at least incorporating an objectivist concern into the framework.

The Contingent Careers of Social Problems

The constructionist approach assumes that problems are interpretations that are "built" or "made" by people. A claimsmaker must point out the troublesome condition or behavior. Then the media may publicize the claim. Opinion leaders and the general public may ignore or legitimize the claimsmaker's concern. Policymakers may or may not decide to hold hearings, establish committees, and formulate new rules or laws. New agencies or occupations may or may not be created to deal with the issue.

At any point in time, the existence of a problem—from a subjective perspective—is in jeopardy. People can always stop thinking and talking about an issue. They can get distracted by another event or news story. They can decide that the issue is not as bad as previously thought. They can decide that a problem is "solved," or even that it is "unsolvable," and hence turn to other matters.

When constructionists say that a problem is *contingent,* they mean that problems "depend" on a great many things. A social problem exists because people do things to ensure that the problem continues to be an ongoing concern. Problems have "careers" or "histories" that develop over time: problems emerge, gain or lose attention, become categorized in one way or another, undergo debate, are addressed with policies, and so on. At every stage, the perceived nature of a problem is not automatic or inevitable; it is contingent on how people choose to think and talk about it. Over centuries, decades, or even days or minutes, what starts out as a normal part of life (e.g., smoking near your children) may come to be seen as immoral or perhaps illegal. It depends on the choices people make, within the constraints set by their cultures, economies, political contexts, and other social factors.

Adopting the constructionist framework, then, requires that you form a particular style of questioning. You develop an inclination and ability to ask:

- Where is this problem within the social construction process? Is it just emerging? Is it being newly discovered, or rediscovered? Is it being categorized for the first time? Is its perceived nature being shaped and reformed by new or recycled claims?
- Is claimsmaking about this problem increasing, decreasing, or remaining stable? How much attention has the problem received over time? What might explain this level of attention?
- Which claimsmakers and which audiences are paying attention to the problem? What social factors may be influencing the actions of those who are attempting to promote, undermine, or redefine the problem?

These kinds of questions draw your attention to the subjective experience of social problems among various groups in a society. Rather than trying to determine the true nature of a problem—or even whether it exists—a constructionist's first impulse is to collect and analyze examples of the claimsmaking that may occur at one or more points in the contingent career of a social problem. The constructionist's goal is to understand how (and why) problems are noticed, interpreted, discussed, and acted upon.

What's to Come in This Book:
A Series of Case Studies

It takes practice to fully learn and appreciate the constructionist perspective. It's not enough to read a theoretical explanation (such as this book's introductory and concluding chapters) or to read one or two studies of specific social problems. Instead, what is needed is repeated exposure to the practice of constructionist analysis across a wide range of social issues. After a while, the perspective sinks in, and you develop the knack for applying the perspective in your everyday life—if not to a research project of your own. The recurring thought—"Ah yes, I see how this problem too could be interpreted in different ways"—will be replaced by a firm habit of thought: an enduring sensitivity to the social construction of problems, to the processes by which bothersome behaviors and conditions become viewed and acted upon in particular ways.

To help you develop this habit of thought, we present a series of case studies in this book. Topics run the gamut from teen suicide to natural disasters to our current financial crisis. Each chapter is intended to provide an interesting, succinct, and clearly written example of constructionist analysis. While they share this theoretical perspective in common, the chapters do tend to emphasize different dimensions of the social construction process. Thus we have separated the chapters into five parts, covering claims, claimsmakers, experts, the media, and policy outcomes. Each part is preceded by its own introduction to help orient you to the theme and to highlight the contribution each chapter makes.

Part 1

The Nature of Claims

Every social problem begins with a claim. Basically, we can think of every claim as offering an answer to the question: "What's the problem?" At first glance, this may not seem to be an interesting question, because the answer appears obvious. When we think of familiar social problems, we think we know a lot about them: we know what sort of problem it is; we understand why it should be considered a problem; we probably have ideas about what its causes are; and we may even have strong opinions about what ought to be done to solve it. It is easy to take this knowledge for granted, to view what we know as just common sense.

But once we think about it a bit more carefully, it becomes obvious that most of what we know about most social problems has been learned from other people. As children, we leaned about social problems by watching the reactions of adults; later, we gained more knowledge from exposure to the news. The sources for most of our apparently common-sense knowledge are claims made by other people.

What may be less obvious is that all of these claims reflect choices about how social problems should be constructed. Any social problem can be understood in lots of different ways. Take poverty. We might think of poverty as an individual failing: people who are poor just don't work hard enough, maybe they lack ambition, or they're lazy, or they waste what money they do have—if people are poor, it is basically their fault. Or we might think of poverty as a societal failing, as caused by social arrangements that limit the opportunities of individuals to improve themselves, by systems that ensure that the rich get richer, even as the poor get poorer, or by patterns of discrimination that keep poor people from getting ahead. At different times, different claims have constructed poverty as God's will, as Karma, as a form of social injustice, as an inevitable byproduct of capitalism, and so on. There isn't one way to think about poverty; it can be constructed in lots of different ways, and the same can be said for every social problem.

The chapters in this first part of the book all point to choices made when people try to specify just what the problem is when they make claims. In Chapter 2, Marguerite O'Leary and Joel Best examine how two communities, not all that far apart geographically, constructed the same problem. Both Needham and Nantucket are in eastern Massachusetts; residents in both communities identified teen suicide as a serious local problem. However, far from sharing a single construction of teen suicide, each community focused on different causes, and each devised different solutions. People in each town understood teen suicide rather differently than their counterparts in the other community. Claims can vary, even when they are made at the same time, and in nearby places.

In Chapter 3, Peter Parilla examines shifting claims about a new technology—cell phones. As new technologies spread, they often alter social arrangements and become the focus for new claims. There have been lots of social problem claims related to cell phones, such as complaints about the noise from people's conversations impinging on others' ears, and warnings that phone companies' ability to track a phone's movements may constitute an invasion of privacy. Parilla focuses on another issue: whether using a cell phone while driving ought to be considered a problem. As he notes, driving while using a cell phone has actually inspired a series of different claims and different constructions of just what the problem is—or whether there is a problem at all.

In other words, both of these chapters focus our attention on the fact that any problem—such as teen suicide or talking on cell phones while driving—can and often will be constructed in different ways, through the use of different claims.

2

Teen Suicide:
A Tale of Two Communities

Marguerite L. O'Leary and Joel Best

We often think about the construction of social problems as a national process—with claims made on cable news shows and the floor of Congress. However, claimsmakers often construct *local* social problems, issues that affect specific communities, such as whether a particular old building should be demolished or preserved as a historical landmark (Lofland 2003), or where a women's shelter ought to be located and how it ought to be staffed (Mann 2000). Often, the same issue can be constructed in very different ways in different communities (Bogard 2003).

This chapter compares how two communities in eastern Massachusetts responded to claims that teen suicide had become a local problem. In each case, local claimsmakers juxtaposed recent reports of local teens killing themselves to construct teen suicide as a local problem. That is, they argued that teen suicide seemed to be concentrated or clustered in their communities, and that it was necessary to understand the causes of this phenomenon and to take action to do something about it. However, the two constructions that emerged differed in important ways: the two communities identified different causes of teen suicides, and they devised different policies to address teen suicide. In other words, although the two communities both defined the same phenomenon—teen suicide—as a local problem, they constructed it in very different terms, and they devised different policies to address it.

13

Needham, Massachusetts, is a wealthy suburb about twenty minutes southwest of Boston. Nantucket is a small island off the coast of Cape Cod; although it is a popular summer vacation spot for tens of thousands of New Englanders, the island's year-round population is much smaller. The two communities are less than a hundred miles apart. Besides their geographic proximity, they share something else: in recent years, both came to define teen suicide as a local problem. Between November 2004 and February 2011, Needham experienced six teen suicides, while Nantucket experienced four in an eighteen-month span during 2007–2008. Teen suicide is of course not limited to these two towns; a 2005 Massachusetts survey of risky behaviors among youth found that "27 percent of high school students felt sad or hopeless for more than two weeks, 13 percent seriously considered suicide, 12 percent made a plan to kill themselves, and 6 percent actually tried" (O'Brien 2008). However, both Needham and Nantucket experienced several teen suicides within relatively short periods of time, which inevitably led to widespread local concern. Despite this, the social differences between the two communities led to very different constructions of what might at first glance seem to be the same social problem.

Contrasting Constructions of the Problem

Needham

Needham is a prosperous suburb, home to upper-middle-class families. With roughly 30,000 residents, Needham had a median household income of $117,650 in 2009, nearly double the state's median of $64,081 ("Needham Demographics" 2011). Its residents are well-educated; 64.9 percent of those aged twenty-five or older have received a bachelor's degree or higher and 33.5 percent have earned graduate or professional degrees, compared to the average levels for Massachusetts of 21.2 percent for bachelor's degrees and 14.6 percent for graduate or professional degrees ("Boston Education" 2011; "Needham, Massachusetts [MA] Profile" 2011). Obviously, the community values education; its young people are groomed for college as a gateway to future success. As one *Boston Globe Magazine* article put it, "Kids study. A lot. Roughly 95 percent of them are going to college—it's just a question of where" (O'Brien 2007, p. 44). The community hardly seems like a place that would be characterized by serious social problems.

The reports that several students at Needham High School had killed themselves were shocking; news reports described the students as smart, athletic, friendly, and popular—not at all the sort of people who might be expected to commit suicide (O'Brien 2007, p. 44). People at the school and in the town began to ask themselves what had caused the suicides. This self-reflection led to the construction of a "Needham teen suicide" profile, in order to understand what it was about Needham that might have led promising youths to kill themselves.

Eventually, Needham residents constructed teen suicide as a problem caused by a demanding, overly stressful high school environment. Needham High School had become notorious for its academic demands and pressure. The *New York Times* described it as having "an ethos of super-achievement . . . [with] extreme competition over college admissions," and quoted a Needham High teacher as saying: "The culture here has always been about rigor" (Hilton 2007). The view of the high school as especially demanding was widely held throughout the town, so that linking high academic stress and suicide was an easy and natural connection for concerned parents and town officials to make.

Having linked the school's academic demands with suicide, the Needham High administration was forced to look into the causes of this stress and examine how the students were responding to the pressure. According to the *New York Times* reporter who interviewed Needham High's principal Paul Richards, "many students were so stressed out about grades and test scores—and so busy building résumés to get into the small number of brand-name colleges they equated with success—that . . . they could not fully engage with school" (Hilton 2007). A survey at Needham High supported Richards's contention:

> A 2006 survey of more than 1,100 students at the school revealed that stress from academics and parental expectations contributed to some students cheating, drinking, and even physically hurting themselves through "cutting," or self-mutilation. Fifty-seven percent of the respondents labeled the school's culture as "sink or swim," and nearly three quarters of students said they took time off from school to cope with stress. Forty-four percent said they were willing to "suffer" in high school to get into a good college. (Ramirez 2009, p. 1)

Put literally, that means 75 percent of respondents, or 825 students, at some point "took time off from school to cope with stress." Further, the fact that 44 percent of the respondents said that they were willing to "suffer" to get into a good college highlights the level of expectations attached to academic achievement and suggests that potentially unhealthy stress may have resulted from this environment. The danger of this environmental stress was best described by a former Needham High student, Michael Hass, whose own battle with depression was described in a *Boston Globe* article. According to the article, Hass had "cut himself with razor blades and at times thought he would rather die than show up for class at Needham High School" (O'Brien 2008). Although Hass's experience might be considered extreme, surveys at the high school suggest that his experience was hardly unique.

In fact, these concerns were formally addressed in a "community needs assessment" commissioned by the Needham Coalition for Suicide Prevention. The report was based on "census data, statistics from the Department of Public Health, town records . . . [and] in-depth interviews with 39 community leaders, school staff, students, families, human service departments, police and fire department personnel, and Emergency Room and Psychiatric Hospital staff" (Needham Coalition for Suicide Prevention 2008, p. 11). The assessment found frequent areas of concern: "There is a culture in Needham that puts too much pressure on children to succeed academically, socially, and athletically . . . [and] families who 'snowplow' their children (paving the way for their children's futures without allowing their kids to make mistakes)."

As a further means of surveying the community, the coalition convened focus groups that asked Needham residents about a variety of aspects of the town. The results confirmed the coalition's concerns: "Life in Needham was called too competitive, too much about 'keeping up with the Joneses.' . . . Parents talked about feeling isolated in 'a very, very busy town.' . . . Teachers talked about the intense pressure that kids faced at school and at home. 'The parents went to Harvard,' said one, 'and their kids are going to go to Harvard'" (O'Brien 2007, p. 44). The focus groups weren't just limited to adults, either; according to one student who participated: "It seems like we're only statistics—how many of us will get into college, no one really cares about who we are" (O'Brien 2007, p. 44). The assessment's findings reinforce how community members were conscious of the pressured culture that students were experiencing. This awareness of the demands for success led to concern over the effects of this culture upon students and its correlation with the spike in teen suicides.

Nantucket

Nantucket is a small island about fourteen miles long and three and a half miles wide, located off the coast of Cape Cod, Massachusetts. It is self-described as "a Mecca for the tourism industry," having a year-round population of just over 10,000 that expands to 50,000–60,000 during July and August ("About Nantucket" 2011, p. 1). The median income of residents is $72,547, slightly higher than the average income in Massachusetts ("Nantucket Demographics Summary" 2011). Educationally, Nantucket also resembles the state as a whole, with 25.6 percent of adults having obtained a bachelor's degree and 13.1 percent a graduate or professional degree, compared to 21.2 percent and 14.6 percent, respectively, for the state ("Nantucket Demographics Summary" 2011; "Boston Education" 2011).

As news of its teen suicides spread throughout this small community, Nantucket began to ponder the causes of the problem, much as Needham had. As one news article put it, "for an island that hasn't suffered a teen suicide in over 60 years, and in the course of a year has three teen suicides, you can imagine the questioning and second guessing everyone is doing" (Grohol 2008). Well aware of the island's sharp decline in population during the winter, the town attributed its teen suicide problem to causes that were unique to its community. According to its construction of the problem, the suicides had resulted from the teenagers attending an isolated high school on a confining island.

Indeed, for this small winter community, the shock and effects of the teen suicides left many wondering if isolation was a factor. This thought process can be seen in comments by a Nantucket High student, Schuyler Shepherd, about the death of a friend, Benjamin Rives, who committed suicide in 2008. Shepherd characterized his friend as a smart, laid-back, and well-liked kid who "felt the island's young people need something to do" (Bragg 2008, p. 1). One idea that began receiving attention was that of suicide as "coming in clusters"— meaning that one suicide might increase the likelihood that others would follow. According to a Department of Public Health official, "Such copycat phenomena are more likely in tight knit communities such as Nantucket, where the high school has only 400 students" (Badkhen 2008). As a local antiques dealer and father, David Place, put it, "Everybody's going, 'Is my child next?'" And it was not just the parents who were concerned. Fifteen-year-old Nantucket High sophomore Rachel Foulkes asked, "What if it is somebody I'm close to? It's kind of scary, because they talk about chain reactions" (Badkhen 2008).

Just as Needham found the causes of teen suicide in its stressful high school, Nantucket looked at the effect of its isolation upon students and island residents. In 2008 the *Boston Globe* reported that the island's residents had "higher rates of alcohol and drug use, depression, and seasonal affective disorder than statewide rates" (Baxter 2008). The effects of these factors were "multiplied because of the isolation and long winters" (Grohol 2008). Furthermore, *ABC News* found: "While each suicide has its own set of circumstances, parents of teens who killed themselves in Nantucket and South Wales have cited isolation as a possible motivator. On Nantucket, where a summer population topping 55,000 drops to just 10,000, teens are literally locked in by the ocean" (Schoetz 2011). Finally the *Globe* noted that many Nantucket students described feeling a sense of isolation and hopelessness on the island, "where jobs are few and adult expectations of academic success are high" (Baxter 2008). As one student described it, "The two-hour boat ride that separates the island from the mainland seems to take an eternity, and the remoteness adds to the sensation of hopelessness" (Badkhen 2008). Teens across the country are faced with stressors and anxieties and many consider suicide an outlet; however, for Nantucket islanders, their remoteness was seen as contributing to these stressors and maybe even as the trigger for suicide.

Different Communities, Different Constructions

Needham and Nantucket, two communities that share little more than proximity, were both struck by the same problem of teen suicide. And for both, this problem sent the communities reeling and searching for answers. Residents asked themselves why their town, their island, had been affected, and what was unique about their culture that might have caused these tragedies. Needham responded by focusing on the unique environment of academic stress, rigor, and demands that had become characteristic of the town. Nantucket, likewise, looked at its own distinctive characteristics for answers. For community members such as Jill Page, who recalled her high school years on Nantucket as "the darkest time of my life" and explained that "it's hard enough being a teenager, but being a teenager on this island was really trying . . .

[because of] the darkness, the isolation" (Badkhen 2008), answers were easy to find, and they were found in the confining island and its small winter population.

Differing Policymaking

Once Needham and Nantucket had constructed answers to why this problem of teen suicide had hit their respective communities, both had to determine how they were going to respond. Just as each had looked to its own unique characteristics when constructing causes for the problem, each would devise policies and solutions that would accommodate and reflect those different constructions. "Policies . . . involve yet another reconstruction of the troubling conditions—this time by policymakers who must devise a plausible causal story, depict a suitable target population, and so on" (Best 2008, p. 220). While both communities constructed causes for the social problem, policymakers reconstructed the problem so that solutions would be feasible and effective and focus on those in need.

Needham

Needham town officials realized there was a significant issue in November 2004, when two Needham High students committed suicide on the same day in separate incidents: both hanged themselves. The Needham community would experience another four suicides over the following several years. Each suicide captured the town's attention and heightened the sense of urgency to understand and address this crisis. As George Johnson, director of Needham High's student development, noted: "Communities will have to examine their identities to find their own approach. . . . There was a lot of anxiety in the community, and people wanted us to respond right away with programs responding to grief. We had to take a step back and look at how we could prevent future instances of suicide, and do the research on what would make a difference and what would fit in with Needham" (Noonan 2007). Through this assessment process, Needham constructed its social problem of teen suicide as stemming from a stressful high school environment that placed intense pressure on students to perform well academically. Identifying solutions required understanding why this stressful environment existed, how it had evolved, and how it could be remedied and monitored to become healthier.

The town's initial formal step was the development of the Needham Coalition for Suicide Prevention. A number of awareness programs and service offerings were widely publicized in the high school community. Relationships with existing programs such as Samaritans Inc., a local suicide prevention and support services organization, were strengthened and broadened. Needham took remedial actions while continuing to study and evaluate the issue.

The Needham Coalition for Suicide Prevention spearheaded these efforts by combining a public health approach to the study of the problem of suicide "with what we know about Needham's unique traits and values as a community" ("Needham Coalition for Suicide Prevention" 2011). Understanding teen suicide as a complex issue, the prevention group sought to learn and confront the associated environmental factors by "working within the fabric of the community." It addressed a portion of this challenge by sponsoring educational training programs for adults who worked with children and teens, developing public awareness campaigns, and educating youths on coping skills (Noonan 2007). One example of the town's suicide prevention awareness campaign was the widespread distribution of posters in "Needham's storefronts, restroom stalls, and school hallways" that featured the haunting statistic: "In Needham more than 135 youths in grades 8 to 12 made a plan to commit suicide . . . and more than 60 made a suicide attempt" (Meade 2007). The coalition also worked toward the continuation of suicide prevention programs, including SOS (Signs of Suicide) for students, and QPR (Question, Persuade, Refer) for teachers (Needham Coalition for Suicide Prevention 2008, p. 5).

In addition, the high school eliminated class ranks and stopped publishing the honor roll in Needham's local newspaper. This move was intended to decrease the competitiveness and academic comparisons that such measures allowed students and parents to make. Though considered controversial at the time, even drawing national attention, this move, spearheaded by Principal Richards, was one of many initiatives "to reduce stress at the high school" (Ryan 2008, p. 1). Andy Shapiro and Ruth Bonsignore, parents of Kyle Shapiro, who was considered the town's "fourth suicide" when he killed himself in his junior year at Needham High in April 2006, supported Richards's move: "They never really thought about it before their son took his life. But now, too late, they recall him reading the honor roll—'the local list of who's who'—and walking away disappointed, knowing he had not made that list" (O'Brien 2007, p. 44).

Additionally, the high school began incorporating relaxation yoga instruction into physical education classes as an added effort to provide students with coping tools and forms of stress relief during the school day. Further, the Youth Education Subcommittee of the coalition developed a "wellness" campaign" designed to spread positive messages throughout the high school, while also developing wellness-related activities. Some examples of these were the revision of the high school identification tag to include a list of suicide prevention resources and the development of connections with existing student groups to strengthen awareness and participation (Needham Coalition for Suicide Prevention 2008, p. 6).

In an effort to further assess the health of the student body and school environment, a survey at the high school was implemented to gather data on student responses to teen suicide and monitor the response of the school and community to the issue. Some additional suggestions came out of this survey. For example, students "commented on the high level of stress they feel in school and offered a number of suggestions on how to lower it. . . . [They suggested] that their teachers could be more watchful about 'overloading' school work" (Needham Coalition for Suicide Prevention 2008, p. 10). It's evident that students felt that school work and stress were key sources of the problem. The survey's findings were "presented to the Needham High administration," which developed its activities for the 2008–2009 school year based on those findings (Needham Coalition for Suicide Prevention 2008, p. 9).

In addition to the response of town officials, a number of students took part in Samaritans Inc., a local suicide prevention organization. Nick Galatis, a Needham High graduate who was attending the University of Massachusetts at Amherst, responded to a question about the "haven" that Samaritans provided for students by saying, "There is an enormous amount of pressure put on teenagers to fit the high expectations set by friends, parents and society. It is extremely stressful to get through this and teens find themselves feeling suffocated and isolated." One event that Samaritans hosted was a fundraising dance called "Make Noise to Save a Life." Galatis noted that it was "a great way for students to take a break and release some stress" (Wachtler 2010, p. 1). As a recent Needham graduate, Galatis noted stress as a trigger—acknowledging the pressure that students felt coming from all sides—and highlighted activities that could help relieve that stress.

In summary, Needham began to address the issue of teen suicide by forming an organization, the Coalition for Suicide Prevention, which helped organize the town's efforts. The resulting collaboration by school officials, students, and the community helped Needham to make significant changes and modifications designed to reduce the likelihood of future teen suicides. Note that these responses—while attributing the teen suicide problem to the community's high academic expectations—sought to reduce some unnecessary pressures (such as publicizing the high school's honor roll), but did not challenge the high expectations themselves. No one, for example, suggested that the community not encourage its youth to pursue admission to selective colleges. Thus the policies that emerged were intended to address what were defined as the causes of teen suicide without challenging the community's culture.

Nantucket

In a span of eighteen months between 2007 and 2008, four Nantucket students took their own lives. Amid the clamor for something to be done, policymakers reconstructed the causes of teen suicide, moving away from an emphasis on Nantucket's winter isolation and toward social issues such as high rates of drug and alcohol usage as well as high rates of seasonal depression. Although community members initially constructed the problem of teen suicide as resulting from the island's isolation, policymakers argued that this isolation fostered an increase in drugs, alcohol, and depression, and that these in turn led to the social problem of teen suicide. By redefining the nature of the problem, policymakers were able to devise attainable solutions designed to reduce the risk factors of drugs, alcohol, and depression.

Nantucket's efforts to remedy its teen suicide problem focused on increasing awareness and resources for residents about drugs, alcohol, and depression. The initial actions were intended to provide students with more services both in and out of school. At Nantucket High, new programs for students included a drop-in center with a full-time clinician and adjustment counselor as well as new training courses for staff to help them recognize indicators of suicide (Baxter 2008). Additionally, in recognition of the strain of the long winter, the local Boys & Girls Club extended its hours to accommodate more students (Schoetz 2011, p. 1).

For the larger community, the Nantucket Suicide Prevention Coalition and the Alliance for Substance Abuse Prevention Coalition were developed. Both were composed of school and town administrators, mental and public health professionals, members of faith-based and civic organizations, members of parent and youth groups, and public safety officials (Bragg 2008, p. 1; Nantucket Alliance for Substance Abuse Prevention 2008, p. 21).

One notable development was "dances and other events on weekend nights in the winter" held by the Suicide Prevention Coalition ("Family Planning Response" 2010, p. 2). The intent was to provide safe activities for students during the winter. These activities involved collaboration between the two coalitions, whose goals were to "incorporate recreational, enrichment, and leisure activities into our approach to prevention . . . [and] help create alternative opportunities for youth whose leisure time may lack the supervision, stimulation, or positive outlets for self-discovery that s/he needs" ("Family Planning Response" 2010, p. 44).

The Alliance for Substance Abuse Prevention Coalition also emphasized a correlation between isolation, suicide, and teen drug and alcohol use in devising its strategic plan for youth. In its evaluation of Nantucket's risk and protective factors, the alliance noted that there was an "early initiation of problem behavior" combined with an "availability of alcohol, *no place for kids to go,* [and] few consistent, dedicated, youth-directed recreational venues and activities for youth development" (Nantucket Alliance for Substance Abuse Prevention 2008, p. 13, emphasis in original). The alliance's strategy to deal with these problems was the implementation of the Communities Mobilizing for Change on Alcohol program, whose primary goals were to obtain "youth prevention" grant funds, to engage with local youth groups, as well as to "facilitate focus groups to gather more information regarding underage drinking behaviors on Nantucket and continue to build community relationships" (Nantucket Alliance for Substance Abuse Prevention 2008, p. 17).

Nantucket initially constructed the problem of teen suicide as relating to the island's unique and isolated winter culture; of course, little could be done to increase the island's winter population, or reduce its geographic isolation. However, policymakers argued that this winter culture led to a cycle of negative effects—a connection to high rates of drug and alcohol use and depression, which in turn led back to teen suicide. By focusing on suicide prevention techniques—as well as trying to reduce drug and alcohol use and increase awareness of seasonal depression—policymakers sought to address what they defined as the distinctive aspects of their community's social problem.

Different Constructions, Different Solutions

Teen suicide can be attributed to a wide range of stressors on the individual. Some are unique to the individual; others are linked to more common environmental stressors. Defining teen suicide as something that had become a local problem in their communities, Needham and Nantucket sought to find ways to reduce the environmental stressors thought to contribute to teen suicide. Each community identified stressors that were specific to its own environment and sought to implement initiatives and policies to minimize these stressors. For the communities of Needham and Nantucket, this required looking at their own ideas and images and using them to shape their own specific responses to the social problem of teen suicide.

Conclusion

Any social problem can be constructed in different ways. A psychiatrist is likely to view teen suicide very differently than, say, a religious fundamentalist. But just as the claimsmakers' viewpoints make a difference, so does geography. Social problems are often constructed as national problems. Presented in books and magazines or on network television, national constructions identify general causes for teen suicide, such as characterizing adolescence as a tumultuous, stressful stage in life. But social problems can also be constructed in particular localities. When several teen suicides occurred in both Needham and Nantucket, local residents found themselves trying to understand why this problem was occurring in their communities and why their teenagers seemed particularly likely to kill themselves.

Note that the fact that a community experiences several teen suicides within a few years need not be constructed as a local problem. Teen suicides are relatively rare events, but even if they occur randomly, we would expect to find instances of some suicides occurring near one another in time and space. It might be possible to view these as coincidences, as simply the normal variation of events. However, since teen suicides are defined as especially tragic because they cut young lives short, people are likely to notice these deaths and to assume that, when two or more teen suicides occur in the same community within a couple years of one another, this is a "cluster," a troubling pattern—one that demands not just an explanation, but also some sort of action.

In both Needham and Nantucket, residents argued that multiple teen suicides indicated that their communities were especially troubled. These constructions raised questions that, in turn, forced the two communities to consider how they might be different from other communities and why their teens seemed especially at risk. Needham and Nantucket answered these questions in different ways and, in turn, devised policies that reflected the different ways they had constructed teen suicide as a local problem.

3

Cell Phone Use While Driving: Defining a Problem as Worthy of Action

Peter F. Parilla

In 1984 the reader of a magazine or newspaper might run across an ad featuring an image of a well-dressed businessman behind the wheel of an expensive-looking automobile. He is clearly making an important call on his new Western Union cellular phone. The caption: "Can your secretary take dictation at 55 MPH?" The ad declared that those in business would benefit "because now you can take your office and its support systems anywhere you drive." The obvious message being conveyed is that success, status, and productivity all come with using a phone while driving. Turning a few pages, the same reader might find a second ad. This one includes a drawing of dozens of cars gridlocked in a traffic jam. The drivers have dour expressions as they sit and stew—with one exception. A smiling driver is happily chatting on his Radio Shack cell phone—apparently oblivious to the pain that his fellow travelers feel. The tag line for the ad: "Get into the fast lane with Radio Shack's new car telephone" (see *New York Times* 2009 to see these ads and others).

Both ads appeared in 1984, only months after the first commercial cell phone call had taken place (CTIA 2011). The cost of early phone service was prohibitively expensive for most Americans. Not surprisingly, the early ads targeted relatively well-to-do persons. To justify the cost, a major selling point was the ability of owners to use their phones while on the road either to conduct business or to catch up with family and friends. Early newspaper articles about cell phones

27

captured this benefit as well. In a 1988 article in the Minneapolis *Star Tribune,* a realtor is quoted about using his phone on the road, "The more phone calls you can make, the more successful you will be." In the same article, a business consultant claims: "It's another way I can say to my clients, 'You are important to me, and I am even more available to you than I was before'" (Marcotty 1987). In a similar vein, a 1988 article in the *New York Times* offers the following coverage of cell phone use:

> "Do you know how many times I've driven with an architect or somebody else and we get a good idea and you want to call someone with it, but you're not in your office?" said Mr. Leonard, who also has a phone in his boat. "The whole key to success in business is to react fast to what your clients want. I've found a million things to do with my car phone, like working on my way to work and when I'm traveling. Everybody I know has a car phone, and you don't have to be a millionaire to own one anymore." (Bass 1988)

It would be unthinkable today to market cell phones by emphasizing that owners should use them to talk or text while driving. In recent years, a drastically different image has emerged. In place of a successful businessperson increasing productivity, we envision the scene of a traffic accident where a distracted driver, often a teenager, has killed himself or others due to the irresponsible use of a phone while driving. Today, we are more likely to measure the impact of cell phone use while driving in terms of fatalities and injuries rather than in terms of hours saved at work.

Driving and Using a Cell Phone as a Social Problem

The change in imagery about driving while on the phone is not happenstance. There has been a concerted effort to shape the public's perception of this behavior as an extremely risky one that must be controlled. The concern begins with the realization that driving an automobile is a complex, multitask activity requiring the driver to simultaneously coordinate physical movements to operate the automobile (e.g., steering or braking) while also needing to constantly monitor instrumentation within the car (e.g., speed or climate control) as well as maintain awareness of changing circumstances in the external environment (e.g., other traffic, pedestrians, or road signs). The problem is that using a phone while driving is a distraction that can divert the driver's attention from the primary task of driving. The result is increased risk of serious injury or death for the driver, passengers, and others in the vicinity. According to the National Highway Traffic Safety Administration, in 2009 nearly a thousand persons were killed due to cell phone use while driving (NHTSA 2011). The sense of urgency about the problem is rising for several reasons. First, there are more phones than ever before—subscriptions now number over 300 million in the United States (CTIA 2011). Second, as almost everyone sees on a daily basis, many drivers are on the phone when they drive. During any given daylight hour, 9 percent of drivers are using their phones (NHTSA 2011). Third, the popularity of texting has grown enormously, as has the willingness to text while driving. Nearly one in three drivers under the age of thirty have admitted to texting while driving in the preceding month, while 9 percent of older drivers have admitted to texting while driving (LaHood and Guest 2011, p. 2). This is viewed as especially problematic because texting is more distracting than conversing.

Those in the movement to curtail phone use while driving come from a variety of arenas and include law enforcement officials, legislators, and other governmental officials. Also involved are organizations with a stake in highway safety (e.g., insurance companies and the American Automobile Association), victims' groups like FocusDriven, and celebrities (e.g., Oprah Winfrey, and Click and Clack of *Car Talk*). They seek to mobilize support to "do something" about the problem, which research shows is as risky as driving with a 0.08 percent blood alcohol content, the legal threshold for drunk driving. Their efforts to stop the behavior have taken many forms, ranging from educational efforts (e.g., changes in driver training curricula and public service announcements) to moral appeals for drivers to stop cell phone use while driving (e.g., Oprah's "no phone" pledge) to a wide variety of legislative activities (e.g., over thirty states have enacted laws prohibiting cell phone use while driving).

Those seeking to ban cell phone use while driving face an uphill fight. Their claims about the dangers of this activity have been frequently contested. Many in the telecommunications industry have resisted efforts to prohibit phone use while driving, arguing that cell phones are just one of many distractions that drivers face and are certainly not the worst; they should not be singled out. More important, there is significant resistance from the tens of millions of drivers in the United States who routinely use their phones without harm. The challenge facing those who advocate banning the use of cell phones while driving is to devise ways to convincingly portray the harmfulness of an activity that has become so much a part of Americans' daily lives.

This chapter analyzes the efforts to transform the behavior of driving while on the phone into a social problem that is worthy of public action. The role of the media is vitally important in this process. If the media ignore efforts by claimsmakers to publicize claims, their ability to persuade the public is greatly diminished (although in the age of the Internet, this may be less true). Thus, a crucial step in the creation of a social problem is for the media to consider the topic worthy of coverage. For those matters deemed worthy, the framing of the issue becomes critically important. Which claims are reported and which are not? Which version or versions of reality are portrayed? Are all sides represented? How the media define a topic can shape their audience's understanding of whether a condition is a problem and, if so, what needs to be done. On some occasions, the media may shift from "neutral reporting" to editorializing on the topic—joining the debate as a proponent or opponent. In short, the media have an influential role in shaping how the public and policymakers define problems. Media constructions of social problems can evolve over time. This chapter examines changes in claims regarding cell phone use while driving as reported in the print media. Specifically, it analyzes the coverage of this behavior as problematic over the nearly three decades since commercial cell phone use began. Drawing upon the model proposed by Joel Best (2008), the goal is to explore how the issue has been defined and redefined in efforts to convince the public that driving while on the phone is indeed a problem in need of a solution.

For the purposes of this study, driving while on the phone includes the use of a cell phone to either converse or text while driving. Newspapers are analyzed because, unlike national magazines, they report on legislative activity at the state level, which is where most highway safety legislation originates. The two newspapers analyzed are the *New York Times* and the Twin Cities–based *Star Tribune,* published in Minneapolis and St. Paul, Minnesota. The *New York Times* is often considered to be a "newspaper of record." It has the third largest daily newspaper circulation and the largest Sunday circulation in the United States (Rosenthal 2011). It is also thought to be an authoritative source of information that influences leaders and policymakers (Saguy and Gruys 2010). The *Star Tribune,* while not possessing the scope or influence of the *Times,* is viewed as a strong regional paper. It has the seventeenth largest daily newspaper circulation and the tenth largest Sunday circulation in the United States, and is the most widely read paper in the state of Minnesota (Rosenthal 2011). In addition, both publications have the method-ological advantage of being available in electronic archives for the period of interest.

In an effort to conduct a comprehensive search of articles pub-lished in the two papers, three different search engines were used to scan electronic archives—Proquest, Lexis-Nexis, and each newspa-per's own archive. The dates covered in the search range from January 1, 1984, to September 21, 2010. The first date roughly coincides with the creation of the first commercial cellular phone network. Searches were conducted using a variety of keywords, including terms such as "cell phone and driving," "texting and driving," "talking and driving," "car phone," "hang up and drive," "distracted driving," "cellular and drive," and "cellular and vehicle." For an article to be included, it needed to be long enough to deal with the issue substantively. Thus, articles shorter than 200 words were eliminated. Letters to the editor were also excluded. Not all articles that addressed cell phones and cars are part of this study. Substantively, the article needed to be "about" driving while on the phone, and it needed to approach the issue from the perspective that such behavior could be problematic. For example, articles that compared mobile phones or phone systems in terms of cost or quality of reception were excluded. Articles devot-ed to describing the details of a traffic fatality in which cell phone use may have played a part were not included unless the article also included additional and more general information about the dangers of driving while on the phone.

Analysis

Extent of Newspaper Coverage

Figure 3.1 shows the number of *New York Times* and *Star Tribune* arti-cles about driving while on the phone, that met the aforementioned criteria for inclusion, published between 1984 and September 2010. Several patterns are immediately discernable. First, the *Times* published many more articles that met the criteria for inclusion than did the *Star Tribune*. In the twenty-seven years covered in the study, the *Times* published 135 articles compared with 65 for the *Star Tribune*. Given the reputation of the *Times* for comprehensive coverage of topics, this difference is unsurprising. It is worth pointing out that in 2009, the year the difference is most noticeable (a ratio of three to one), the *Times* ran an extensive series titled "Driven to Distraction," investigating the problem of driving while on the phone.

It is also clear from Figure 3.1 that the articles were not published at a consistent rate over the period of the study. In the eleven-year span from 1984 to 1994, the *Times* published only four articles on the topic and the *Star Tribune* none. If one compares the first eleven years of coverage with the last eleven (2000 to 2010), the difference is 4 articles compared to 171. Clearly, media coverage of the topic increased over time. Because of the sheer volume of articles in the *Times,* a 50 percent sample of these articles was selected for the content analysis. Articles were placed in chronological order of publication and a coin toss was used to decide whether to start with the earliest published article or the next earliest. Then every other article was selected for coding. Thus, the findings of the content analysis are based on 68 *New York Times* articles rather than 135.

Figure 3.1 Number of *New York Times* and *Star Tribune* Articles About Driving While on the Phone, 1984–2010

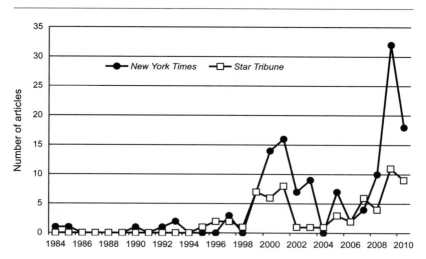

Identifying the Problem

The first step in the claimsmaking process is the identification of an issue or condition that is troubling. Those seeking to convince others that a problem exists must first stipulate grounds—statements of facts that document that the issue is problematic. These grounds are the foundation for the ensuing discussion and debate about the issue and its eventual resolution (Best 1987, 2008). As can be seen in Table 3.1, the vast majority of the articles in the study included content asserting the claim that driving while on the phone is a risky behavior that increases the likelihood of traffic accidents. In the *New York Times,* 56 of the 68 articles (82.3 percent) addressed the link between safety and driving while on the phone. A similar proportion of *Star Tribune* articles (84.5 percent, 55 of the 65 articles) included such coverage. In those articles where the linkage to accidents was made, most (46 of 56 in the *Times* and 48 of 55 in the *Star Tribune*) offered information on only one side of the issue—that driving while on the phone increased the chance of an accident. In 9 *Times* articles and 6 *Star Tribune* articles, the claim was made that driving while on the phone caused accidents alongside a counterclaim that driving while on the phone was not a major factor in accidents. Only one article in each paper provided a one-sided presentation of the issue claiming that driving while on the phone did not cause accidents. Those articles that did not include any mention of accidents tended to be focused on legislative action regulating cell phone use while driving and did not directly address why the legislation was needed.

Table 3.1 *New York Times* and *Star Tribune* Coverage of Cell Phone Use While Driving as a Cause of Traffic Accidents, 1984–2010

	Percentage of *New York Times* Articles	Percentage of *Star Tribune* Articles
Article contains the claim that driving while on the phone causes accidents, but no counterclaim	67.6	73.8
Article contains only the counterclaim that driving while on the phone does not cause accidents	1.5	1.5
Article contains both the claim and the counterclaim	13.2	9.2
Article contains neither the claim nor the counterclaim	17.6	15.4

The claim that driving while on the phone causes accidents was supported with different kinds of evidence in the various articles. One common approach was to use anecdotes about incidents where cell phone use had led to erratic driving and accidents. About one-third of *New York Times* articles and half of *Star Tribune* articles included such an anecdote. Often the anecdote took the form of a "horror story"—a particularly tragic incident (Best 1987; Johnson 1995). One example comes from a letter published in the syndicated column *Car Talk:*

> My 2-1/2-year-old daughter, Morgan Lee, was killed as a result of an auto accident that occurred on Nov. 2, 1999. My vehicle was hit broadside by a man who admitted that he did not stop at a stop sign because he was distracted while dialing his cellular phone. Cause of death—blunt head trauma. He ran into the rear passenger door at 45 miles per hour, right where Morgan was sitting. He received a total of $50 in fines. I need to speak out on this issue. I cannot live with what happened to my daughter. I was not aware prior to the accident just how dangerous the roads have become with the saturation of cell phones. I now know . . . I am just one woman, putting myself out there in the hopes of creating public awareness. I am working with my local senator to get legislation through. Please tell people what they can do to help me fight for my daughter. (Magliozzi and Magliozzi 2000)

Reliance on such "horror stories" is a common rhetorical device in efforts to convince the public that some behavior is worthy of public concern (Best 1987, 1989; Johnson 1995). Typically, horror stories are positioned at the beginning of an article and act as a "grabber" seeking to capture the reader's attention and provoke an emotional reaction such as anger, outrage, or fear in response to the issue being described. Such stories are often distortions, not because they are untrue but because they are atypical. The reader is drawn to make several inferences. First, describing the most tragic cases conveys the impression that the practice of driving while on the phone is extremely dangerous. Victims, often children, suffer terrible injuries. Second, such stories are likely to elicit a strong emotional reaction; their goal is not just to inform but to arouse. Third, horror stories imply that such tragedies can happen to anyone at any time. In each case, the victims were doing nothing out of the ordinary and yet they suffered deadly consequences. No one is safe if they are on the road. Finally, the horror story is directly linked to the need for legislation to protect other innocents from such tragedies.

In addition to using such anecdotal information, claims that driving while on the phone caused accidents were commonly supported with references to evidence from either governmental traffic statistics or scientific studies. Over half of the articles (58.8 percent of *Times* articles and 53.5 percent of *Star Tribune* articles) contained some reference to statistical evidence regarding the risks of driving while on the phone. Thus, a *Star Tribune* article reports on a study published in the prestigious *New England Journal of Medicine:*

> Talking on a cellular telephone while driving quadruples the risk of having an accident, making it as dangerous as driving while drunk, Canadian scientists report today. The first large study of the wireless phones also found, to the authors' surprise, that so-called hands-free phones are no safer than conventional hand-held phones. "This may indicate that the main factor . . . is a driver's limitations in attention rather than dexterity," said Dr. Donald Redelmeier of the University of Toronto. (*Star Tribune* 1997)

It is worth noting that the *New York Times* published a similar report on the same day. In the early 2000s, this *New England Journal of Medicine* study was cited repeatedly in articles published in both papers. The claim that driving while on the phone bears similarities with drunk driving took on special importance, showing up in 24 percent of the articles in the two newspapers either to demonstrate the dangerousness of the behavior or to endorse the need for a public campaign to change public attitudes, as had been done in the 1980s with driving while intoxicated.

In most cases, the statistical evidence bolstered the case that driving while on the phone was risky behavior. However, in articles where counterclaims were found, these were also supported with empirical data demonstrating that the behavior was not particularly dangerous. Often spokespersons from the Cellular Telecommunications Industry Association (CTIA), the trade association for the cellular phone industry, provided this information. A 1996 article provides an example of the early position taken by the organization:

> Tim Ayers, a spokesman for the Washington, D.C.–based Cellular Telecommunications Industry Association, points to myriad studies that he says show that cellular phones are safe in cars, including a survey by the University of Michigan Transportation Research Institute reporting that drivers rank reading a map and changing cassettes as more distracting than car phones. "Reading a map,

drinking a cup of hot coffee, doing your makeup, combing your hair or talking on the phone are all unwise things to do while driving," Ayers said. "But you can call 911 on a cell phone, and two-thirds of the people buying them say they do so for safety reasons." (Brown 1996)

A similar view is expressed in a 2005 article in which the CTIA offers its position on the merits of cell phone legislation:

John Walls, the vice president of public affairs of CTIA, the Wireless Association, a trade organization representing wireless interests, said it was unfair and unnecessary to create hands-free laws. "We question the need for a law singling out behavior that apparently is pretty far down the pecking order of accidents in the first place," Mr. Walls said. He cited statistics showing that before the New York law was enacted, fewer than one-hundredth of 1 percent of New York City accidents were related to cellphones. (Radsch 2005)

Framing the Issue over Time

The key claim identified with driving while on the phone was that it was unsafe and could cause traffic accidents. However, how the issue was framed or portrayed in the newspaper coverage varied considerably over time. While the earliest articles tended to examine the topic generically, as time progressed the coverage moved away from general discussion and focused on particular dimensions of the problem to the exclusion of others. In other words, patterns emerged in the definition of the problematic condition. In some years, the focus was on restrictions for handheld phones but not hands-free ones; in others, it was on banning cell phone use for new drivers but not for experienced drivers; while in the more recent past, the target has shifted to texting. In Figure 3.2, the articles from both the *New York Times* and the *Star Tribune* are combined to make an analysis of the dimensions of the problem more straightforward.

Handheld phones as the problem. Examining Figure 3.2, one can see that articles published between 1999 and 2001 tended to focus attention on the use of handheld phones as the problem. Holding a phone in one hand leaves only one free hand for other driving-related tasks such as steering, shifting gears, and adjusting controls. Framed in this manner, the problem is a biomechanical one. The obvious solution is to require the use of hands-free devices. As one industry official

**Figure 3.2　Framing the Issue of Driving While on the Phone,
New York Times and *Star Tribune* Coverage, 1997–2010**

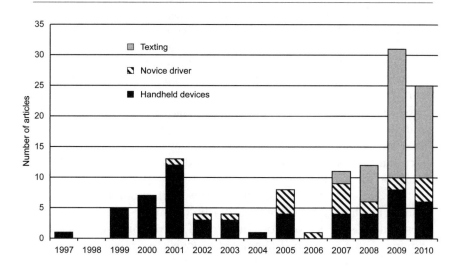

commented: "'There are no hard studies that say you're better off if you use a hands-free device rather than not using one when driving,' said David Clevenger, a spokesman for Verizon Wireless in Chicago. 'But we think it's common sense that you're a better driver with both hands on [the] wheel than if you're trying to hold a phone to your head and drive with the other hand'" (Alexander 2001).

Over the course of this three-year period, twenty-four articles dealt with efforts to restrict the use of handheld phones. Many of the articles reported on regulations approved by local governments (e.g., cities and counties) in New York and in surrounding states that prohibited drivers from using handheld phones. This led to a patchwork of laws within the New York vicinity. In July 2000 the *New York Times* published an editorial on the topic of handheld phones:

> There was a lot of debate about the safety implications of car radios when they were developed over 70 years ago. A similar debate is under way now about the use of hand-held cell phones in cars. On the face of it, cell phones are a much bigger potential distraction than radios. They require more concentration by the driver and tie up one hand that ought to be on the steering wheel. A few small

American municipalities, most recently Marlboro, N.J., have banned the use of hand-held cell phones by drivers. . . . [O]ur instinct is that Marlboro and the other communities are on the right track. We would go so far as to recommend state legislation to guarantee uniformity. (*New York Times* 2000)

Given the location of these events, one might expect that the vast majority of articles included here would have come from the *New York Times* rather than the *Star Tribune*. Surprisingly, this is not the case. Of the twenty-four published on handheld bans between 1999 and 2001, ten appeared in the pages of the *Star Tribune,* which covered activities in the eastern United States as national news due to the fact that they were the first efforts to address the problem of driving while on the phone.

In 2001 the state legislature in New York prohibited the use of handheld phones by drivers. From one vantage point, this was a tremendous success for those in favor of restricting phone use while driving. Other states had attempted to legislate against the behavior and had failed. New York's passage of a ban on handheld phones was the first such statewide law in the nation and, as mentioned, received national attention. At the same time, some might view the ban as more a symbolic victory than real progress toward traffic safety. After all, research had found that hands-free devices were not safer because the distraction caused by a phone conversation is largely cognitive, not biomechanical. Even advocates for a ban on handheld phones acknowledged this fact. For example, the *New York Times* editorial supporting a ban on handheld phones noted:

A 1997 Canadian study published in the New England Journal of Medicine found that the risk of an accident increases fourfold if the driver is on a cell phone. . . . One technological answer could be hands-free or voice-activated cell phones, which are growing in popularity. But the Canadian study suggested that these phones do not confer a safety advantage over hand-held units. (*New York Times* 2000)

In the years since New York passed its ban, eight other states and the District of Columbia have approved similar bans on handheld phones (Governors Highway Safety Association 2011).

New drivers as the problem. By about 2005, the cost of cell phones had plunged drastically and they were affordable to many more Americans, including teenagers. Concerns about teenager driving while on the phone led to a second framing of the problem. Between 2005 and 2010, eighteen articles appear in which there is discussion of a ban on cell phone use for new drivers, although the focus is invariably on teenagers. Unlike coverage of handheld bans, there is less balance between how the two newspapers covered this framing: fourteen of the eighteen articles appeared in the *Star Tribune*. The likely reason is that in 2005 the Minnesota legislature approved a law banning cell phone use by those with provisional driver's licenses and by all drivers under the age of eighteen. Only emergency calls could be made by these drivers. During this period, a regular reader of the *Star Tribune* might have developed a very different perspective on the issue, interpreting driving while on the phone as primarily a problem for novice drivers:

> A new national study shows [that seventeen-year-old] Max is far from alone when it comes to distracted teenage drivers. While they're getting the message to refrain from drunken driving, the survey shows that cell phones, iPods, text-messaging and rowdy friends are combining to make driving more perilous than ever for teens. That's why a new national series of public-service TV ads launched Thursday tries to urge kids that it's cool to complain when their peers are driving recklessly. (Brown 2007)

The issue for teen drivers went beyond immaturity and rowdiness. The belief underlying the ban was that teens and other new drivers did not possess the wherewithal to deal with the variety of distractions to which experienced drivers were accustomed. Thus, targeting restrictions on new drivers was the logical solution:

> [Two legislators] held a State Capitol news conference Thursday with State Patrol and traffic safety officials to highlight the law, similar provisions of which are already in effect in seven other states. Heightened risks faced by young and inexperienced drivers warrant their special treatment under the law, the officials said. For example, traffic crashes are the leading cause of death for teenagers in Minnesota and the nation, and 16-year-olds have an accident rate three times that of drivers only two or three years older. "That's why we targeted them." (deFiebre 2005)

Restrictions on new drivers, who are largely teenagers, were not unique to Minnesota. By 2011, thirty states and the District of Columbia had passed similar prohibitions (Governors Highway Safety Administration 2011). It is likely that bans on cell phone use for new drivers could save lives; teenagers already have higher than average accident rates, so preventing them from using phones when they drive should improve traffic safety. At the same time, such bans affect only a relatively small minority of all drivers. Politically, implementing a ban on teens is also safer because those under age eighteen cannot vote. Politicians do not need to fear the consequences of restricting their behavior.

Texting as the problem. Beginning in 1993, a new form of communication developed using mobile telephony—the short message system (SMS), better known as texting (Ling 2008). Initially this new use of cell phones was limited to the hearing-impaired due to expense. However, in the new millennium, the use of texting began to increase dramatically. Data from the CTIA, the trade association for the wireless industry, indicate that over 2.1 trillion text messages were sent in the United States in 2010 (CTIA 2011).

As texting increased in popularity, this became yet another frame for the problem of driving while on the phone. By about 2010, texting while driving dominated coverage of the overall problem. Between 2007 and September 2010, the *New York Times* and the *Star Tribune* published a total of forty-four articles that included some discussion of banning texting while driving—twenty-five in the *Times* and nineteen in the *Star Tribune*. These articles depicted texting as riskier than conversing on the phone while driving because of the greater attention that needs to be given to writing and reading text messages. Newspaper readers of this time would likely have formed the impression that texting while driving was especially dangerous:

> The first study of drivers texting inside their vehicles shows that the risk sharply exceeds previous estimates based on laboratory research—and far surpasses the dangers of other driving distractions. The new study, which entailed outfitting the cabs of long-haul trucks with video cameras over 18 months, found that when the drivers texted, their collision risk was 23 times greater than when not texting. The Virginia Tech Transportation Institute, which compiled the research and plans to release its findings today, also measured the time that drivers take their eyes from the road to send or receive texts. In the moments before a crash or near-crash, drivers typically spent nearly five seconds looking at their devices— enough time at typical highway speeds to cover more than the length of a football field. (Richtel 2009b)

Britain's Transport Research Laboratory found texting more dangerous than substance use: Text messaging lowered drivers' reaction time by 35 percent, while people high on marijuana slowed down 21 percent and those who were legally drunk slowed down by 12 percent. (Ward 2010)

Although both newspapers focused on texting while driving during the late 2000s, their emphasis was not identical. In Minnesota, the legislature passed a bill prohibiting texting while driving for all drivers, so some coverage in the *Star Tribune* was devoted to this legislation. New York did not legislate against texting during this same time period; however, the *Times* did run its series "Driven to Distraction," which included extensive coverage of the dangers of texting.

Of the efforts to control cell phone use while driving, one would think that the arguments for banning texting would be easiest to make. Texting places cognitive, manual, and visual demands on a driver, reducing their ability to concentrate on the main tasks of operating a vehicle. It is unsurprising that, as of 2011, thirty-four states and the District of Columbia have banned texting while driving for all drivers. More surprising is that seven other states have outlawed texting while driving only for new drivers; experienced drivers are not affected by these laws and are free to text while driving. In addition, nine states have no laws regulating texting while driving (Governors Highway Safety Association 2011).

Distracted driving as the problem. In each of the preceding three framings, the threat of driving while on the phone was not about using the phone per se, but about some particular aspect of the behavior. It was a problem only for (1) those with handheld phones, (2) novice drivers who lacked the experience needed to multitask while driving, and (3) persons who texted while driving. With the exception of bans on new drivers, coverage in the two newspapers was quite consistent in the patterns of how the issue was being framed, leading one to believe that their coverage was not solely the result of local legislative activity. It is likely that these claims were being made beyond the individual states where the newspapers were published.

At the same time that attention was being directed at texting while driving, a more significant reframing of the issue presented itself. Instead of subdividing the issue into the different types, the new approach treated driving while on the phone as a subset of a larger problem—"distracted driving." In articles about this topic, cell phones were invariably mentioned as the prime example, even though conversing while driving is not statistically as dangerous as other behaviors such as eating and drinking while driving (Stutts et al. 2001). This change in the characterization of the issue occurred in both newspapers. As can be seen in Figure 3.3, articles mentioning distracted driving were fairly uncommon prior to 2008—no more than two articles appeared in any prior year. Yet in the two-year period of 2009–2010, the *Star Tribune* published thirteen articles mentioning the term, and the *New York Times* published seventeen.

Consider the lead *Times* article in its series on the topic:

> Extensive research shows the dangers of distracted driving. Studies say that drivers using phones are four times as likely to cause a crash as other drivers, and the likelihood that they will crash is equal to that of someone with a .08 percent blood alcohol level, the point at which drivers are generally considered intoxicated. Research also shows that hands-free devices do not eliminate the risks, and may worsen them by suggesting that the behavior is safe. A 2003 Harvard study estimated that cellphone distractions caused 2,600 traffic deaths every year, and 330,000 accidents that result in moderate or severe injuries. Yet Americans have largely ignored that research.

Figure 3.3 Coverage of "Distracted Driving" in the *New York Times* and *Star Tribune*, 1999–2010

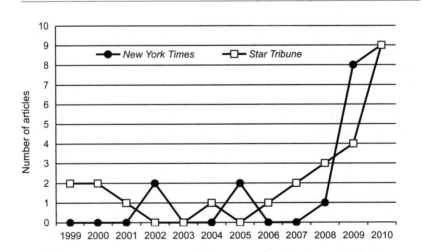

Instead, they increasingly use phones, navigation devices and even laptops to turn their cars into mobile offices, chat rooms and entertainment centers, making roads more dangerous. (Richtel 2009a)

The National Highway Traffic Safety Administration (NHTSA) and Transportation Secretary Ray LaHood became key players in the campaign to address distracted driving. The *Star Tribune* reported on it in the following story:

> "Hang up and drive" could be much more than a bumper sticker if U.S. Transportation Secretary Ray LaHood gets his way. On Tuesday he supported banning all cell-phone use by drivers. . . . The national drive includes a new federal website, http://www.distraction.gov, and a new nonprofit organization called FocusDriven, modeled on Mothers Against Drunk Driving. . . . LaHood said the new group and federal website are among the fruit of last fall's first-ever distracted driving summit. . . . We're not going to sit around, and we're not going to wait around for Congress," LaHood said. "We're moving ahead. . . . We're on a rampage about this." (Foti 2010)

While a number of factors may have led to this new way of conceptualizing the problem, two claimsmakers stand out as being particularly important. One is the *New York Times* itself. Its series "Driven to Distraction" received national attention and eventually earned reporter Matt Richtel and the *Times* the Pulitzer Prize for National Reporting in 2010. The citation praised the award winners for "stimulating widespread efforts to curb distracted driving." The second is Transportation Secretary Ray LaHood, who became an outspoken champion for the cause against distracted driving, making it a priority of the NHTSA.

Joel Best (2008) writes that an important part of claimsmaking is the ability to "name" the problem so that it is looked at differently. For example, "road rage" is catchier and more threatening than "bad driving." He further states that naming the behavior is not the same as defining it. Indeed, having a vague or loose definition may be desirable in the claimsmaking process. "Distracted driving" is such a concept. It encompasses a wide variety of problematic driving behaviors, including driving while on the phone, which is the most-cited example. Yet it is a term that is extremely difficult to define precisely (see Lee, Young, and Regan 2009) and could include almost any objectionable driver-related behavior (e.g., drinking coffee, changing CDs, disciplining children). By reframing the issue of driving while on the phone and calling it "distracted driving," it becomes a behavior that is much easier to attack and more difficult to defend. While someone might reasonably argue that they should legally be allowed to use a phone and drive at the same time, it is more difficult to make the case that they should be able to engage in "distracted driving," a term for which the connotation is entirely negative. Interestingly, one indicator of the ascendancy of this new formulation of the problem came from *Webster's New World Dictionary Online,* which in 2009 named "distracted driving" as its word of the year.

Conclusion

Distracted driving is as old as driving itself. Ever since the first automobile hit the road, drivers had experienced periods when their attention strayed from the primary task of driving. They had eaten burgers, put on makeup, and yelled at children in the backseat for decades with little public attention being paid to the dangers associated with such behaviors. There were no organized campaigns or targeted legislative initiatives. And then came cell phones. The proliferation of this new technology and its widespread use by drivers has led to a concerted effort to ban their use by drivers. What is special about the problem of driving while on the phone? One explanation would be that this behavior is so much more dangerous than any previous distraction that action is needed. However, there is little evidence to support this contention, at least for conversing on the phone (see Stutts et al. 2001). A more plausible explanation relates to the popularity of driving while on the phone and its high level of visibility (Sundeen 2007). The fact that so many persons find it irritating to see another driver on the phone is also relevant.

The purpose of this chapter has been to examine efforts to ban the use of cell phones while driving by analyzing how the issue has been framed in the pages of two major metropolitan newspapers. The challenge facing those seeking to mobilize support for a ban is to convince the public that a behavior they many engage in on a daily basis is actually a very dangerous activity. In the past decade, newspaper accounts of the issue show that how it has been portrayed has shifted considerably as various efforts have been made to mobilize the public and policymakers to ban the behavior. One argument is that those seeking to end cell phone use while driving realized that their chances of a total ban were remote and so they settled for an incremental approach, passing laws that were achievable even if they were ineffective at lessening accidents (such as bans on handheld phones) or only targeted particular segments of the driving public (such as teens). Equally plausible is that the movement sought to find a rhetoric that would win the support of the public. In a sense, different definitions were hoisted up the flagpole to see whether anyone would salute, whether they were a way to gain support for the issue. Whatever the reason, in the course of the discussion, the framing of the issue changed multiple times, as claimsmakers searched for a construction that would effectively persuade the public and legislators of the dangers of driving while on the phone. With the reframing of the issue in terms of "distracted driving," the claimsmakers seem to have succeeded. It is a catchy phrase that has clearly entered the popular lexicon. It is also a way of defining the issue so that it is difficult to oppose—no one can reasonably argue in favor of distracted driving. Ironically, this way of defining the problem has an inherent limitation. By broadening the definition of the problem to include anything that might distract a driver, it encompasses so much that the problem may be impossible to address effectively.

Whether the campaign has been successful is open to debate. As mentioned, a number of states have passed laws regulating cell phone use while driving. Certainly, the greatest gains have been made in prohibiting texting while driving. The majority of states now ban this, although some only for novice drivers. One national poll found that 97 percent of respondents believed that text messaging while driving should be illegal (Connelly 2009). Of those who held this view, 50 percent believed that the penalty should be the same as that for drunk driving and 2 percent wanted the punishment to be more severe. Although many states have regulated certain aspects of driving while on the phone, no state has passed a ban outlawing the behavior completely.

Poll data on public attitudes regarding talking on the phone while driving show little change. One poll found that 70 percent of respondents said that it should be legal to use a hands-free phone while driving. This figure is similar to the one in the 2001 poll that found that 72 percent of respondents thought it should be legal (Connelly 2009). A 2010 poll revealed mixed evidence about the effect of the movement to reduce distracted driving. On the one hand, 78 percent of respondents said that they had reduced or stopped activities related to distracted driving, with two-thirds of those saying that they made the change because of reading or hearing about the dangers. Yet the poll also showed that both talking and texting while driving remain common occurrences. Nearly two-thirds of respondents under thirty years old admitted to using a handheld phone while driving during the preceding month. Nearly one-third admitted to texting while driving during the same period. For those over thirty, 41 percent admitted to having used a handheld phone and 9 percent to having texted. As far as whether people have been convinced of the dangers of the behavior, the same poll found that for those under thirty years old, only 30 percent thought it was "very dangerous to use a handheld phone" while driving (LaHood and Guest 2011). The fact that younger respondents are more likely to engage in driving while on the phone and think of it as safe raises questions about the long-term prospects for the campaign to reduce distracted driving.

Part 2

Claimsmakers

Claims cannot exist by themselves; every claim needs a claims-maker, someone to present the claim. The obvious example of a claimsmaker is a social activist, a person conducting public protest demonstrations to draw attention to a cause. Traditional activism relied on such demonstrations—picket lines, protest marches, and the like. Activists such as civil rights leader Martin Luther King Jr. used demonstrations to attract media coverage to their causes, in order to sway public opinion and press for policy changes.

These attention-grabbing protest tactics were needed at a time when there were relatively few media outlets, when activists depended on coverage by newspapers, magazines, and primarily just three television networks to bring widespread awareness to their causes. Today, of course, the media landscape has changed: the circulation of newspapers and magazines has declined, just as the share of the television audience commanded by ABC, CBS, and NBC has shrunk. Today, there are many more venues for making claims—dozens of channels on cable and satellite television, all manner of online sources, including websites, blogs, Facebook pages, and discussion groups, to say nothing of emerging media such as Twitter.

Claimsmakers can now choose how they want to promote their claims. Traditional demonstration remains an option, but online claimsmaking is relatively inexpensive, and it has another key advantage. The Internet offers a means for causes that have relatively few proponents—people who in the past might have had trouble finding others who shared their concerns—to organize and rally around their issues. Individuals who only a couple of decades ago might have wondered whether they were alone, can now locate like-minded people and make a common cause with them. The three chapters in this part of the book illustrate different aspects of claimsmakers in our contemporary world.

In Chapter 4, Nancy Berns reminds us that claimsmakers need not be disinterested advocates. In fact, many claimsmakers have a vested interest in their causes; they speak out about what they consider troubling conditions in their own lives. If their claims succeed, not only are their own lives likely to improve, but they also stand to gain visibility, status, and influence from being recognized as successful claimsmakers. But other claimsmakers have an even more direct interest—they construct social problems in order to increase the demand for goods or services that they sell. Berns analyzes one set of interested claimsmakers—businesses that use websites to depict the grief that people experience when their pets die as a serious social problem, in order to sell pet grief–related products and services.

In Chapter 5, Victor Perez examines people who might seem to be more traditional claimsmakers—the parent activists who formed a social movement claiming that vaccines cause childhood autism. This movement faced considerable resistance from the medical establishment: most scientists and physicians agreed that the scientific evidence discredited the activists' claims that vaccines cause autism. Nonetheless, the movement continued to promote its cause, in spite of experts challenging its claims. Perez argues that the Internet played a key role in maintaining the movement; interlocking websites provided an electronic environment where the activists' claims could receive support, and where their opponents' counterclaims could be dismissed.

Finally, in Chapter 6, Tiffany Jenkins describes the success of an unlikely group of claimsmakers. In recent decades, there have been various calls to remove human remains from museum collections. Most often, these are skeletal remains found by archeologists and used by museums to show the physical characteristics or burial practices of different civilizations. In recent decades, protests by various tribal groups have called for the restoration of the remains of their ancestors. But what about those remains that might not have identifiable descendants? British museums contained many skeletal remains from ancient British sites, remains that had no identifiable descendants. However, a small group of self-identified pagans began to speak on behalf of some of those British remains, and Jenkins describes how some museums came to take these claimsmakers seriously.

These chapters illustrate the role of claimsmakers, but of course all of this book's chapters are in some sense about claims made by particular claimsmakers. It is useful to compare how different sorts of claimsmakers achieve more or less success in influencing what people think about different social problems.

4

The Pet Grief Industry: Framing the Problem of Pet Death

Nancy Berns

In your time of sorrow, may it comfort you to know, that on your heart remains an eternal paw print—and on your pet's is a hand print of love.
—New York Regency Forest Pet Memorial Park

Feeling bad that a pet has died is not a new emotion and caring for a pet's remains is not a new task. Generations of people have been burying pets in backyards or choosing other means to take care of an animal after death. However, the expectations for what you should do after a pet dies have changed dramatically in the past decade. A booming pet grief industry has shaped the death of pets as a particular social problem in need of specific services—those sold by professionals. Businesses attempt to frame pet death and subsequent grief as a problem involving moral, cognitive, and emotional factors that requires professional services and products to solve.

In the 1990s, Patricia Boyce (1998) conducted a qualitative analysis of pet loss. As if writing a blueprint for the future pet grief industry, Boyce explained the arguments for what soon became main themes in the construction of pet grief as a social problem. She argued that people lacked three important things related to pet loss: information on human-pet relationships, permission to grieve for a pet, and resources for grieving for a pet. The pet grief industry has tapped into these concerns in constructing the problem and framing it in a way that requires professional solutions. And this has happened relatively quickly. Although there were some businesses and cemeteries catering to pet owners in the past, most current pet grief businesses selling cremation, burial services, and memorial products started after the year 2000. In this chapter, I break down three components of the pet grief frame: grounds, warrants, and conclusions (Best 1990, 2008). The grounds identify the troubling condition, warrants tell us why we should care, and the conclusions explain what should be done about the problem.

Although individual pet owners, media, counselors, and others voice opinions about pet grief and death care, I focus on businesses that sell pet grief products and services. This study is based on an in-depth qualitative analysis of twenty-seven pet grief businesses, which were chosen based on the following criteria. First, they specialize in pet grief memorial products or disposition (burial or cremation) services. Second, they offer urns or caskets as part of their product line, which weeds out some of the smaller businesses that only offer a limited product such as a single pet memorial picture frame. The final criterion is geographical diversity. Using the nine US census regions, I chose three businesses from each area. In general, the analysis focuses on their websites, which are extensive in marketing their services and products.

The Grounds: Here Is the Problem

When constructing an issue as a social problem, claimsmakers need to establish the grounds that help define it. What harm is there? What kind of problem is it? Constructionist scholars have uncovered several strategies that claimsmakers use for framing a problem, including the construction of familiarity through piggybacking (Best 2008; Loseke 2003). Piggybacking is "when a new problem is constructed as a different instance of an already existing problem" (Loseke 2003, p. 61). By piggybacking onto the problem of bereavement over human death, claimsmakers can use familiar language and solutions to frame pet grief.

In the pet grief industry, an overarching theme is that pets are like people and are part of the family. The United States is not the only culture to treat pets as family. Elmer Veldkamp (2009) explains how pet funerals in Japan are increasing along with the idea that pets are family. There are two components to this claim that establish grounds for the social problem. First, pet grief is normal, natural, and devastating. Because pets are like family, losing them results in grieving for them that is similar to grieving for humans; second, pets need dignified endings that they may not currently be receiving.

Pets Are People Too

Pet grief businesses explain to pet owners that their grief is normal and natural. Memorials.com claims: "Grieving over a beloved pet is perfectly natural and should never be minimized or dismissed." The New York Regency Forest Pet Memorial Park states on its website: "It is important to understand that feeling sad over the loss of a pet is normal. The degree of pain we feel is different for each of us. We may experience some emotions such as grief, shock, anger, guilt, and loneliness. It is essential to recognize that any of these feelings are a normal response to loss."

Related to the argument that pet grief is normal and natural, many businesses claim that it is the same if not worse than grieving the loss of a human loved one. For example, according to Dignified Pet Services in Oregon: "Many times the loss of a pet companion comes as a shock to those who have shared in that life. A loss this significant can become one of the most devastating experiences we encounter in our lives, even as devastating as the loss of a close human family member." According to Georgia-based Dream Land Pet Memorial Center: "Most families feel the loss of a pet in the very same way they would feel the loss of a human family member, and sometimes more. Why? Because your pet's love was unconditional."

The main reason given for why pet grief is normal and as difficult, if not worse, than grieving for humans, is that pets are part of our family. "Pets are family too" or "pets are people too" are claims repeated persistently in the pet grief industry. One business in Illinois even uses such a claim in its name: Pets Are Family Too Cremation Service. Arizona-based Fairwinds Pet Loss and Memorial Services refers to its potential clients as "pet parents" and "pet families" and claims that people grieve for pets as much as they do for any other family member. Fairwinds invites clients to bring other "pet members of the family" to the funeral service.

Rolling Acres Memorial Gardens includes this question on its website: "Is it stupid caring this much for a pet?" The answer: "Absolutely not!! Many times in our lives a pet may have been the only one who really understood us or may have been with us at a time when no human was there for support. In many cases our pets are the only children we have and even the only family we have."

Pets Deserve Dignity After Death

Since pets are part of the family, they deserve the same respect and dignity after death that we give people. The founders of Heavenly Paws Pet Cremations in Kentucky reassure pet owners that they too are animal lovers and then instruct them with this message: "They [pets] are family members and dear friends. It is only right that we treat their passing with the same respect and dignity we reserve for our family members." Best Friends of Mississippi gives a similar message on its website: "Remembering the years of love and care given to our pets, and the lifetime of companionship and devotion returned, we cherish their memories long after their brief lives have ended. So when their lives are over, we want their final tribute to be as loving and dignified as possible."

These claims explicitly state that it is the responsibility of pet owners to make sure pets receive dignity and respect after death. The pet grief industry constructs pet grief as a social problem partly because, it is claimed, we cannot trust just anyone to take care of our pets. There is a sense of urgency and importance in these claims because "our pets deserve the best." Tennessee's Yeargan Pet Cremation Services tells potential clients that because pets cannot make final arrangements, "their final resting place depends entirely upon their owner's wishes to provide dignity and memorialization in return for the years of unquestioned love and devotion."

The pet grief industry has grown because of the assumption that people need to use professional services to properly take care of their pets. Constructing grounds for why pet grief and death care is a social problem includes the warning that more traditional ways of caring for pets after death are not proper for "family members."

Coleen Ellis is a leader in the pet grief industry and the owner of Two Hearts Pet Loss Center in Indiana. Ellis's story about why she started her business is described in an online article:

> It was then she [Ellis] discovered her veterinarian, like most throughout the United States, put euthanized animals in garbage bags and stored them in a freezer for up to one week. A disposal

company then picked up the bodies and brought them to a landfill, or crematory. "Those [pets] do not deserve to be in trash bags," Ellis said. "When we go pick up babies [pets], they are wrapped in blankets and put in caskets and treated like little people. Their body is given dignity and respect all the way through." (Mott 2007)

Rolling Acres Memorial Gardens also points out the problems with some methods of caring for dead pets.

> If you bury your pet in the back yard, you might consider that your backyard might not always be your backyard. It could be somebody's swimming pool or an apartment complex. Some people leave the disposition of their pet up to their veterinarian or the city. But there is no magical burial ground. Those pets are generally mass cremated (congregate cremation). In some areas of the country, they are taken to the landfill or the rendering plant.

The grounds for a problem assign blame and responsibility. In the case of pet grief, partial blame is placed on society at large for not offering enough support for pet owners. More traditional ways of disposing of pets' remains are framed as part of the problem. In the rhetoric of some businesses, veterinarians and local city ordinances are blamed for allowing the dumping of animal remains. However, the primary responsibility rests on individual pet owners to utilize the services offered through the pet grief industry. Pet owners are responsible for giving pets "proper endings" and for taking care of their own emotional health.

The Warrants: Why We Should Care

In framing the problem, the warrants tell us why we should care. Claimsmakers frame issues in a way that makes connections with peoples' emotional lives. Advocates for any issue need to elicit emotions and frame a social problem as a combination of cognitive and emotional factors (Berns 2011; Goodwin, Jasper, Polletta 2001; Loseke 2003). Arlie Hochschild defines feeling rules as "standards used in emotional conversation to determine what is rightly owed and owing in the currency of feeling" (1983, p. 18). Building on Hochschild's research, Donileen Loseke (2000) shows how advocates construct claims that can be easily recognized through widely circulating feeling rules.

Claimsmaking about pet grief draws on a range of emotional themes including love, hope, grief, fear, regret, and guilt. Industry insiders are not so much focusing on why owners should care about their pets, but rather on why owners should care about offering the particular "proper" and "dignified" services and products that the businesses provide. There are three main warrants constructed: (1) pet owners need proper services and support to help with grief and to find closure and peace of mind, (2) pet owners will regret it later if they do not take proper action now, and (3) pets can be kept forever.

Pet Owners Need Closure and Healing

The pet grief industry claims that pet owners will not heal properly without taking the proper actions after a pet dies. California-based Angel Ashes tells pet owners that the memorialization of their pet is a "basic human need." Owners of Memorials.com in Texas make an even more explicit connection to the pressure to spend money and a family's emotional health. "So today's experts—and just those who speak from experience of having lost a pet—highly recommend that, when you have lost a pet, the best thing to do for your families [*sic*] emotional health is to invest a few dollars in some sort of memorial and give your cherished friend a memorial befitting the treasured memories."

"Basic human need" and "emotional health" are general concepts. Most pet grief businesses refer to specific concepts within these broader categories. Frequent buzz words in this frame are "closure," "healing," "peace of mind," and "comfort." For example, Fairwinds says its services will "bring peace of mind to you and your family." Dream Land promotes "healing by providing professional services and quality products."

Sometimes closure is promised through a specific service or product. Angel Ashes states: "A memorial pet urn can help you achieve closure and give back a little of what your companion gave to you." Owners of Dignified Pet Services say: "A funeral, memorial service, burial, or placement of the ashes encourages healthy closure to the loss process." Pet Dignity Pet Funeral Services in Ohio informs visitors to its website that "pet visitation does not have to be a formal event although it may help people bring closure to the loss of your pet."

Pet Angel Memorial Center in Indiana offers an online "planning ahead guide" for pet owners who want to plan their pets' services before the pets (or owners) die. In this guide, "pet parents" are told that a ritual or ceremony will not end grieving but will help with healing. "It can provide a sense of closure, and help turn one's focus to the positive—to reinforce the wonderful memories, as a way to stem the tide of pain that comes from loss." In another online planning guide, from DeJohn Pet Services, "pet parents" are advised to prepare for the emotional toll that will follow the death of their pet. "Certainly none of us likes to think of that day, the day our heart will be broken into a million pieces. . . . Take this time to reflect upon what your pet will need in respectful death care treatment, as well as the support you will need as a grieving pet parent."

Pet Owners Regret Decisions About Pet Death Care

Horror stories and cautionary tales are common rhetorical strategies used in claimsmaking. These types of stories use extreme and disturbing circumstances to frame a problem. These strategies are found in pet grief claimsmaking, although not all pet grief businesses use them. The most common horror stories involve dead pets being disposed of in landfills, garbage bags, dumpsters, and rendering plants (places that recycle dead animals into products such as pet food). I gave a few examples of these horror stories in the section discussing grounds for the social problem. In warrants claimsmaking, similar stories are used but focus specifically on the regret and pain that the pet owner will experience later if proper action is not taken now.

In encouraging people to pre-plan how they will take care of their pets' remains, Tennessee-based Yeargan Pet Cremation Services shares a generic horror story to caution others about the risk of not planning:

> We have talked to many people who after recovering from their grief are extremely upset to discover that there are no magical burial grounds for pets. They do not know what has become of their little friend, or are fearful to ask. Perhaps in their moment of grief, a hasty decision was made and later could not be changed. We mention this fact simply because we want you to know that all of these decisions can be made in a period of calm . . . not crisis.

Other businesses warn pet owners to be careful whom they trust with their animal's remains, lest those remains end up in undesired places. This attempt at arousing fear may be combined with the claim about familial ties. Forever Pets in Minnesota claims: "Our pets are family members. If we don't bring them home, they are forever lost to landfills and other unfamiliar places." In the following quote, Nevada Pet Cremation combines fear and love in warning pet owners:

> Several who have had pets cremated recently cite discomfort at the thought of a dear pet's body being taken to the section of the local landfill that is reserved for such organic refuse. "It's the last ultimate service you can do for the animal you love," claims Las Vegan Ruth Jessop, 63, who recently ordered her fourth pet cremation. Vet services will tell a client they'll "take care of" a deceased pet, according to Jessop. "They'll tell you, 'We dig a communal grave.' They won't tell you, 'We put them in a big sack and take them to the dump.'"

PA State Pet Memorial & Cemetery has a link on its website to a horror story about an owner who regrets how he handed over two pets to a local veterinarian. Later, when opening his own pet crematory, he sent surveys to the veterinarians in the area:

> As I was reading through these surveys, one response hit me in the face like a sledgehammer. It was a response from the veterinarian who had euthanized [my pets] Brandy and Keasha. She had written a note at the bottom of the survey that stated that what we were providing sounded like a nice service but she didn't think she would have many clients who would be interested because most of them allow her to handle the disposition of their pet's body and that she disposes of the bodies by sending them to a rendering company. Most of us know these companies as "glue factories" where dead farm animals, road kill, waste from butcher shops or any other source of animal body parts, are cooked down and sold as protein for animal feed or used as fertilizer. I was horrified to know that this was the final end for my loyal companions. I blame myself for allowing this to happen, but at the time, I was very naive and trusting. I cannot change what happened to my pets but I can assure you this will never happen to my pets again. If it is important to you that your pet's final disposition be handled with dignity, respect and integrity, then you need to read this web site to educate yourself so this does not happen to one of *your* beloved pets. (Pet Owner Alert)

Similarly, owners of Memorials.com in Texas use graphic language to warn people about potential disposal methods. For example, they state "some reports say that many bodies of pets end up in rendering plants where they are mechanically stripped of their fur and flesh (sometimes while still wearing their collars and other such items), and each part ground up and churned into a variety of other products, ranging from fertilizer to, yes, pet food."

Horror stories are one way to connect emotionally with potential clients. Another emotion used is hope. After provoking fear for what might happen to a pet, businesses offer options for keeping a pet "forever" or having a happy reunion later.

Pets Can Last Forever

The promise of eternal life for pets is another emotional claim found in pet grief rhetoric. There are two general ways this promise is used. First, you will see your pets again in heaven, so you should treat them properly at death. Second, you can keep your pet with you forever if you choose the right products now.

The owner of Beloved Pet Cremation Service in Maryland tells pet owners that they will see their pets again: "If they were a tail wager [sic] before, you will see that again. If they purred on your lap before, you will have that again. And, in some manner, they will impart to you the feeling that you handled their passing away all right." The last part of this claim imposes more responsibility (and at least tries to raise guilt) for how pet owners treat their pets after death.

Some businesses explain that the actual memorial products will make eternal life happen. At Memorials.com, pet owners are told that pet memorials help families remember the legend about an animal's afterlife. The following quote from its website explains the legend and connects it to the products that pet owners can buy:

> Tradition has it that, when a pet dies, it travels across the legendary Rainbow Bridge, and ends up in a beautiful meadow where it frolics endlessly with all of the world's other deceased pets. When the pet's owner dies, then, his or her first stop on the way to heaven is across this same rainbow to the same meadow, where he or she is reunited with the pet. The two companions travel to heaven where they live together for eternity. A comfortable looking, inviting, pet memorial, no matter its form, will help bring this legend to life for a grieving pet owner, reminding the pet's owner that, as he or she buries the special friend, the two will one day be together again forever.

The pet grief industry offers hundreds of memorialization products specific to pets. I discuss specific claims and products in the next section, but point out here that the industry motivates people to buy products because this will allow them to "keep their pets with them." The claims raise the question: Why should you let go of your pet completely? The answer implies that through professional services and products you can keep your pet in your heart or even in your home forever. Testimonials from satisfied customers are posted on websites to reinforce the industry's claims. Pet Urns Unlimited in Michigan includes this quote from a customer: "I had my cat when I was in high school, he was such a good friend to me. He always talked to me everyday and I miss him dearly. Now I can look at him everyday when I am in the kitchen where he sits everyday. Thanks!"

Professionals in the pet grief industry target a genuine love that many owners have for their pets. I am not arguing that the pet grief industry created the bond between humans and pets. However, this industry is instrumental in changing what owners see as "proper" ways to treat pets after they die. The "proper" solutions are framed to show that professionals are needed to solve the problem.

The "Conclusions": What Needs to Be Done

Claimsmaking in the pet grief industry constructs pet grief as normal because pets are part of the family. Owners are told that this problem warrants their attention because they need to learn how to "properly" take care of pets who died in order to have closure and peace of mind, and because they cannot simply trust just anyone with this responsibility. These claims lead us to the question: What, then, should we do for our pets when they die? We already have been told that pets deserve the same kind of dignity and respect that we give other family members. But what specifically constitutes dignified and proper treatment for pet remains? How can I know that I gave my pet the very best care? And whom can I trust to help me through this difficult process? In their "conclusions," claimsmakers in the pet grief industry outline the answers to these questions. In general, their claims describe "dignified endings," the proper type of memorialization, and trusted and caring professionals.

Dignified Endings

In the marketing of the pet grief industry, people are told repeatedly that pets deserve a "dignified ending." Ohio-based Pet Dignity Pet Funeral Services reminds us "it is only right that we treat their passing with the same respect and dignity we reserve for our family members."

There is remarkable similarity within the marketing rhetoric in what constitutes "dignified" ways to treat pet remains. Dignified treatment, according to pet grief businesses, involves private cremations, formal services, quality caskets or urns, memorial products, and professionals who care. Handling of animals should be individual, intimate, caring, gentle, respectful, and loving. Undignified treatment would be communal cremation, informal backyard burials, landfills, plastic bags, cardboard boxes, or professionals who do not care. Handling of animals that is casual, anonymous, indifferent, or impersonal reflects disrespect for pets. In general, dignified endings are characterized as those that involve individualized care, superior products, and professional service.

The central theme in discussing dignified endings involves the choice of final disposition: what to do with a pet's dead body. Pet grief businesses emphasize the need to have a private cremation instead of a communal cremation in order to ensure a dignified ending for a pet. Of course, this is also the more expensive choice compared to other cremation options. As part of their description of private cremation, these businesses try to outdo one another in terms of the level of privacy they provide. Pet Dignity Pet Funeral Services offers only private as opposed to communal cremations. It highlights its personal delivery service as part of its claim for being more private, and thus more dignified, than other pet grief businesses:

> For many pet owners, cremation is a sensible option. We at Pet Dignity do *not* endorse *nor* practice "community cremation." Each cremation is a single cremation. Your pets cremains are 100% your pets [*sic*]. Pet Dignity offers service in which we do not use a postal service nor carrier to deliver your pets [*sic*] cremains. We make the delivery ourselves by our hearse to your home or cemetery. (emphasis in original)

Similarly, Pet Angel Memorial Center, though offering partitioned and group cremations in addition to private cremations, emphasizes the dignity of the latter. It claims that a pet deserves dignity and respect and therefore provides "personalized cremation services, featuring Truly Private Cremations in a compassionate, supportive setting."

Other pet grief websites choose their words carefully to persuasively frame their services. Angel Ashes tells owners to "request a 'private cremation' which indicates you do not want your pet's cremains commingled with other animals." In this example, "commingled" does not sound as loving as "private cremation." Forever Pets also uses specific language to place judgment and value on the different cremation options. Communal cremation is described as disrespectful: "Communal cremation is when multiple pets are simultaneously cremated and their ashes disposed of on private cemetery grounds or taken to a local landfill." Forever Pets's version of what it calls "private cremation" is the cremation of two to four animals at a time in a chamber, but with the animals separated by bricks. Added to the description is this: "the cremains are then generally processed in a commercial blender to attain a fine ash consistency and eliminate visible bone fragments." This is an accurate description of the process that is generally used after cremation, including the cremation of humans. However, it is interesting that the website provides this graphic detail for the group cremation option and then describes its most expensive and most individualized option differently: "Individual cremation, or Priority Cremation, is one pet in one cremation unit at a time. Pure and simple, it is what most pet owners expect."

Fluke's Aftercare in Maine warns pet owners about private cremation from other places: "Sadly, many owners, though having chosen private cremation, are not totally convinced that the cremains received are solely of their pet or are their pet's cremains at all." Fluke's then explains that it "allows attended cremations to alleviate any of these fears as well as offer emotional support during a very difficult time." Attending costs extra. Fluke's goes on to warn owners about what happens if you call the veterinarian's office:

> You leave your pet behind. Your pet will be picked up during a route, possibly several days after their passing. Ashes will be returned to you the next route day. For preservation purposes and because it may be several days before they are tended to, your pet will be placed in a chest freezer. They may be placed over other beloved pets or ultimately under other pets who are awaiting cremation.

Owners of Beloved Pet Cremation Service in Maryland provide a "certificate of cremation" to prove that a pet had an individual cremation. They describe this certificate as a very important document that needs to have very specific details such as a "real pen and ink signature" by the person who did the cremation with the exact times the cremation started and ended. They, of course, provide all this and say that anything less is not trustworthy.

Heavenly Paws Pet Cremations in Kentucky offers six different cremation options. For $350 you can purchase "The Tribute Package," described as "a perfect way to show your love for your lost family member," which includes a special urn, an engraved nameplate, a "Heavenly Paw" plaque, a picture frame, and a decorative cremation certificate. The price drops to $75 for the lowest-cost package, called "Communal," for which only this description is provided: "This option is a disposal service with no ashes or certificate returned."

Sometimes a business will gently warn pet owners about other issues to consider when choosing a final disposition. For example, Pet Angel Memorial Center poses a question in its "planning ahead guide" that raises concern about outdoor burials: "If we are considering burial, and my pet was an inside pet, will I/we be comfortable having my/our pet outside?"

Costs of pet cremation vary widely depending on the type of cremation and the weight of the pet. For example, a private cremation for a pet under 15 pounds might cost around $125, while for a pet over 200 pounds the cost can be more than $400. Pickup of animals and delivery of ashes cost extra, ranging from $75 to $400 depending on distance and time of day. The pet owner will also need to provide or buy an urn. There are opportunities (and extra fees) to attend a cremation or hold a viewing, memorial service, or candlelight vigil. Some pet grief businesses have an official "pet minister" for conducting a funeral or offering counseling, which is an extra charge. The pet owner can choose to have "professionals" scatter the ashes. Beloved Pet Cremation Service offers this service: "Our fee for the scattering of your pets [*sic*] ashes, using our special scattering urn, is $150 per hour, computed to the tenth of an hour. There is a $350 minimum fee for this service."

For those pet owners who do not choose cremation, some pet grief businesses offer burial services. In this case, many businesses advise owners to take elaborate precautions in preserving their pet's body. Pet owners are told to look for material that is "impervious to the elements" or "restricts seepage of water and the intrusion of air" in order to provide peace of mind. Best Friends of Mississippi offers a durolon casket and vault combination made from composite technology. It claims that "seamless construction creates a leak proof enclosure and the high impact material has a longer lifetime than metal or wood because it is impervious to the elements."

Pet Heaven Express in New Jersey says this about its caskets: "Each luxury pet casket is water proof and non-biodegradable. Our elegant luxury pet caskets will not deteriorate! They will protect your dogs and cats for eternity!" It offers four lines of caskets: Choice, Deluxe, Royal, and Imperial. The least expensive is the Choice pet casket and includes this description: "Plastic pet caskets. Cat dog rabbit caskets. Economy, cheap." Of course, even some of the caskets costing over $100 are labeled as "economy, cheap." The higher-end caskets, ranging from $250 to $650, are described using words such as "luxury," "elegant," and "velvet." The Imperial pet casket is the most expensive and is described as worthy of "the most special cat or dog." New York Regency Forest Pet Memorial Park offers several lines of caskets as well. Pet owners can choose among Deluxe, VIP, Beloved Pet, Oak Royal, Monarch, and Simplicity. The company's website, at the bottom of its casket page, reminds pet owners that "your pet deserves the best."

Memorialization:
Keeping Memories and Keeping Remains

Pet owners are told that they can keep their pet forever in their hearts and, in some cases, in their homes. The suggestions for memorialization focus primarily on the products and services that these companies sell. As Dignified Pet Services defines it: "The term 'memorialization' implies any number of ideas that help you cope with your loss and embrace the memory of a special relationship."

Products on the websites generally have descriptions that include the price but also the "priceless" things you receive along with the tangible item. For example, Fairwinds in Arizona offers a special "memory box" for $55:

> With the Pawprints Memory Box, you can create and beautifully exhibit an impression of your pet's paw in an elegant display that also stores and preserves his or her most precious keepsakes. Everything is meaningful when it comes to your pet. Use the Pawprints Memory Box to store those significant mementos including items such as their first collar, special photos, favorite toys, and the sweater they take their walks in. Keep them safe in this elegant display that is sure to be a part of the family for generations.

This description includes language that reflects care and beauty, such as "beautifully exhibit" and "elegant," and emphasizes the ability to keep a pet forever as "a part of the family for generations."

Pet grief businesses offer a range of memorial products with the claim that pet owners need these products in order to keep their pets forever in heart and memory. But why stop with just memories? Also offered are products that allow owners to keep pet cremains with them. The most common method is to keep pet cremains in an urn. An unimaginable number and variety of pet urns are available in wood, marble, glass, rock, plastic, or metal. Biodegradable urns are also available for purchase. There are even more options for the shape of an urn. If your pet had a sense of humor, you might want to choose a lightheartedly themed urn in the shape of a fire hydrant or a wooden box displaying a ceramic picture of dogs playing poker. The cost of an urn can vary from $50 to over $1,000, although typical urns cost around $100.

In addition to the urns, creative methods for carrying pet cremains have emerged. Pet Dignity Pet Funeral Services has one such new item: the key chain urn. The description states: "It is a way to carry your pets memories close to you. It is an honor, pets ask nothing and give everything. Choose a key chain urn to keep your pet family memories close to you and they will live on." At $20, pet owners are offered the ability to carry their pets wherever they go.

Alaska Bridge Veterinary Services advertises LifeGem, which is a company that turns pet remains into gems. "Wow. These gorgeous gems express visibly, the enduring love and memory of your pet in a manner quite unlike any other that we have seen. Please contact us for ordering details. These are real diamonds and their cost reflects that: $2,500 and up depending on carat." A newer item on the market is "DNA keepsake jewelry." Pet Urns describes the jewelry: "DNA is purified into a fine, silky web that captures a luminescent color tincture of your choice. You choose the color to reflect your pet's unique personality." Other businesses sell DNA jewelry, too, at prices ranging from $125 to $360.

Good Shepherd Pet Services, located in several Southern states, sells "memories" of pets. Memory glass—hand-blown glass pendants—hold pets' cremains inside and come in several forms. Because Good Shepherd only needs a small amount of ashes for each pendant, pet owners are encouraged to buy each member of their family a different pendant. Memory glass pendants start at $144. Other glass artwork that holds cremains costs between $250 and $350. Good Shepherd's "crystal companions" are created by turning cremains into crystal. Describing the crystal, the business states: "what a great way to treasure your pet and keep it safe forever." They also claim that owners can "crystal gaze" at their pets: "You can enjoy the special bond that you feel whenever you crystal gaze, knowing that your Crystal Companion is totally unique." The crystal companions cost between $700 and $1000.

Forever Pets in Minnesota offers Teddy Bear urns; now pet owners and their entire families can cuddle with deceased pets every night. "These beautifully made Teddy Bear urns are the perfect urn for those individuals looking for a huggable memorial which they can display and remember with daily affection." They can be purchased individually for $45.96 each, or as a "family pack" of three for $99.98.

Freeze-drying is another way to make pets last forever. Perpetual Pet in Florida offers such a service, and explains what to expect from a freeze-dried pet:

> Even from a distance of a mere couple of feet or so, it will be difficult to tell any difference at all, save the lack of movement. For this reason, we highly recommend a sleeping or at least lying down posture, which looks the most natural in the absence of movement. However, we will work with you to accommodate any other pose or special considerations you would like. Your pet will retain its original size and the shape in which it posed indefinitely. However, it will weigh much less than it did, due to the removal of the water and other liquids which account for the majority of an animal's weight. If not subjected to subsequent damage (dirt, spills, stains, weather, mistreatment, etc.) there should be no further change or deterioration. With a little care, your pet can be held, carried, transported, and even gently petted.

Freeze-drying is not cheap. According to Good Shepherd, which also offers freeze-drying, it costs $995 for a pet up to ten pounds and $70 for each additional pound. Freeze-drying the pet's head in an upright position costs an extra $340.

Freeze-drying businesses offer testimonials from customers to reinforce the notion that you can keep your pet forever. Here is one from another freeze-drying company, Anthony Eddy's Wildlife Studio: "She [Minnie] looks so perfect! I can't believe how perfect she looks. She's not messed up or dead looking at all. I can't wait to get Chip back and see him again. It's like we never lost Minnie at all in a way."

Trusted and Caring Professionals

After explaining what to do, most pet grief businesses construct explanations for why they are the perfect people to help. Claims focus on the need to have a professional who loves animals, has also experienced pet grief, and will treat pets with gentleness and respect. Personalization of claims is a common strategy used in claimsmaking. Rhetorical strategies of personalization within pet grief claimsmaking include owners' personal pet stories, customer testimonials, and assertions that the owners "care," "understand," "treat pets as their own," and offer "compassion."

Language that emphasizes gentleness and respect is important in not only describing these services but also in planting fears of alternative treatment. Dream Land Pet Memorial Center does not rely on pet owners making that connection on their own. On its website, Dream Land highlights its own delicate treatment of pets while discussing horror stories about how other people use plastic bags and group cremations: "Our staff will gently wrap your pet in their favorite blanket, always caring for them in a delicate manner. You can be assured that your beloved pet will never be placed in a plastic bag, treated with disrespect, or cremated with other pets. Your pet is special in our eyes and will receive the same treatment that we would expect for our pet during this painful time."

Frequently, pet grief businesses cite their own "pet ownership" and "pet love" as proof that they can be trusted. Louisiana-based Heaven's Pets tells people that every staff member "is not only a pet owner but a pet lover as well." Many of the owners of these businesses give specific examples of their own grief to lend credibility to their services.

Final Thoughts

This analysis has focused on the claims found in the pet grief industry for what people should do when pets die. There are other sources that broaden the scope of "dignified ways" to take care of pets after death. For example, some pet grief articles and advice columns advise people on how to do a home burial for a pet without needing any "professional" help. The resources that explain "do it yourself" options are not selling particular services or products related to pet loss but rather are typically only disseminating free information. In the same way, a broader analysis of pet grief resources reveals a wide-ranging list of memorialization ideas. And significantly, many of those suggestions cost little to no money. Some examples include planting flowers or a tree in memory of a pet, making a charitable donation, holding a family funeral service (without professionals), drawing a picture, making a clay sculpture, doing needlework, placing a pet's nametag on a key ring, writing a poem, composing music, creating a memorial photo album, writing a letter to the deceased pet, or framing a pet's photograph.

Although it is possible to find other narratives about pet grief and ways to take care of a dead animal, the claimsmaking within the pet grief industry is gaining a powerful presence on the Internet and in other self-help resources. Pet death care is following the path that our culture took with human death care. At one point, families used to take care of their loved ones in the home after death, but now the overwhelming majority of people rely on professional funeral directors to manage human death care. Those in the pet grief industry claim that professional pet death care is the sensible direction to go, since pets are people too. Professional organizations such as the Association for Pet Loss and Bereavement and the Pet Loss Professionals Alliance are growing in number and scope, which has further institutionalized the professionalization of pet death care.

In addition to the professionalization of death care, the industry shapes other "feeling rules," which are informal lessons we learn about how we are supposed to feel. One of the ways we learn about feeling rules is through cultural narratives found in stories and advice passed along through media, professionals, family, or friends. We use these narratives to make sense of our own lives and emotions. We attempt to manage our emotions and actions in an effort to look and feel the way we think we are supposed to feel and act in any given context. In the case of pet grief, businesses that sell products and services for pet death care shape expectations for how people should feel and act after a pet dies. People who read the claims made by the pet grief industry might come to believe that only professional services and products can provide dignified and respectful ways of caring for a pet after death. Furthermore, if we choose not to use these services or cannot afford them, the implication is that we do not (or did not) love our pets enough. And we are led to believe that failure to use these professional services may not only damage our own healing process but also jeopardize the mental health of our entire family.

Not everyone grieves the loss of a pet, but many do. The pet grief industry did not create the bond that some humans have with animals, nor has it caused people to feel sad about pets dying. However, the pet grief industry is shaping specific expectations for what are proper, loving, and dignified ways to care for a pet after death. This claims-making seems to be good for business, and the pet grief industry shows no signs of slowing down.

5

The Movement
Linking Vaccines to Autism:
Parents and the Internet

Victor W. Perez

Refusing to give up on our son, my husband and I spent hundreds of hours talking to any and all parents of a child diagnosed with autism, reading dozens of recommended books, watching countless hours of educational videos, and of course, surfing the internet constantly. We were determined that our beloved son would grow far beyond his label and that he would have a future that was wonderful and amazing despite his autism diagnosis. Early on, the most important step for us was to get busy. It was up to us, his parents, to make a difference for his future.
—Lisa Ackerman (2011),
founder of Talk About Curing Autism (TACA)

The Internet is a burgeoning source of information for persons researching health-related issues (Hardey 1999; Koch-Weser et al. 2010). After the primary-care physician, the Internet increasingly functions as the principal informational resource for parents committed to learning more about their children's health—including childhood autism spectrum disorder (ASD), the role of vaccines in its etiology, and possible treatments (Baker 2008; Poltorak et al. 2005; Sabo and Lorenzen 2008). Access to this online information has been hailed: "Families are now far more aware, well-informed, and self-empowered. They can utilize such tools as the Internet to inform one another of how to get a diagnosis and increase services for their children" (Marcum 2009, p. 34). However, parents who go online encounter a diverse, often contradictory array of information, claims, and counterclaims about ASD (Coates 2009; Hardey 1999, p. 821). While autism may in fact be "a complex syndrome without a uniform etiology" (Poulson 2009, p. 42), considerable attention online has nonetheless been given to the hypothesis that childhood immunizations cause autism.

This chapter explores how the Internet emerged as an invaluable resource for a populist social movement that challenged scientific consensus and framed autism as an instance of medically induced harm. Given the overwhelming scientific evidence debunking the vaccine-autism link, how do claims that vaccines cause autism persist and what is the role of the Internet in their perseverance? I argue that the networking capacity of the Internet allows unbridled, unfiltered claims-making across websites (Maratea 2009) and allows parents to validate their experiences with the onset of autism by sharing their stories online with others. The Internet serves as a venue for vaccine-critical parent organizations and nonexpert claimsmakers, who function as "movement entrepreneurs" (Earl and Schussman 2003, p. 157), to catalyze and sustain opposition to scientific consensus with their own forms of evidence supporting their claims that vaccines cause autism.

Background to the "Autism Epidemic"

Initially made visible by a vocal minority of vaccine-critical parents, the "autism epidemic" is known to a wide audience of parents and the general public. For readers who may not be familiar with the issue or the purported relationship between vaccines and autism, a brief summary is provided here.

Childhood autism gained considerable attention recently because of rapid increases in diagnosis and the controversy over the causes of these increases. Research suggests that current rates of childhood ASD are between three and four times higher than three decades ago, with some estimates ranging from 1 in 500 to 1 in 150 children diagnosed with an ASD (NIMH 2004; Perez 2010). Some recent reports suggest rates as high as 1 in 91 for US children ages three to seventeen in 2007 (Kogan et al. 2009); an average rate of 1 in 110 in 2006 was recently reported by the Centers for Disease Control (CDC 2010). This precipitous rise in prevalence fueled a debate over its cause; in particular, there has been disagreement about whether autism is a genetic disorder, the product of environmental factors, or a combination of both for susceptible children

(Poulson 2009), and about whether the increase in diagnoses reflects a real increase in the disease, greater awareness and expanding diagnostic criteria (Grinker 2007; Steiman et al. 2010), or diagnostic substitution for other mental disorders (King and Bearman 2009).

Though scientific evidence doesn't point to any single cause of autism, considerable popular media attention has focused on one particular group of claimsmakers: parent activists who argue that vaccines have caused the dramatic increase in ASD diagnoses (Matson and Minshawi 2006). In particular, concerns link the rise in autism diagnoses to the use of the measles-mumps-rubella (MMR) vaccine, the vaccine preservative thimerosal (containing a form of ethyl mercury), which was used in several vaccines until 2001 (but never in the MMR), and the concurrent increase in the number of vaccinations children receive early in life. It is important to understand that there is considerable scientific consensus that none of these explanations are sound, that vaccines do not cause autism. Nonetheless, activists claim that the MMR vaccine causes "gut inflammation and the release of autism-causing proteins into the blood and the brain," while also proposing that "the mercury [from thimerosal] in childhood vaccines damages the immune system and, possibly, the brain" (Begley 2009, p. 45).

Still other claimsmakers argue that the increase in the total number of vaccinations that children now receive early in life and in close temporal proximity, relative to thinner vaccination schedules in previous decades, explains the accompanying rise in autism diagnoses. The idea that "the simultaneous administration of multiple vaccines overwhelms or weakens the immune system [in young children] and creates an interaction with the nervous system that triggers autism in a susceptible host" has gained popularity in vaccine-critical organizations and across some online communities (Gerber and Offit 2009, p. 459). All of these claims, however, are rejected by prestigious medical institutions and have met resistance from scholars suggesting that the rise in autism diagnoses is actually a result of the broadening definitions of autism and the increasing readiness to apply autism as a label (Perez 2010).

Online Vaccine-Critical Claimsmaking as Popular Epidemiology

Though claims that the increase in ASD is attributable to vaccines garner almost no mainstream scientific support (Institute of Medicine

2011), some parents and professionals still avidly maintain this hypothesis (Fitzpatrick 2009):

> The Centers for Disease Control and Prevention, the Food and Drug Administration, the Institute of Medicine, the World Health Organization and the American Academy of Pediatrics have all largely dismissed the notion that thimerosal causes or contributes to autism. . . . Yet despite all evidence to the contrary, the number of parents who blame thimerosal for their children's autism has only increased. And in recent months, these parents have used their numbers, their passion and their organizing skills to become a potent national force. (Harris and O'Connor 2005)

The movement linking vaccines to the onset of autism promotes its claims through a variety of cyber-arenas (e.g., websites, message boards, blogs) (Kirby 2005; Mooney 2009). Online communities devoted to the issue of childhood autism span hundreds of sites, each providing a venue for claimsmaking and information dissemination, while also facilitating communication among members and prospective advocates (Maratea 2009). In short, parents who believe that vaccines cause autism find, in the Internet, the perfect venue to promote their claims, because it permits the perseverance of their claims even when they lack support from mainstream science.

The online activities of vaccine-critical organizations and parents resemble what Phil Brown calls "popular epidemiology,"

> the process by which laypersons gather scientific data and other information, and also direct and marshal the knowledge and resources of experts in order to understand the epidemiology of disease. . . . Further, it involves social movements, utilizes political and judicial approaches to remedies, and challenges basic assumptions of traditional epidemiology, risk assessment, and public health regulation. (1992, p. 269)

Vehement online claims that vaccines can cause the onset of childhood autism are largely based on evidence that comes from a confluence of parents and sympathetic professionals, at times working in tandem, investigating the issue through various advocacy organizations (Russell and Kelly 2011). In online venues, anecdotal evidence from parents becomes an integral component for understanding the causes of autism (ARI 2009a; Kerr 2009). This evidence has the propensity to obscure the boundaries of expertise. For instance, one parent posted online:

I had Christian when I was 19 years old. For the first year of his life I couldn't imagine anything being wrong with my baby. He smiled; he laughed; he rolled, crawled and walked on time. At age one he had a massive overload for his little immune system. He had two ear infections, a high fever, back to back treatment of major antibiotics and he was given his MMR, varicella and HIB [influenza] vaccines while he was still very sick. Christian faded away for the next 6 months. (TACA 2009b)

This example illustrates the sort of experiences shared online, with parents describing a typically developing child who "regresses" into autism after immunizations (Novella 2007), although critics note that such experiences are not typical for the vast majority of parents of children with autism (Fitzpatrick 2004, p. 72).

Parents, then, are key catalysts to vaccine-critical protest online. While opportunities exist for any movement to form online even around scientifically discredited ideas, claims about a vaccine-autism link rely on parents' embodied experiences with their children, which are given credibility. Framing autism as an injury caused by vaccinations, parents can share their experiences with each other online regarding their children's descent into autism. The structure of Internet networking allows for laypersons' involvement in the production of this alternative evidence that circumvents external scientific validation (Brown 1997; Pitts 2004).

Historically, there are several prominent cases of popular epidemiology in which laypersons' activities in identifying health risks in their communities steered the direction of science and informed scientific discoveries. Classic cases include toxic contamination of water wells in Woburn, Massachusetts, where some local residents claimed that this contamination caused higher-than-expected rates of leukemia in children; and the famed "Love Canal" case in upper New York state, where contaminated water seeped into basements and was subsequently inhaled by residents, causing illness (Gatrell and Elliott 2009, p. 213; Legator, Harper, and Scott 1985). In these cases, residents noticed that something was "out of the ordinary" about their community's health and took steps to find the causes; these were examples of successful citizen science movements.

These examples provide precedents for nonexperts within the autism community who make pronouncements to reaffirm each other's experiences and to persuade others that their parental experiences are valid. Though the social processes of prior environmental health movements resemble the movement linking vaccines to autism, one key difference is locale: parents who suggest that vaccines induced their children's autism are found across vast geographic spaces, but can easily connect to each other and to those who hold similar beliefs via the Internet. This, in turn, allows for ordinary citizens across an expansive area to fortify a shared allegiance to their cause and validate each other's perceived experiences with their children, further obfuscating the lines of expertise.

The Autism Collaboration as an Online Opportunity Structure

The Internet offers an online opportunity structure for the construction of social problems. Not only is it a venue with theoretically unlimited space for unrestrained claimsmaking, but social movements also benefit from the unique networking and organizational properties that the Internet provides (Maratea 2009). Hyperlinks that connect websites represent shared ties through social networks, even if the sites do not explicitly endorse each other or necessarily accept the information contained on one another's sites (Burris, Smith, and Strahm 2000; Maratea 2009; Park, Thelwall, and Kluver 2005). For example, one website that served as a collection of sites for this purpose was called the Autism Collaboration (AC), located at http://www.autism.org.[1] This page served as a central gateway or "digital hub" (Kahn and Kellner 2004, p. 87) to an elaborate network of interconnected webspaces, which together presented a unified front in the vaccine-critical movement, a collaborative effort to control and manipulate information pertaining to the dangers of vaccines, and an electronic vehicle for worldwide claimsmaking (Maratea 2009). This network offered a working partnership of sites that framed vaccines as one of the causes of autism, while advocating for parent-oriented and parent-driven research into vaccines' role in the onset of the condition.

Studying the Autism Collaboration as a Gateway Hub

Examining the online network of the Autism Collaboration will answer a few questions about the role of the Internet in the social problems process. First, how does a network of sites forge a collective identity and common purpose among its organizations and participants? It insulates them within an interconnected lattice of sites with shared perspectives and goals; this is a foremost consequence of the network. Second, how do sites within the collective control information about vaccines and autism? An important aspect of hyperlinking across sites is that sites can present selective information that supports their position while providing relatively few (if any) links to information contrary to their shared position. Third, how does corroboration between parents within this digital hub build solidarity among them and validate their experiences with the onset of autism in their children? Sharing stories validates the personal experiences of parents and, within the network of sites, these claims escape external validation by experts. Fourth, how does the Internet provide a forum for the investigations of nonscientific experts into their presumed causes of autism? As a deregulated forum, the Internet is the ideal place to marshal and disseminate lay investigations into troubling conditions and publicize, unfiltered, their findings.

My analysis identifies fifteen interlinked websites (including the AC hub) that promoted the view that vaccines cause autism.[2] Table 5.1 displays the name of each organization and website included in the research sample. The principle hyperlink structure of the AC, presented in Figure 5.1, indicates how sites were connected, if only by at least one hyperlink, to each other through the AC hub (i.e., as a mediating

Table 5.1 The Autism Collaboration: Analyzed Organizations and Websites

Organization	Website
Autism Canada Foundation	www.autismcanada.org
Autism One	www.autismone.com
Autism Research Institute (ARI)	www.autism.com
Autism Society of America	www.autism-society.org
The Autism Trust	www.theautismtrust.com
Generation Rescue	www.generationrescue.org
Medigenesis	www.medigenesis.com
Mindd Foundation	www.mindd.org
National Autism Association (NAA)	www.nationalautismassociation.org
SafeMinds	www.safeminds.org
Schafer Autism Report	www.sarnet.org
Talk About Curing Autism (TACA)	www.tacanow.com
Treating Autism	www.treatingautism.com
Unlocking Autism	www.unlockingautism.org

Figure 5.1 The Autism Collaboration: Hyperlink Network Structure

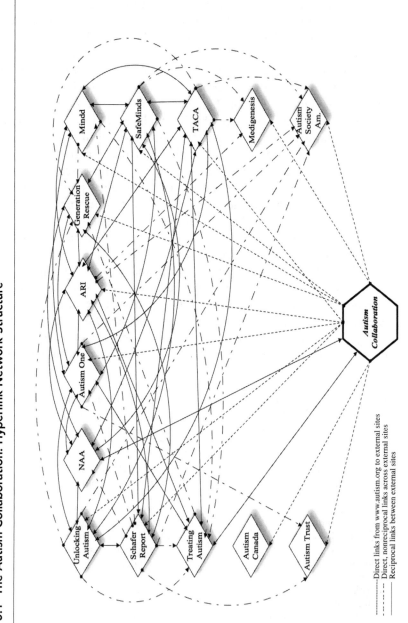

------ Direct links from www.autism.org to external sites
— — Direct, nonreciprocal links across external sites
——— Reciprocal links between external sites

site). The figure also demonstrates how individual sites were interconnected through their own direct hyperlinks to each other.

The hyperlink connections presented in Figure 5.1 reveal several important interorganizational features of the collaborative network of webspaces. Among the fourteen direct hyperlinks emanating from the AC to sites contained within the collaboration, there were only two sites (the National Autism Association [NAA] and Treating Autism, a United Kingdom–based site) that had direct connections back to the collaboration's hub, while a substantial number of interconnections between individual sites within the collective were present. As such, the AC functioned mostly as a gateway or "digital hub" for the sites included in the partnership (Kahn and Kellner 2004, p. 87; Maratea 2009).

Establishing a Collective Identity and Common Purpose Online

Supporters of a vaccine-autism link are likely to have some direct experience with autism spectrum disorder through an affected child (Baker 2008); online discussions, through hyperlinked sites and shared personal experiences, help establish a sense of collective identity and promote a communal position and purpose regarding the issue (Maratea 2009). Though several sites in the AC did not explicitly make the claim that vaccines cause autism, they often provided a profusion of information on studies that investigate the vaccine-autism link, informational guides regarding administration of vaccines, and recommendations for what needs to be done in order to correct what activists see as major problems with childhood vaccination regimens. For example, Talk About Curing Autism didn't dedicate substantial webspace for openly making claims that vaccines cause autism, but it provided resources suggesting the possibility that vaccines can play a role in the onset of the condition, contained resources on safety interventions for parents when considering vaccination, and had hyperlink connections to advocacy organizations (such as SafeMinds and Generation Rescue) that explicitly claimed that vaccines can cause autism.

The Internet facilitates communication across large geographic areas. This is particularly important because groups that organize for collective action use social networks as a means of uniting individuals with shared experiences and beliefs and strengthening ties among them

(Burris, Smith, and Strahm 2000; DiMaggio et al. 2001; Maratea 2009). This is visible in a statement from the Autism Research Institute, on its "our partners" page, regarding the Autism Collaboration:

> The Autism Research Institute (ARI) and the following organizations share common goals, objectives and dedication to the autism community. In an effort to expand outreach efforts and services to the autism community, ARI has agreed to establish working relationships with each of these organizations to achieve goals that they believe are important in improving the lives of those with autism. The goal of this collaborative effort is to capitalize on each organizations' [*sic*] strength, coordinate programs and services and to promote unity within the autism community. (ARI 2009c)

Instead of unaffiliated, disparate websites making claims in isolation, the collaborative network of sites allowed for a quasi-alliance to form (Clare, Rowlands, and Quin 2008; Maratea 2009, p. 76; Van Aelst and Walgrave 2002) that could support a social movement that stands in opposition to mainstream scientific evidence through "shared values, a common discourse, and dense exchanges of information and services" (Keck and Sikkink 1998, p. 2).

Though most sites did not direct users back to the gateway AC hub, several external webspaces included in the collaboration shared reciprocal ties to each other via hyperlinks, thus bypassing the need to use http://www.autism.org as a mediating link. As shown in Figure 5.1, in all, there were thirty-one reciprocal connections between sites, while there were also twenty-two direct, nonreciprocated hyperlinks across sites. Several individual websites, including ARI, the Schafer Autism Report (SAR), Autism One, Unlocking Autism, Talk About Curing Autism, and SafeMinds, though not sharing reciprocal links with the AC, did contain areas on their websites where they displayed a succinct list of most of the sites contained in the AC (largely including each others' sites) where users could navigate to these affiliate sites directly. For example, the site for the parent advocacy organization SafeMinds, along the side of its homepage, listed (as hyperlinks) several of the sites included in the AC, while TACA, introducing its affiliation as a "proud member" of the collaboration, employed a similar approach.

This grouping of hyperlinks together on a page allowed users to move directly to other sites within the AC rather than having to go back to the central gateway hub. This is a very important characteristic for the social problems process, allowing for multiple access points into the collaboration and its partnership of sites. This benefits sites that are not prominently displayed in more general Web searches, and allows for the presence of similar claims across these connected sites. The collection of sites reinforced their shared ties (explicitly stated or not) and subsequently fortified a collective strength by listing partners and collaborative allies in the vaccine-critical ASD social movement (Maratea 2009).

Controlling Information Online

Key advocacy organizations within the Autism Collaboration shared multiple reciprocal ties. Unlocking Autism, the NAA, Autism One, the ARI, Generation Rescue, SafeMinds, and TACA all had at least five reciprocal connections with other sites in the collective. In this way, the AC was used by claimsmakers to limit the variety of information received by users, highlighting the potential for users to receive all of their information within sites sharing the perspective of vaccine-induced childhood autism (Hardey 2001; Maratea 2009, p. 78). The outcome is that the advocacy organizations restrict audiences to searching for additional resources within the affiliate sites (a finite set of options), where member organizations can exert total control over not only the content, but also the claims that are presented and the ways in which these issues are framed (Maratea 2009, p. 78). Talk About Curing Autism, Generation Rescue, SafeMinds, and the ARI, all connected by reciprocal links, presented both information critical of mainstream science and information specifically supporting their cause, but had few links to other websites with information contradicting their shared point of view. Moreover, some of these organizations would include vaccine-critical information from another group's website in documents presented on their own. For example, TACA included in its own report of "Autism Studies & Related Medical Conditions" a press release from SafeMinds that was highly critical of the 2004 Institute of Medicine report denouncing any credible vaccine-autism link:

> In response to the failure of the Institute of Medicine-Vaccine Safety Committee to fulfill their duty to protect America's children, SafeMinds will be posting several press releases, studies and comments to highlight the flaws and failures of the commit-

tees [*sic*] report. Please feel free to search through the rest of this website to educate yourself to the scientifically proven dangers of Thimerosal/mercury in medical products, especially vaccines, and learn how your voice can be made heard to help remove this threat to America's children. (TACA 2009a)

Some suggest that the Internet is having a democratizing effect on the public sphere (Drezner and Farrell 2004; Rodman 2003); any individual with an online connection, in theory, has the ability to distribute problem claims and supporting information to widespread audiences at all hours of the day (Maratea 2009, p. 77). Although some research suggests that people seeking information about vaccines in general are likely to encounter antivaccine or vaccine-critical sites early on with popular search engines (Davies, Chapman, and Leask 2002), vaccine-critical advocacy groups ultimately have little to no control over where an individual chooses to explore the Internet for desired information. Nonetheless, by creating a compelling and informative protest network, such as the AC, vaccine-critical advocates can maximize the likelihood that audiences will be exposed to and internalize their message by creating multiple access points for receiving claims, raising awareness of core issues concerning vaccines and childhood ASD with selective information, and attempting to influence where users proceed for further information via hyperlink connections (Maratea 2009, p. 77).

Though it is unclear how users may react to attempts at information control, the presentation of claims within the partnership of websites suggests the likelihood of selective exposure (Klapper 1960): the more one acquires information about ASD from a single activist network, or from individual sites therein, the narrower an overall breadth of knowledge one is likely to obtain about the issue (Maratea 2009, p. 79). For example, critiques of mainstream medical institutions, such as the CDC, were present on several websites within the Autism Collaboration. Reprinting an editorial from 1999 on its site, the Autism Research Institute noted:

The CDC is deeply committed to increasing the number of vaccines that young children receive—about 35 doses of vaccines are already given before the child enters school. The MMR vaccine is in particular highly suspect, in both the U.S. and the U.K. In the U.K. there is a large class action suit underway by parents of vaccine-injured children. Asking the CDC to look into vaccine safety is like asking the fox to guard the chicken coop. (ARI 2009b)

Because activists cannot actually control where audiences search online for content, the existence of a unified protest network of inter-linked websites may serve to fortify allegiance to the larger movement among users who are particularly inclined to sympathize with the cause (e.g., parents of children with autism). By increasing the exposure to claims that vaccines cause autism and decreasing the need to search outside the network for more information, strategies of information control are potentially most effective among people who are already predisposed to support the movement (Maratea 2009, p. 80).

Although some sites did provide links to Internet sources that do not necessarily share their point of view, it was often in order to critically challenge the information presented on those sites. For example, the advocacy group SafeMinds published critical response papers denouncing peer-reviewed scientific studies that did not support a relationship between vaccination and the onset of ASD (see http://www.safeminds.org/research/commentary.html) (Maratea 2009, p. 78). In addition, vaccine-critical sites would often pit "our science" (i.e., vaccine-critical evidence) against "their science" (i.e., peer-reviewed scientific evidence) concerning the hypothesis that vaccines cause autism. Much of this began with the now retracted 1998 *Lancet* paper by Andrew Wakefield and colleagues:

> Most scientific opinion continues to dismiss the causal hypothesis. The Wakefield study was criticized for its scientific weaknesses; better-designed studies have failed to produce any evidence of a link between the vaccination [MMR] and autism. But Wakefield's supporters still offer lists of research besides his to support their position, and criticize the negative studies for *their* methodological weaknesses. (Richardson 2005, p. 132, emphasis in original)

Other sites that had similar reporting critical of science and public health agencies included the ARI, Autism One, TACA, and Generation Rescue. SafeMinds shared reciprocal ties with each of these other member organizations of the Autism Collaboration, facilitating the sharing of information and controlling perspectives—a key component of online protest (Keck and Sikkink 1998).

Corroborating and Validating Lay Experience

Popular epidemiology involves a process of nonexperts investigating the presumed causes of some illness affecting their community (Brown

1992). This type of community activism is the result of an affected individual (or individuals) noticing ill-health outcomes or conditions in themselves or their children. With a condition or diagnosis such as autism, one that has a relatively unknown etiology, claims that vaccines can cause autism likely resonate with parents who may have noticed the onset of their child's condition soon after a vaccination (Offit 2008). They perceive changes in their children analogous to the symptoms of autism and find others within the online community who report similar experiences (Poltorak et al. 2005). Although scientific evidence to the contrary is available from mainstream scientific outlets online, these parents "hypothesize something out of the ordinary" (Brown 1992, p. 269) as a result of their online encounters with vaccine-critical organizations and their members, and subsequently launch investigations into the issue.

Thus, an integral component of popular epidemiology is the lay contribution of experience and understanding as *evidence* to explain the onset of autism, as well as fostering lines of scientific inquiry in line with this anecdotal evidence (Brown 1992, 1997). In the movement linking vaccines to autism, the backdrop for parents' involvement in the causal understanding of its etiology lies in their shared, lived experiences, namely concerning the coinciding onset of the condition and immunization (Hardey 2001; Novella 2007). For example, Jenny McCarthy, a prominent activist and celebrity spokesperson for Generation Rescue, described the experience in one of her books by stating: "We [mothers] had healthy beautiful children who climbed up stairs perfectly until one stair caused them to fall. We have witnessed the neurological downfall of our children after certain vaccinations, but when we tell the doctors what we saw, they don't believe us" (McCarthy 2008, p. 21). For most parents, however, this involvement relies heavily on the Internet and its opportunity structure for claimsmaking. On the website for Generation Rescue, there are proclamations similar to McCarthy's about the shared personal experiences of parents, corroborating and validating their anecdotal evidence about the onset of autism: "Thousands of parents believe their child's regression into autism was triggered, if not caused, by over-immunization with toxic ingredients and live viruses found in vaccines. The Centers for Disease Control and the American Academy of Pediatrics dispute this but independent research and the first-hand accounts of parents tell a different story" (Generation Rescue 2009a).

Though concerned parents have been successful in encouraging epidemiological studies of immunizations and ASD (Offit 2008) and have produced research of their own (see Perez 2010), the great majority of peer-reviewed scientific evidence invalidates their beliefs about the onset of autism. Thus, many vaccine-critical claims coming from parent and professional autism activists are framed in ways that openly challenge mainstream medical and scientific evidence and authority. The Internet has been an integral venue for disseminating this anecdotal evidence, such as the personal narratives posted online by parents. The decentralized nature of the Internet makes it better suited than traditional media formats for promoting radical medical and health perspectives (Fox, Ward, and O'Rourke 2005; Gillett 2003). Individual webspaces in the Autism Collaboration allowed activists to collectively validate their experiential evidence (i.e., affirm their knowledge or belief of the cause or causes of childhood ASD) and thus openly challenge at least some mainstream sources of scientific information (see Barker 2008; Furedi 2006).

Whether sites shared reciprocal links within the collaboration, or simply were included in the collective (i.e., some sites did not share many links to other sites), users may have gained a sense of cohesiveness and solidarity when navigating the AC (Maratea 2009). When users can read about others who may have had similar experiences, and also obtain a variety of other vaccine-critical resources from these affiliate sites, there is potential for their subjective understandings of autism onset to become "truth" (Schaffer, Kuczynski, and Skinner 2008). Much of this anecdotal knowledge, though, falls outside of the parameters of scientific standards of proof (Brown 1992; Schreibman2005). Within the virtual community of the AC, the ability to disseminate activist-generated anecdotal experiences provided for corroboration and, subsequently, validation of users' shared experiences of watching typically developing children regress into autism after vaccinations. In turn, this likely served to legitimize the contention that there is a causal relationship between vaccination and the onset of ASD symptoms. For example, the UK-based advocacy organization Treating Autism provided a page for "Parents' Stories," where it stated:

> Most of the parents of Treating Autism began the process of helping our children by listening to the stories of other parents, noticing similarities with our own children and our own experiences and proceeding from there to explore possibilities in treatments and therapy optons [*sic*]. We gain insight and direction from each

other's stories, and also hope, as well as admonitions and warnings. The parents' stories here have been generously shared by people who have seen improvements in their children's overall health and behaviour through the use of various biomedical interventions. (Treating Autism 2010)

Similarly, Mindd and Generation Rescue had areas within their webspaces for users to read about parents who may have had similar experiences concerning their children's autism and its treatment, and sometimes areas for users to contribute narratives, while Autism One had an interactive blog and a dynamic community forum facilitating user input. All of these sites are within the AC network, denoting their shared, mutual affiliation (even if only because they're included), and are connected to each other by both one-way and reciprocal hyperlink ties.

Nonexpert Marshaling of Science

Mercury. Aluminum. Formaldehyde. Ether. Antifreeze. Not exactly what you'd expect—or want—to find in your child's vaccinations. Vaccines that are supposed to safeguard their health yet, according to our studies, can also do harm to some children. (Generation Rescue 2009a)

In the early to middle 2000s, some parents who espoused the hypothesis that vaccines cause autism were not only critiquing the existing scientific literature, but also conducting and promoting their own studies reinforcing the plausibility of this claim (see Bernard et al. 2001; Blaxill 2004; Blaxill, Redwood, and Bernard 2004). Several of the groups included in the AC, such as SafeMinds, Generation Rescue, and the ARI, were founded by or included key members who are parents of children with autism and have been involved with actively producing or gathering research. Though some of the early investigations and claims were being published in a handful of printed journals, a significant amount of information produced by vaccine-critical organizations and activists was and continues to be disseminated through the Internet.

On its website, Generation Rescue had available several visual displays illustrating their position that vaccines can overload a child's body with toxins and induce neurological problems. One chart, in the form of two parallel hypodermic needles, compared the number of vaccine administrations given in 1983 relative to the number given in

2008 to suggest that contemporary vaccination regimens, which include more vaccines and administrations than in previous decades, caused the increase in autism diagnoses (Generation Rescue 2009a). In another visual display, a bar chart compared numerous countries and the total number of vaccines children receive in each, and concluded that the United States has "the most bloated vaccine schedule" with the most number of vaccines relative to all of the other twenty-nine countries listed (Generation Rescue 2009c).

A substantial effort at more rigorous research by Generation Rescue involved working in tandem with an independent opinion research group surveying families in California and Oregon. Deemed the "Cal-Oregon Vaccinated vs. Unvaccinated Survey," the organization performed a telephone survey of both families whose children had been vaccinated and those whose children had not and compared the neurological health outcomes of these children (Generation Rescue 2009b). Ultimately, based on data on more than 17,000 youth aged four to seventeen in selected California and Oregon counties, Generation Rescue suggested that vaccinated boys are more likely to be diagnosed with autism, as well as other neurodevelopmental disorders, relative to those who are unvaccinated. This survey, though of questionable item validity, sample generalizability, and utility in drawing epidemiological conclusions, is a genuine example of direct involvement of parent-oriented advocacy organizations in ushering scientific inquiry, encouraging others to follow suit, and using the Internet as a forum to promote their claims. As Generation Rescue stated on its website in discussing the findings:

> Generation Rescue is not representing that our study proves that the U.S. vaccine schedule has caused an epidemic in neurological disorders amongst our children. We are a small non-profit organization. For less than $200,000, we were able to complete a study that the CDC, with an $8 billion a year budget, has been unable or unwilling to do. We think the results of our survey lend credibility to the urgent need to do a larger scale study to compare vaccinated and unvaccinated children for neurodevelopmental outcomes. (Generation Rescue 2009b)

These efforts at producing evidence to demonstrate the viability of the hypothesis that vaccines cause autism are in line with discussions of activists being intimately involved in the search for and production of knowledge, "pressing for official corroboration" of their findings (Brown 1992, p. 272) while seeking widespread acceptance of their beliefs (Furedi 2006, p. 15; see also Ryan and Cole 2009).

Conclusion

Given the overall lack of mainstream scientific support for claims that vaccines induce childhood autism spectrum disorder (Institute of Medicine 2011; Novella 2007), it is particularly important to better understand how the Internet played a central role in the development and persistence of these claims, and subsequently in the success of this issue as a social problem. Vaccination rates have dropped for some groups, which is plausibly attributable to the successful claims-making activities of vaccine-critical organizations and activists on the Internet (NCQA 2010).

My analysis of the Autism Collaboration shows that hyperlink networking capacity played a fundamentally important role in the development of the vaccine-critical ASD movement online, and that it facilitated most aspects of what Phil Brown (1992) called "popular epidemiology." Of chief importance is the ability for professional and parent activists to strategically produce, disseminate, and exchange—online—alternative information, experiential accounts, and other claims supporting their hypothesis. In a network of interconnected webspaces, the authority of scientific evidence is pitted against the personal experiences of some parents, where the "network has the potential to allow lay people to mount a challenge to the medical profession's control over information and resources" (Lupton 2003, p. 140). As such, the Internet provides a conduit through which parents of children with an ASD diagnosis and professionals who work with them can collaborate from locations all over the globe to actively communicate, establish relationships, construct identities, and foster scientific investigations in line with their beliefs about the causes of autism (Gurak and Logie 2003; Maratea 2009, p. 60; Nip 2004).

By exploring the online presence of one area of vaccine-critical activism, this research suggests that online technology can help unorthodox, niche movements persist by utilizing organizational tactics of hyperlink connections among advocacy webspaces that coalesce online into an informal, yet unified, collective of claimsmaking entities dedicated to a mutual cause (Maratea 2009). In particular, examining the Autism Collaboration offers a historical case study to demonstrate the role of the Internet in helping protest movements that oppose scientific consensus persevere. We might expect to find similar patterns in other claimsmaking campaigns, including those regarding climate change, intelligent design, creationism, HIV denial, and others.

There is a tendency for "medical victims" to catalyze the social problems process by lobbying for action in relevant ways; for the vaccine-autism issue, that involves the pursuit and production of alternative health data, and the Internet is increasingly vital for this (Conrad 2007). Often, those involved in such movements favor anecdotal evidence over traditional epidemiological evidence that does not validate their experiences (Gatrell and Elliott 2009). Ultimately, the social movement to keep the vaccine-autism link in the public spotlight and regarded as a legitimate hypothesis was able to advance because of the underlying structure of the Internet and its capacity for networking and information dissemination. Providing a needed catalyst to evolve vaccine-critical protest into a social movement and full-fledged social problem, the Internet served as a conduit for independent organizations and vaccine-critical parents to organize into something of a unified, online protest network (Maratea 2009, p. 68).

Notes

Earlier versions of this work were presented at the 2009 annual meeting of the Society for the Study of Social Problems and at the 2010 annual meeting of the Eastern Sociological Society. I thank R. J. Maratea, Melinda Goldner, and Annette Lareau.

1. Principal analysis of the Autism Collaboration network took place in November and December 2009, but some preliminary browsing and limited data collection were performed periodically earlier in 2009 and also in 2010. When this research was performed, http://www.autism.org was the Web address for the Autism Collaboration. After the data were collected, the Autism Collaboration updated its site and changed its organizational name to the Global Autism Collaboration, although its Web address remained the same. Data presented here are relevant to the time period in which the analysis was conducted, but do not include the current organizational structure of the Global Autism Collaboration. As such, this is a historical case study.

2. A complete description of the design, procedures, and limitations of the analysis is available from the author. Though attempts were made to update Web links when needed, some of the referenced links may no longer be functional.

6

Old Skeletons, Pagans, and Museums: Why Ancient Human Remains Are a Bone of Contention

Tiffany Jenkins

Since the 1990s, human remains in British museum collections have been the focus of numerous controversies, with activists demanding that bones and bodies be repatriated to the indigenous groups with which they are considered to be affiliated. Thus a tribe might have returned to them remains in an institution once taken from some ancestral gravesite. In the late 1990s, the debate over the ownership of human remains came to dominate the museum sector in Britain, and received extensive coverage in the national media, before achieving changes in museum practice and legislation. A pagan group, Honouring the Ancient Dead (HAD), subsequently formed and claimed ownership over ancient British remains. Campaigning for respectful treatment, as well as for reburial, HAD was able to achieve some success in changing museum practice.

I begin the chapter by discussing the background to the controversy over human remains and explain how it developed into a prominent issue. I focus on an important group of activists who were from the museum sector, their use of rhetoric, and how they associated their cause with other high-profile issues, giving it a sense of urgency. I then examine a different group of activists—those from HAD—and how they were able to achieve significant influence over the treatment of human remains in museums, despite not being recognized as legitimate activists by broader society, nor by many in the museum profession. Under the right conditions, even pagans, an otherwise marginalized minority, can shape organizational policy.

Human Remains in Museum Collections

Museums have collected, studied, and displayed human remains since the eighteenth century. Before the nineteenth century, collection of human remains was eclectic. They were exhibited as curiosities obtained by explorers, colonial officers, and traders. Throughout the nineteenth century, greater numbers of human remains were gathered by scientists on collecting expeditions, or from the British colonies, motivated in part by a desire to preserve material from what were considered to be vanishing races (Greenfield 2007). The specimens in museums were categorized and presented as part of scientific, ethnographic, archeological, or medical classification systems, through a shift in an idea of what the purpose of the museum should be. With the Enlightenment, the museum developed into a rational authoritative space. This, together with the emergence of the scientific view of the body, permitted human remains to be treated as research objects. Human remains held in British museums today are diverse in kind and purpose. A study showed that of the 148 English institutions surveyed, 132 held human remains (DCMS 2003b). Overall, these numbered approximately 61,000, although the individual numbers varied widely from institution to institution. The Natural History Museum in London held the greatest number: a research collection of 19,950 specimens, ranging from complete skeletons to a single finger bone, and representing the global human population and a timescale of 500,000 years. The majority of other institutions mostly held small collections: sixty-four museums had fewer than fifty items each. Of the 61,000 human remains in British collections, roughly 15,000 were from overseas; the remainder were from the British Isles. Of the institutions surveyed, thirty-five stored most of their collections, whereas eighty-nine had most or all on display. Of the historical human remains from the period 1500–1945, the most common on display were organized and exhibited in contexts that included archeology, anthropology, anatomy and pathology, and Egyptology, which overlap but have distinct approaches. These exhibits have included excavated burials and cremations, as well as shrunken heads and objects such as drinking vessels made from skulls.

The Emergence of Claims over Human Remains

Despite their common use, since the 1980s human remains in collections have become subject to a growing number of claims and controversies in different countries. Indigenous groups in North America, Australia, Canada, and New Zealand started to demand the repatriation of human remains that were considered culturally affiliated or associated to them. Many—including physical anthropologists and scientists who research the material professionally—forcefully opposed the repatriation requests for the human remains, because they are important and even unique evidence of the past. Beginning in the late 1980s, however, despite opposition from scientific quarters, codes, policies, and laws were instituted that advised a sympathetic response to claims of ownership. For example, with the passage of the National Museum of the American Indian Act of 1989 and the Native American Graves Repatriation Act of 1990 in the United States, legislation compelled the inventory of human remains (and associated material) from all federally funded institutions and their transfer to lineal descendants.

The contestation over human remains in collections in Britain became prominent in the late 1990s. It had different influences over the controversy in other countries. One of the most important observations is that there was significantly weaker external pressure on British institutions compared to those in Australia, the United States, and Canada, which did respond to claims for repatriation from indigenous groups. In Britain, a survey conducted for the Human Remains Working Group, a government-appointed committee formed to advise on change to practice and legislation regarding treatment of human remains, characterized ownership claims from overseas indigenous groups as "low" (DCMS 2003a, p. 16) and found that only thirty-three such claims had been made in the United Kingdom, seven of which had already been agreed to, and some of which were repeat claims from the same indigenous group. This lack of significant pressure from overseas indigenous groups partly explains why it took longer for the issue to become important in Britain compared to elsewhere.

To understand why it did become prominent when it did, we have to look to causes other than pressure from overseas indigenous groups.

Museum Professionals: Unlikely Claimsmakers

It is important to first examine who the campaigners were. Before the pagans, there was another set of campaigners who became influential—professionals from the museum and heritage sector. These included Tristram Besterman, a museum director; Cressida Fforde, an archeologist; Maurice Davies, deputy director of the Museums Association (the professional body for the sector); Jane Hubert, an anthropologist; and Moira Simpson, a museologist. Indeed, one the most important observations about the contestation over human remains in Britain was that it was waged less by campaign groups external to the sector than by insiders. Senior curators, directors, and policymakers within the sector have been instrumental in constructing various aspects of the holding, display, and treatment of human remains as problems.

This is especially interesting because museum professionals are an unlikely group. In campaigning for repatriation, senior professionals participate in activities that result in the removal, at times, of highly valued material from research collections. They appear keen to highlight the negative historical legacy of colonialism, its deleterious impact on communities, and the role that museums have played in this. But until recently, members of the sector would not advocate the removal of valued material from museum collections, nor would they critically question the role of the museum sector. They were the gate-keepers of such institutions, guarding the collections. What, then, did these activists hope to achieve by questioning the role of the museum and promoting repatriation—an act that appeared to alter, even undermine, their own role and status? Why did they participate?

Those examining the construction of social problems identify and explore the claimsmakers' interests in promoting an issue. Joel Best (1990) observes that claimsmakers may stand to acquire more influence, or that there may be indirect symbolic benefits that contribute to explaining their activism. In the case of human remains, we have to look at broader trends in museums and society to understand why the activists are campaigning the way they are.

Traditionally, museums play a role in affirming ideas about the pursuit and organization of knowledge, for reasons that are historically constituted. While aspects of the museum as an institution can be traced back to the medieval Schatz, a treasury of goods collected by the Habsburg Monarchy, or to private collecting in the Renaissance, it is the development of public collections in the eighteen and nineteenth centuries that rationalized the transformation of private collections into public. And with the Enlightenment, ideas developed about the absolute character of knowledge, discoverable by the methods of rationalism and its universal applicability, that informed the purpose of the museum and the rationale of the display of artifacts. But since the 1960s, the traditional justification of museums has been criticized.

The central tenets of the Enlightenment, which informed the remit of the museum in the eighteenth and nineteenth centuries, have been called into question (Bauman 1987; Foster 1985). While there was always hostility toward the principles of this period, a number of intellectual trends since the late 1960s have consolidated this critical outlook, challenging the claims to objective knowledge and the idea of the museum as a distinct realm removed from social and political forces (Furedi 2004). Postmodernism, cultural theory, and postcolonial theory have variously challenged the traditional justifications of the museum. With the rise of postmodern and postcolonial theories, culture and science came to be viewed not as universal or objective, but as a damaging reflection of the prejudices of European cultures. Major debates over objectivity, truth, culture, and relativism were rapidly assimilated into museology by theorists and practitioners. Until the 1980s, examination of the social and educational role of museums was marginal. This shifted dramatically later in the decade when a body of work developed criticizing the idea that museums are value-free, arguing instead that they are inherently political. Pierre Bourdieu's 1984 book *Distinction: A Social Critique of the Judgement of Taste* was a catalyst for this approach. Bourdieu developed the idea that cultural discernment was a marker of class position and that visiting galleries was a way to indicate taste and class. Cultural tastes were really influenced by primary and secondary socialization processes rather than a response to universal values of truth or beauty, he argued.

As a consequence of these intellectual shifts, the outlook of the earlier period that informed the role of museums—to validate the superiority of modern reason, to make judgments, to pursue the truth, and to claim to pursue the truth—has been discredited. The development of museums in Western societies, it has come to be argued by a wide group of museologists and practitioners, occurred in specific historical circumstances and actively supported the dominant classes, thus maintaining the status quo as natural, which is a problem because this serves the interest of only a narrow elite. While there are significant variations in this approach, I argue that the challenges to the historical claims to objectivity and truth have been internalized and promoted by academics and professionals. This is why many are involved in critiquing their institutions' past. The creation of controversy over the repatriation of human remains is one of the ways these academics and professionals are trying to find a new role. By repatriating human remains, museums are distancing themselves from a mission that is research-centered and moving toward a purpose that is more about helping communities and involving diverse groups of people.

Effective Use of Rhetoric

The campaigners had to convince other, resistant professionals as well as figures in cultural and political circles that the retention of human remains was a problem and that these remains should be repatriated to their communities. In order to do so, the campaigners used language effectively to make their demands seem urgent and important. Returning human remains to their communities, it was argued, would make amends for the dreadful circumstances of how they were taken in the first place. Claimsmakers spent considerable time outlining how the original acquisitions had been harmful. Activist Moira Simpson described "the removal of bodies from battlefields, the theft of bodies from mortuaries, graves, burial caves and other mortuary sites" (1996, p. 176). Tristram Besterman argued that "the collections in our Western museums derive, at their most innocent, from grave robbing, and at their worst, from wholesale slaughter" (IoI 2003, p. 3). A submission to the Working Group on Human Remains read: "The Working Group, may, for example, wish to examine as a case study . . . remains such as those currently held by a UK museum that are Australian Aboriginal individuals killed in a "'punitive expedition'" in 1920. The leader of the expedition boiled down the bones of the massacre victims after slaughter was complete in order to prepare them as museum specimens" (Fforde 2001, p. 4). In this excerpt, archeologist and activist Cressida Fforde uses an especially graphic case to illustrate the treatment of individuals whose bones were then given to museums. The words "boiled," "massacre," "victims," and "slaughter" were all forcefully employed to suggest that this is how museums obtain their collections. The use of the word "specimens" implies that people are killed in order to be used as objects in museums.

A similar account, which appears to refer to the same case and employs the use of numbers, was included in a newspaper article in the important national newspaper the *Guardian.* Statistics or numbers are often an important element in building an argument. This excerpt shows how the number of remains in museums became a rhetorical tool for campaigners: "The Natural History Museum's collections (of 20,000 body pieces) include a skull and leg bone from a 25-year-old man shot in 1900 in a punitive expedition near the Victoria River, Australia. The bones were prepared for a collector on the spot, with the skin boiled off in a pot" (Morris 2002, p. 15). Here, the author—who at that time was the editor of the *Museums Journal,* the magazine for the Museums Association, describes the remains using empathetic and emphatic language—"body pieces" instead of "specimens"—in highlighting a relatively recent artifact. A striking comparison is the following description of the same collection, produced by the Natural History Museum: "The Natural History Museum holds the national collection of human remains, comprising 19,950 specimens (varying from a complete skeleton to a single finger bone). The remains represent a worldwide distribution of the human population and a timescale of 500,000 years. The majority of the collection (54 percent) represents individuals from the UK" (NHM 2006, n.p.).

Activists referred to the large number of body parts in institutions, instead of the small number of requests for return, to suggest that the scale of the problem was great. Crucially, there was no mention of the small number of recorded requests (thirty-three) from communities seeking repatriation. The implication in the *Guardian* article is that the 20,000 body pieces are suspect and may have been acquired in a fashion similar to that of the skin that was boiled off the body of the twenty-five-year-old man. The reference to "body pieces" in the *Guardian* article, as opposed to the Natural History Museum's use of "human remains," was rhetorically more effective.

Creating Links to Prominent Political Issues

Campaigners linked the issue of human-remains repatriation to other issues that were commonly accepted as problems and portrayed prominently in the media and public arena. This linkage suggested that the issue of human-remains repatriation was of comparable worth and merited the same concern and attention. In the early 2000s, those campaigning for the repatriation of overseas remains associated their cause with the Holocaust and the work of plastinator and bodies exhibitor Gunther von Hagens, whose exhibits of human bodies had caused a stir and met with divided reaction (Jenkins 2010). However, the event that had the greatest impact on the debate was the association of human-remains repatriation with the controversy over the retention of children's body parts at Alder Hey hospital in Liverpool and at other hospitals. In early 2000 there were a number of controversies over the retention of children's body parts by hospitals, after a medical scientist who gave evidence in 1999 to the Bristol Royal Infirmary Inquiry, set up to investigate the quality of pediatric cardiac surgery, made reference to a large collection of children's hearts stored at the Royal Liverpool Children's National Health Service Trust (the Alder Hey hospital). The storing of children's body parts was picked up by the media and presented as a scandal, and a major controversy broke, including a group of parents who protested about the retention of their deceased children's hearts, of which they were previously unaware. Subsequently the Bristol Royal Infirmary Inquiry (2000) and the Royal Liverpool Children's Inquiry (2001) investigated the circumstances leading to the removal, retention, and disposal of human tissue, including children's organs. The inquiries established that organs and tissues had been removed and used without what was considered proper consent. The controversy dominated the media and political debate for months.

Repatriation advocates associated their cause with this prominent issue, high on the political and media agenda, which raised questions about how contemporary body parts were acquired, stored, and used by the medical profession and by artists. In the early 2000s, campaigners began to refer to the body-parts controversies in their writing, papers, and speeches on the need for repatriation, focusing on events at Alder Hey. The parents had been treated with a great deal of sympathy, and activists tried to suggest that indigenous groups felt the same way as the parents, implying they shared a common cause.

Campaigners Cressida Fforde and Jane Hubert wrote that "this desire to bury the remains of a relative appears to echo the responses of indigenous people, who have for many years been trying to take home the various human remains of their own dead, to dispose of them with due rituals" (2002, p. 14). This, in turn, is recognized in the official report from Britain's Working Group on Human Remains, a government group appointed to advise on legislation changes, which also suggests equivalence between the "distress" experienced by parents and that experienced by indigenous groups: "The Working Group feels that there are strong resonances between the recent distress suffered by the relatives involved in the Alder Hey revelations and the distress of those indigenous peoples who are still mourning the loss of their ancestors taken from them decades ago" (DCMS 2003a, p. 81).

Linking to these controversies gave the issue of human-remains repatriation greater weight and credibility as a problem. The Working Group's description of the removal of remains as having happened "decades ago" is noteworthy. This description is not wrong in a formal sense, but it makes it seem as if the remains were taken more recently than 200 years ago, which is the correct timeframe. It is more dramatic to give the impression that the remains were taken in recent times.

Pagan Claimsmakers

Paganism is understood to encompass several recognized sets of beliefs. Graham Harvey and Charlotte Hardman (1995) explain that the important shared ideas are the centrality of nature and the limits of one authority. Sociologist Jon Bloch echoes this observation about the perceived limits of authority and a critique of dualistic thinking, positing that the self is considered to have final authority as to what to believe in countercultural spirituality, which legitimates a "pick and choose" attitude toward different beliefs and religions (Bloch 1998, p. 33). Hardman and Harvey (2000) identify contemporary cultural influences, explaining that while paganism has had, for at least a century, an environmentalist philosophy and a romantic view of the land, this has become more coherent in the twenty-first century, influenced by broader environmental thinking. Many pagans describe themselves as polytheistic, worshipping a number of gods and goddesses. Pagan worldviews may include belief in spirits, goddesses or gods, nature as an entity, or an animist outlook. The best-known paths are wicca, druidry, heathenry, and goddess spirituality, with individuals often identifying with more than one at a time. Contemporary paganism, then, comprises a variety of paths, some of which overlap. It can be characterized as a coalescence of individuals around the view that a single authority has limitations, around nature-orientated traditions, and around the rooting of authority in the self, rather than as an organized belief system. But reburial of human remains is not part of pagan tradition. Why, then, did pagans begin campaigning around the issue of how human remains should be treated?

Emma Restall Orr, a druid, in 2004 formed the advocacy group Honouring the Ancient Dead to voice concern about the treatment of pre-Christian remains and to campaign for reburial, ritual, and respect. While HAD has a number of supporters, these have rarely numbered more than twenty at a time, and its campaigning effort cannot be considered large or representative. Honouring the Ancient Dead argues for respect for and, at times, the reburial of human remains. Writing in the magazine *British Archaeology,* Orr stated:

> When Pagans speak of reburial, they are not demanding marked graves lauded over with occultism or magic. They seek simply the absolute assurance of respect. In my opinion, reburial of every bone shard is not necessary: ritual is.
> At Stonehenge, should human remains or burial/sacrificial artefacts be found, priests will be called. Appropriate prayers and ritual will be made to honour the dead, their stories and gifts to the gods. Once finds are catalogued, reburial will be considered by all relevant parties. (2004, p. 39)

According to Orr, when pagans ask for reburial, they are not referring to literal reburial. Instead, they "seek assurances of respect"—which are not defined—and the requirement of ritual. Orr refers to human remains and sacrificial artifacts as a focus, but it is not clear why the pagans believe that these things require respect or ritual. So why would pagans campaign around this issue? Best (1990) observes that newly constructed problems may encourage new claimsmakers. In this case, the prevailing cultural climate in which human remains became objects of contestation cultivated the conditions for various pagan groups to make claims about human remains in order to lend weight to their other concerns. Influencing their claims about human remains was a desire to be recognized and acknowledged as a legitimate group, and to be included in a discussion that has included others. In an interview that I conducted in November 2006, a member of HAD explained that pagans had not gained recognition similar to that of overseas groups, and that this was unfair:

> Aboriginals and Native Americans have helped open up the debate, probably, I think, to a much wider stance . . . it's certainly allowed us to say if you are doing it for them, why can't you do the same thing for us [because] it's that sort of thing, that what's good for the goose is good for the gander . . . you know, hang on a minute, we are here. [T]hey are thousands of miles away, why are they getting special treatment?

These remarks identify the central problem as exclusion of pagans by heritage organizations, in contrast to their treatment of overseas indigenous groups. The statement that this interviewee made—"hang on a minute, we are here"—speaks to strong feelings of nonrecognition, and is reflected in the published demands of pagans. For instance, HAD criticized a code of practice by the UK's Department of Culture, Media, and Sport when the department did not consult with pagans nor include their concerns in writing it. HAD argues that Pagan beliefs need to be recognized and included in the formation of policy:

> The Pagan community's sensitivities towards British human remains must now be heard if bodies are to avoid charges of religious discrimination. While indigenous peoples' attitudes towards ancestry and heritage are now accepted (if seldom comprehended) by those dealing with human remains, British Pagan beliefs continue to be questioned or dismissed. This lack of acceptance is evident in the guidance, where there is no language sensitive to Pagan spiritual and religious concerns. Consultation is needed in order to address and amend this problem. (HAD n.d., n.p.)

The demands were less about old bones than about winning affirmation of the legitimacy of paganism from cultural organizations. These were, fundamentally, claims for recognition and inclusion. The moral privilege rhetorically bestowed on selected and included groups encouraged others to demand equivalent treatment. Those who felt left out protested.

The prevailing cultural climate in which human remains became objects of contestation cultivated the conditions for pagan groups to make claims on human remains in order to lend weight to their existing demands for recognition and involvement in heritage issues. With the contestation about overseas human remains in museum collections high on the political and media agenda, and with professionals questioning the holding and display of human remains, it is no surprise that pagan groups campaigning around other issues gravitated toward the question of human remains, stimulated by the recognition of other groups' demands.

Museum Professionals Find It Difficult to Resist Pagan Activism

What is interesting is how much weight and influence the pagan activists had. Unlike indigenous groups from overseas, pagans are often considered by wider society to be an illegitimate group and their involvement in decisions about human remains cannot be explained as a result of a desire to make reparations for historical wrongs. This involvement can be explained instead by the response of the museum sector, which can be divided into those who were enthusiastic about listening to the pagan groups, and those who were not. HAD did not achieve anything like the recognition or institutionalization of the problem achieved by overseas indigenous groups who suffered colonization. However, HAD did achieve a minor amount of involvement in museum institutions around this problem. Of relevance to this study is why this group received even limited endorsement.

One important response to the group was a strongly positive endorsement in three institutions. Manchester University Museum, Leicester City Council Museums, and Colchester and Ipswich Museum Service responded very positively to HAD. Professionals in all these institutions were "advisers" to HAD, and they all involved the group in a number of activities. Indeed, Emma Restall Orr of HAD and Piotr Bienkowski, the deputy director of Manchester University Museum, forged an alliance to campaign around the problem in general of human remains in museum collections. HAD was also involved by these organizations in consultation on the display, storage, and burial of human remains (e.g., see Levitt and Hadland 2006). In particular, HAD was centrally involved in the removal of a head of a bog body from display at Manchester University Museum, but also in the exhibition of a bog body—Lindow Man—at the same museum. HAD played an influential role and was heavily credited in the publicity and marketing material. These apparently contradictory outcomes—demanding the removal of a bog body head but also shaping the display of another bog body—remind us that HAD's activism was influenced less by a particular aim in relation to human remains and more by the aim of general involvement and recognition.

While Manchester University Museum endorsed HAD and involved it in decisions over the future of human remains and in museum practices, the response of the rest of the museum sector to HAD's claims was far more critical. Some organizations felt strongly that HAD should not be involved and that pagan claimsmakers were not credible. However, the negative response to HAD was difficult to systematically sustain, and many were unable to argue against the inclusion of pagan views. This would appear to be due to, in part, an uncertainty about the role of the museum and the thinking that it is an instrument of recognition; the professionals who do not recognize paganism as legitimate find it difficult to draw a line that excludes pagans but includes other marginalized groups. In one of the interviews I conducted, a curator from a regional museum explained: "I've had to examine my views. I mean I wasn't at all sure when I first heard about this, but really why not, you know? I am not sure I have a good reason for you. . . . We are, you know we are very sympathetic when it comes to certain groups—the Maoris and Aboriginals. We are working with refugees and a Nigerian community . . . really we should be consistent. Who is to say they are not valid?"

In a number of institutions, the claims of the pagans were looked upon sympathetically as part of a wider consultation agenda without a particular interest in the group's beliefs. One of these institutions was Leicester City Museums, which has been broadly supportive of HAD. Its approach is part of a wider consultative approach that takes into account broader concerns from faith groups and issues of multiculturalism. One of the museum's curators explained in an interview: "One of the most interesting changes we have made here is because we have got to know a wider range of our communities. That's been in our attitude because of new considerations about faith and spirituality. The involvement of HAD came about because of the institution's programme of recognizing and involving faith groups." When HAD approached the museum, the group was invited to be part of the consultation process on the content and practices of the institution. This consultation process also included nonfaith groups when competition developed between them for involvement, illustrating that recognition of one group may stimulate antagonism from others.

Another museum director felt strongly not only that HAD should be involved in influencing museum policy and practice, but also that museums should be proactive about this involvement. He took the view that "really excluded" groups won't approach museums, so the museums should go and look for them: "the universal museum cannot simply have a relationship with one interest group. We need to make special steps to give disempowered voices a place. We need to empower them."

The involvement of HAD in museum activities indicates that the difficulty in finding a rationale for exclusion allows the campaigning activity of a small group to have an impact. The rest of the sector finds it difficult to stop this continued challenge from a few individuals, who have a disproportionate effect—not because of their effective advocacy work, but because the context that they are seeking to influence is open and unstable.

Conclusion

Sociologists have demonstrated that effective resistance may minimize the impact of claimsmaking (Lee 2003). In this case, the reverse holds—the lack of effective resistance to the claimsmakers led to them having a disproportionate effect. Although some members of the museum sector do not consider HAD legitimate and do not think it should have a say in the future treatment of human remains, other parts of the profession are unable to articulate this or argue it strongly. Thus, despite the poor and limited claimsmaking abilities of the pagan group, its voice was heard and it affected museum practices. The case study of HAD indicates that difficulty in finding a rationale to exclude claimsmakers may make it possible for even a small group to have an impact. A few individuals can have an effect, not so much because their claims are compelling, but because those they want to influence have trouble agreeing upon standards and policies.

The central conclusion to be drawn is that the shift in the mission of the museum to a more inclusive model, together with the unstable nature of the museum's role and responsibilities, pressures museum professionals to include groups who are asking for recognition even when the professionals are not confident of the legitimacy of these groups.

This means that groups such as the pagan organization Honouring the Ancient Dead can influence museum practice, especially when they campaign around the treatment of human remains—which has come to be a recognized issue in the museum sector—even when they have little support, little credibility, and ill-defined aims.

Part 3

Questioning Experts

The world is a complicated place. Each of us is connected to a great, global web of social relationships, but we cannot observe most of that web and its workings. In order to understand our world, we depend upon experts—people with special knowledge—to explain how it all works. What counts as expertise varies across time and space. In many preindustrial societies, religious authorities were considered the most important interpreters of the world. Social problems—a plague, a bad harvest, any sort of human suffering—might be constructed by religious leaders as caused by supernatural forces, and their solutions usually involved more prayers.

In contemporary developed countries, some people continue to view religious leaders as experts, but there are rival forms of expertise. Lawyers, physicians, scientists, economists, and other such experts are understood to command various bodies of specialized knowledge, and they often work within specialized institutional settings; lawyers work with legal knowledge in courts and legislatures, doctors apply their medical training in clinics and hospitals, and so on. Today, the emergence of an epidemic disease is less likely to be constructed as God's judgment, and more likely to be defined as falling within the domain of physicians who treat the sick and scientists who search for a cure.

Our dependence on expertise means that we consider experts to be particularly authoritative claimsmakers. We are more likely to defer to experts' claims about the nature of social problems, their causes, and the best ways to solve them. At any given moment, experts may have the best available method of assessing problems, and it is easy to imagine that whatever experts say must simply be true. But it is important to remember that all expertise is a product of its place and time. In another country, or at a later time, one set of experts' claims may be rejected while other interpretations are favored. Thus, expertise is a topic that deserves sociological examination.

This part of the book features three chapters that focus on expert claimsmaking (note that other chapters in the book also illustrate experts' claims). In Chapter 7, Liahna Gordon traces the stories of three sets of medical claims about sexual behavior: eighteenth-century warnings about the damaging consequences of masturbation; nineteenth-century constructions of homosexuality as a medical problem; and late-twentieth-century concerns with sexual addiction. The parallels in these three stories are striking: initially, medical authorities construct the sexual behavior as having dire consequences; it takes time for the problem's seriousness—and the previously authoritative claims—to be questioned. The lesson is clear: interpretations viewed as expert today may later fall out of favor. Fields of science rise and fall along with the careers of these experts.

In Chapter 8, Keith Roberts Johnson emphasizes the point that experts have a stake in their claims. When claims are widely accepted, the claimsmakers gain influence, but too much success—the elimination of some social problem—can threaten to make experts irrelevant. Johnson's example is maternal mortality. A century ago, this was a serious problem: it was not unusual for women to die giving birth. However, medical advances have reduced most of the risks of childbirth, potentially making the experts who study maternal mortality unnecessary. In response, those experts have mounted a campaign to redefine the nature of maternal mortality and generate statistics demonstrating that it remains a serious social problem.

Of course, not all experts—not even the most diligent researchers with uncanny powers of foresight—are successful claimsmakers. In Chapter 9, John Barnshaw examines the efforts of what he calls "prophets in the wilderness" to warn about the practices that would lead to the financial collapse of 2008. Even on the eve of the crisis, many officials and financial experts insisted that the economy was in good shape, and they expressed shock as the collapse unfolded. But Barnshaw notes that there were other, highly regarded economic experts who had foreseen what would happen, and who had made claims warning about the danger—claims that government and financial leaders dismissed and ignored. This chapter forces us to ask why some experts' claims aren't more influential.

In short, these chapters share a common theme: the claims of experts should not simply be accepted as true or false. We need to think critically about who is making the claims, what sorts of evidence they bring to bear, and how the reaction to those claims reflects the experts' place in the larger society.

7

Wankers, Inverts, and Addicts: The Scientific Construction of Sexuality as a Social Problem

Liahna E. Gordon

How do social problems get constructed? In the case of sexuality, the process begins with the labeling of a behavior as deviant. In the first volume of his influential book *The History of Sexuality,* Michel Foucault (1990 [1978]) described how, prior to the Victorian era, the Christian Church was largely responsible for defining sexual deviance in the Western world. Such deviance was viewed, however, primarily as an individual problem, not a social one. That is, individuals were seen as sinners, but such sin was not usually defined as having social consequences. At the beginning of the Victorian era, the church's influence over sexuality declined, however, and the burgeoning fields of science moved in to take its place.

It's not just that science took control of sexuality, but that sexuality helped to create the sciences. Psychoanalysis and psychiatry became possible because, in defining sexuality as something problematic that could be solved or fixed, they also positioned themselves as the fields to do that. Sexuality gave them a raison d'être. Certainly there was medicine prior to the medicalization of sexuality, but the burgeoning scientific version of the field (as opposed to healers, midwives, and "witchdoctors") was based at least in part on the premise that sexuality caused all sorts of physical ailments and therefore needed to be attended to and treated. So while sexuality was shaped by science, some fields of science were also able to become well established because they chose sexuality as their subject, and because they convinced the public that some sexualities were in need of fixing.

This chapter applies Foucault's thinking to three historical examples—masturbation, homosexuality, and sexual addiction—in order to better understand the process of constructing sexuality as a social problem. Taken together, we find that the construction of sexuality as socially problematic involves five key steps:

1. Scientists seeking legitimation for their fields stake out areas of expertise by defining some sexual behavior as a new sexual illness.
2. They chart the psychological and physical manifestations of the illness, as well as its consequences.
3. They find treatment for the illness, positioning their own profession or subfield as the most qualified to provide this treatment.
4. Their new construction disseminates through the culture, with acceptance gained for the new definition of the behavior as an illness. In so doing, new sexual identities are created that did not previously exist, leading people to identify themselves as afflicted with the illness, many of whom will seek the treatment offered by the self-proclaimed experts.
5. Eventually, someone within the field (or another subfield of science) will use their expertise to resist the illness construction, thereby helping to normalize the behavior.

As we will see, whether we are talking about masturbation in the eighteenth century or sexual addiction in the 1980s, the process of constructing sexual behavior as socially problematic remains predictable and relatively unchanged over time.

Masturbation

Defining Masturbation as Illness

While there had long been religious and cultural disapproval of masturbation, we first see its emergence as a new social problem in the early 1700s with the publication in London of the anonymously authored *Onania, or the Heinous Sin of Self-Pollution, and All Its Frightful Consequences, in Both Sexes Considered, with Spiritual and Physical*

Advice for Those Who Have Already Injur'd Themselves with This Abominable Practice. "Onania" in the title is a biblical reference, which was not accidental; in many ways, the book was simply a religious and moral condemnation of masturbation. But what makes it important is the book's use of medical discourse, flawed as it was, to support these religious arguments. This book was followed by another in 1769 by Samuel-August Tissot, a Swiss physician who was particularly influenced by *Onania*. He wrote his own book on the health consequences of masturbation. In the century that followed, physicians from all over the United States and Europe spoke out about the physical dangers of masturbation, identifying it as a major health problem.

Germ theory had not yet been developed at this time, and the cause of sexually transmitted diseases (probably the real cause of some of the symptoms physicians attributed to masturbation) had not yet been discovered. That changed in 1879, when the bacterium that causes gonorrhea was discovered, followed in 1905 by the discovery of the bacterium that causes syphilis. With these and other medical discoveries, doctors began to shift their perspective on masturbation from a cause of physical illness to a cause of mental illness (Cornog 2003). Early on, insanity had been identified as a probable result of masturbation because of the damage masturbation was said to cause the nervous system. But as physicians increasingly understood that illnesses were generally caused by germs, they focused more on the mental health effects of masturbation. Emphasis on mental illness, however, made masturbation no less of a health crisis, since insanity was believed to be hereditary; thus, masturbators risked not only becoming insane, but also passing that insanity along to their descendants. Thus psychiatrists were every bit as determined as physicians to deter and cure masturbation.

Manifestations, Causes, and Consequences of Masturbation

As part of the process of defining masturbation as an illness, physicians enumerated the harmful, even deadly, effects of masturbation. The author of *Onania* claimed that the "frightful consequences" of masturbation were primarily due to the strain put on the genitals and the nervous system (Cornog 2003; Stengers and Van Neck 2001; Stolberg 2000). This, in turn, was alleged to cause a whole host of ailments, including weakness, pallor, fainting, epilepsy, tuberculosis, and infertility. In men it also caused a range of penile problems including painful continual erections, impotence, leaking and excessive loss of semen, and excessive wet dreams; for women it caused incontinence, infertility, hysteria, and enlargement of the clitoris (Stolberg 2000). Even worse, *Onania* claimed that the children of masturbators would be born sickly, weak, and likely to die in infancy (Stolberg 2000). Tissot argued that the regret and shame produced by masturbating could cause psychological distress, which in turn produced additional ailments, from digestive problems to paralysis, and "infinite increase in anguish" (Stengers and Van Neck 2001, p. 73). Finally, Tissot asserted that the loss of one ounce of semen was equivalent to the loss of forty ounces of blood, and that masturbation led to the greatest loss of semen of any sexual behavior, making it potentially deadly (Neuman 1975).

The list of physical ailments continued to grow, eventually including such major diseases as epilepsy and tuberculosis, rickets, polio, and cancer; masturbation was also thought to cause nymphomania, especially in blondes, and to either cause or be caused by a whole bevy of perversions, including homosexuality, bestiality, oral sex, anal sex, prostitution, and marital nonprocreative sex (Cornog 2003; Darby 2003). At least one physician argued that because masturbation (and homosexuality) increased the size of a woman's clitoris, it could turn her clitoris into a penis, effectively turning her into a man (Gibson 1997).

In the late 1800s, Richard von Krafft-Ebing, a German psychiatrist, gave a more psychiatric focus for concerns about masturbation. In his influential book *Psychopathia Sexualis: With Especial Reference to the Antipathic Sexual Instinct* (1886), Krafft-Ebing warned that there were possible adverse physical effects from masturbation, but he focused primarily on masturbation as a deterrent to sexual intercourse. Masturbating was likely to cause youth to disassociate sexual feelings from the opposite sex, he wrote, and thus prefer masturbation over intercourse. This sometimes led them to have homosexual sex, but masturbation continued to be preferred even to this. Thus, he worried that by deterring procreative sex, masturbation would eventually decimate the world's population.

Treating Masturbation, Legitimating a Field

Cures for masturbation were many. The author of *Onania* encouraged masturbators to seek help from their physicians for the ailment, but those who were too embarrassed were advised that they could purchase an antimasturbation tonic made by the author or could make a personal appointment with him for a fee, leading some historians to speculate that the author (who remained anonymous) was not a medical doctor at all, but a quack looking to make money (Laqueur 2003; Stengers and Van Neck 2001). As the years went on, cures came to include a range of pharmaceuticals (especially depressants), as well as tying one's hands to the bedposts at night and use of antimasturbation devices that restricted the potential offender's access to their genitals (Darby 2003). The most extreme cures were those requiring surgery. From 1890 to 1925, the Orificial Surgery Society in the United States specialized in both circumcision and clitoridectomies to cure masturbation (Cornog 2003). In the late 1860s in Britain, clitoridectomies were the popular medical treatment for female masturbators (Darby 2003), and they were touted as a cure in the United States not only for masturbation, but also for all the other perversions masturbation might cause (Gibson 1997). Robert Darby (2003) argues that routine circumcision in the United States was adopted to protect boys from not only cancer and syphilis, but also masturbation. Other surgical procedures were also sometimes advocated as masturbatory cures, including cutting the nerves to the penis, castration, and ovariotomy. Commonly, the penis was cauterized to destroy its nerve endings, which would hopefully decrease sexual arousal (and presumably the desire to masturbate or commit other perversions) (Darby 2003).

It should be noted here that although medicine is considered an elite profession today, early in the antimasturbation era there were so many frauds trying to make a quick buck that physicians were often regarded suspiciously. Surgeons were viewed as tradesmen, regarded like carpenters or "internal plumbers" rather than healers. Indeed, surgeons were often viewed as distasteful because they worked with bowels, pus, and other "unclean" aspects of the body. Hence, by constructing masturbation as a social problem that only they were qualified to treat, this helped improve the respect and reputations of the fields of medicine and surgery. The fate of wretched masturbators, and by extension all of us, was, after all, in their hands.

Disseminating the Construction of Masturbation

Fifteen editions of *Onania* were published, and each new edition included an increasing number of letters from readers confessing their masturbatory habits and the horrible consequences of their behavior. It came to be believed that almost anything could arouse the genitals and thus induce masturbation, from trousers to bicycles, feather beds to trains (Maines 1999; Rosenman 2003). For women, working in a department store, being a servant in a hotel, and dressmaking were thought to increase the risk of masturbation (Gibson 1997). The use of sewing machines, particularly those with two foot treadles, was considered particularly dangerous because of the involuntary stimulation they provided (Gibson 1997; Maines 1999). Even the speculum was suspicious. Because it was inserted into the vagina (and therefore likened to intercourse and so viewed as a likely masturbatory aid), it was seen as highly arousing, and tales abounded of women having intense orgasms upon its insertion (Maines 1999). Masturbation came to be seen as almost plaguelike, potentially affecting everyone. John Harvey Kellogg created Kellogg's cornflakes as part of a bland diet that was thought to prevent masturbation, and that was recommended for everyone from school children to housewives to bachelors. Additionally, daily engagement in any type of strenuous physical exercise was recommended so that people would be too tired at night to even think about masturbating (Stengers and Van Neck 2001).

The notion that masturbation was an illness became popularized through the medical texts. Indeed, despite the fact that *Onania* was published at a time when the majority of people still did not read books, 30,000 copies of the fifteen editions of *Onania* had sold by 1730 (Stolberg 2000). Tissot's 1769 book was also a big seller, and was translated into several languages and sold both in Europe and the United States. Krafft-Ebing prefaced the first edition of his *Psychopathia Sexualis* (1886) by saying: "A scientific title has been chosen, and technical terms are used throughout the book in order to exclude the lay reader. For the same reason certain portions are written in Latin" (as reproduced in the tenth edition, 1904, p. vii). By the tenth edition, in 1904, he instead remarked: "Its commercial success is the best proof that large numbers of unfortunate people find in its pages instruction and relief in the frequently enigmatical manifestations of sexual life. The host of letters that have reached the author from all parts of the world substantiate this assumption" (p. ix). The book became so popular among the public that seventeen editions were published between 1886 and 1924 (Oosterhuis 1997).

As the popularity of the construction of masturbation as illness increased, those who masturbated came to view the behavior as problematic and to experience physical and psychological symptoms that they attributed to masturbation, and often sought help from physicians and psychiatrists. The following excerpt from *Onania* is typical:

> Happening to Read your little Book of ONANIA, which I heartily wish I had been so happy as to perused seven Years ago, would prevented that shameful Practice and detestable Sin, I have for so long been guilty of; being ignorant of the heinousness of the Crime and the ill Consequence that now attends it, but hope through GOD's Mercy, and your Assistance, to find Relief in this my unhappy Circumstance. . . . I have now wandring Pains, sometimes in the small of my Back, then in my Breast at times, but generally in my Leggs and Thighs, which seem hot, and makes me very uneasy and unfit for Business, and dull to that degree, that I am ready to sleep as I stand. (Anonymous 1723, pp. 48–49)

In such testimonial letters, the afflicted person usually had not previously thought of the behavior as problematic, then read the book and came to think of it as such. There is still evidence of a strongly religious condemnation of masturbation, but the readers also see it as a medical issue, causing physical symptoms. They implore the author for medical help, which they believe will help both their body and their mind, because they are swayed by the book's author to reinterpret their behavior as causing both their physical and their emotional problems.

Scientifically Normalizing Masturbation

Consistent with Foucault's model, eventually scientists began to use their authority to challenge this construction. In his 1899 book *Auto-Eroticism* (see Ellis 1900), Havelock Ellis not only declared that critics of masturbation had no evidence that it caused either physical or mental damage, but also deemed it a "legitimate source of mental relaxation" (Robinson 1989, p. 12). Ellis maintained that most people masturbate, and that more women masturbate than men, and also pointed to distinguished men who had admitted to masturbation to show that it caused neither imbecility nor insanity (Maines 1999; Robinson 1989). Sigmund Freud once viewed masturbation as the cause of neurosis, but by 1905 had publicly recognized that masturbation was part of a normal stage of psychosexual development in children. It only became problematic, he said, when masturbation continued into adulthood, where it was a symptom of arrested psychosexual development (Makari 1998). In the 1920s, Wilhelm Stekel, a student of Freud's, argued the contrary: masturbation was not harmful to either children or adults, and the ailments thought to be caused by masturbation were actually caused by societally instigated guilt (1950). The neuroses supposedly caused by masturbation were actually caused, he said, not by the act itself, but by giving it up: "Thereupon, through a process of false reasoning, the neurosis is regarded as having been brought about by masturbation. As a matter of fact precisely the reverse is true. The neurosis is a consequence of abstinence" (Stekel 1950, p. 43). Stekel also argued that, far from being a social problem, masturbation was usually a social good, as it kept people from acting out their sexual frustration and fantasies in socially dangerous ways.

Despite Stekel's and Ellis's notions of benign masturbation, popular opinion was slow to follow. The 1927 edition of the Boy Scout handbook, for example, described masturbation as a "bad habit" that "should be fought against. . . . It's important for your life, your happiness, your efficiency, and the whole human race as well" (Rowan 1989, p. 79). Indeed, as late as 1940, the US Naval Academy continued to physically examine prospective students for signs of masturbation, and to refuse masturbators admission to the academy (Cornog 2003). Additionally, circumcision continued to be recommended by physicians until the 1950s as a way of decreasing masturbation (Darby 2003). It wasn't until the 1948 release of the Kinsey Report that the links between mental illness and masturbation were severed in the public mind.

Alfred Kinsey and his colleagues did nearly as much to normalize masturbation as the physicians and psychiatrists of the nineteenth century had done to medicalize it. Kinsey (who was a biologist) and his team conducted nearly 20,000 face-to-face interviews about all facets of sexuality with people all over the United States. Their results, published in 1948 in *Sexual Behavior in the Human Male,* followed in 1953 by *Sexual Behavior in the Human Female,* made international headlines. Kinsey did four things to normalize masturbation. First, he reported that 92 percent of the men they interviewed admitted to having masturbated (Kinsey, Pomeroy, and Martin 1948). The sheer weight of this statistic made the notion that masturbation caused insanity, or even mild mental health issues, untenable. It would amount to saying that everyone in the country was crazy. Second, Kinsey, like Stekel, argued that it wasn't masturbation—no matter how often one engaged in it—but the associated guilt or repression that was likely to cause problems in psychological adjustment (Robinson 1989). Third, he presented statistics correlating masturbation with marital satisfaction, showing that rather than being a threat to heterosexual intercourse, as Krafft-Ebing had claimed, masturbation actually increased both sexual satisfaction in marriage and overall marital happiness. Fourth, Kinsey put to rest the notion that men needed to save up their sperm for reproduction by showing that those men who had ejaculated less frequently in their earlier years were more likely to suffer impotence and other problems in their later years.

William Masters and Virginia Johnson (1966, 1970) also played a significant role in normalizing masturbation. As a team of sex therapists in the 1960s, they set out to understand "normal" sexual functioning in order to treat patients with sexual problems. They legitimized masturbation by identifying the clitoris, not the vagina, as the primary site of sexual pleasure for women, and by asserting that vaginal intercourse in the absence of clitoral stimulation was unlikely to produce orgasms for women. This led them to make two important arguments. First, women needed to masturbate on their own in order to best understand their bodies and sexual arousal (Robinson 1989). Second, they should incorporate masturbation into their lovemaking, either by rubbing their own clitoris during sex, or by showing their partners how to manually stimulate their clitoris during sex. By defining masturbation as a necessary component of sexual satisfaction for women, Masters and Johnson rendered it "respectable." Furthermore, they turned masturbation from an illness into a cure. Their treatment for nearly all of the sexual problems they diagnosed included masturbation as a central component.

Homosexuality

The history of the construction of homosexuality as a social problem is similar to that of masturbation. It goes through all of the same stages: the redefinition of a sexual behavior as an illness by a scientific field seeking legitimation, charting of the manifestations and consequences of the so-called illness, the finding of a treatment by the same field that defined the behavior as an illness, dissemination of the illness construction through the culture, leading to individuals seeking help for their "problem," and eventual normalization of the behavior by those within the scientific field or subfield. Additionally, it also features some of the same key players: Havelock Ellis, Richard von Krafft-Ebing, Sigmund Freud, and Alfred Kinsey among them.

Defining Homosexuality as Illness

One key difference between the constructions of masturbation and homosexuality is that the construction of homosexuality also involves what Foucault (1988 [1986]) called the construction of "the self." Masturbation, as we have seen, was regarded primarily as a behavior, not a "type" of person. While there are references to "the masturbator" in historical medical and psychiatric texts, everyone was viewed as potential perpetrators of the act, and everyone was vulnerable to falling victim to its effects. The construction of homosexuality, on the other hand, was first and foremost a transition from thinking about sodomy as a *behavior* to thinking of "homosexuals" as a distinct *type of person* different from other types of people (Foucault 1990 [1978]; Katz 1995). Although many terms were used to designate this "type" of person—urning, uranian, sexual invert, homosexual, and pervert, among them—the key is the belief that, whatever one calls them, "these people" are intrinsically different than others. This notion was first popularized in 1864 (almost a full century after the publication of Tissot's work on masturbation) not by a physician, but by a German lawyer, Karl Ulrichs. Ulrichs argued that urnings were psychological hermaphrodites: people with male bodies but women's souls (uranians, likewise, were people with female bodies but men's souls). This sexual inversion was caused, Ulrichs theorized, by two "germs" (or what we might call genes). One determined genitals, and the other determined psychological sex. Usually these two germs "matched," so that a person was both physically and psychologically male, but sometimes they did not, causing uranism (Kennedy 1997). Ulrichs argued that because it is natural for people of the opposite psychological sex to desire one another, it is perfectly natural for a man with a woman's soul to desire a man with a man's soul; to desire otherwise would be unnatural. Ulrichs insisted uranism was not a disease, and that urnings were completely "normal" in the sense that they were physically and psychologically healthy (Bullough 1977).

Richard von Krafft-Ebing, who was influenced by Ulrichs, was the first psychologist to write extensively about homosexuality (which he called "sexual inversion"). He came to believe that homosexuality could be either congenital or acquired. He argued that there was a difference between "sickly perversion" and "immoral perversity," the first being a result of biology, the second a result of weak morals (Terry 1997). Krafft-Ebing argued that while the latter should continue to be punished by the courts, the former was a disease and required treatment rather than punishment. This illness, he argued, was a biological inferiority that caused one to inherit a nervous system that was more easily overstimulated by modern society: that is, by "materialism, luxury, urbanization, agitation, absence of religion, unhealthy work, capitalist competitiveness, excessive leisure, food and drink, and immoral habits" (Oosterhuis 2000, p. 54). The result of this propensity to be overstimulated led to homosexual desires and behaviors in afflicted people.

Psychiatry was not well respected when Krafft-Ebing entered the field, in part because even though psychiatrists were charged with helping the mentally ill, they had relatively little success at curing mental illness. Additionally, they were generally relegated to working in asylums, which were overcrowded institutions with poor living conditions, and considered dirty and dangerous (Oosterhuis 2000). In arguing that only psychiatrists were capable of determining whether an act of illegal sodomy was the result of the overly sensitive nervous system (disease) or simply an act of willful immorality, Krafft-Ebing helped to establish psychiatrists as the experts on this matter, thus creating a reason for the courts to need psychiatrists—in this case, to weed out the criminals from the physically and mentally ill (Oosterhuis 2000). Krafft-Ebing also argued that more research was needed on homosexuality (and other sexual behaviors) in order to better understand them and perfect treatment, and in advocating that psychiatrists needed to do this research he helped to establish psychiatry as a legitimate science within universities. Put simply, Krafft-Ebing used homosexuality as his foot in the door to turn psychiatry from a marginalized field into a respected one.

Another new field, sexology, developed in large part to counter Krafft-Ebing's claims. Havelock Ellis and Magnus Hirschfeld, among the earliest sexologists, both considered homosexuality to be a benign variation in sexuality, like left- and right-handedness. They used Darwinism to explain that, just as there are many different types of flowers, all of which are "natural" variations, so too there could be natural sexual variations, and that variation in no way connotes illness or abnormality (Steakley 1997; Terry 1999). They argued that since there was no illness, no treatment was necessary. Hirschfeld created the Institute for Sexology in 1919 to study all kinds of sexual issues, but it was for furthering the understanding of homosexuality that his institute gained members and support. Hirschfeld believed that it was through scientific research and inquiry that oppression of homosexuals (and other forms of sexual repression) would be ended, and therefore he worked hard to gain support for the field of sexology (Steakley 1997).

Thus, in the case of homosexuality, there was no scientific consensus on the status of homosexuality as either an illness or a social problem. Nonetheless, once it had been constructed as such, both psychiatrists and sexologists used homosexuality to legitimate their fields: psychiatry by treating it, and sexology by providing a scientific defense for it. In both cases, this helped to grant some degree of power and authority to those newly developing fields.

Manifestations, Causes, and Consequences of Homosexuality

One thing the psychiatrists and sexologists agreed upon in regard to homosexuality was the need to name it, classify it, and determine its relationship to other forms of sexuality. Ellis focused on classifying "normal" variations of sexuality, including masturbation and homosexual sex, which he did by identifying similar sexual behaviors among animals and other cultures (Robinson 1989). Hirschfeld, on the other hand, categorized sexuality based on four characteristics: sex organs, other biological characteristics, sexual drive, and psychological characteristics. Many variations existed within each characteristic, leading him to calculate that there were literally over 43 million possible combinations, all of which he considered to be normal (Steakley 1997). Krafft-Ebing devoted all of *Psychopathia Sexualis* to classifying sexual disorders. He classified them by four factors: life stage, amount of sexual drive, sexual goal (anything other than penile-vaginal intercourse within marriage he deemed pathological), and the object of sexual desire (people of the same sex, inanimate objects, etc.) (Oosterhuis 2000). Freud, in contrast, classified sexuality by life stage, delineating the "normal" sexual feelings and behaviors throughout the periods of psychosexual development. Even Ulrichs felt the need to categorize homosexuals, focusing on variations within homosexuality and coming up with sixteen different types (Kennedy 1997).

In terms of consequences, homosexuality was not thought to cause physical ailments the way that masturbation did, with the exception of neuranthensia, a type of neurosis popularized in the 1880s. Neuranthensia's symptoms were vast and varied, including everything from weeping and forgetfulness to writing cramps and stomach trouble (Maines 1999). In the case studies that Krafft-Ebing presented on homosexuality, for example, many of the patients were also diagnosed with neuranthensia, though it is not clear whether the homosexuality caused the neuranthensia or vice versa. Many physicians and some psychiatrists believed that there were differences in the bodies of heterosexuals and homosexuals, including size and development of the brain, body type, structure and strength, and genital size and shape (Terry 1999). Additionally, homosexuality was thought to be related to other sexual perversions, especially masturbation, but also fetishism and sadomasochism. Most important, however, was the notion that homosexuality was a form of insanity, and because insanity would inevitably be passed on through the generations, becoming more and more acute with each successive generation, there was great concern among some physicians and psychiatrists that homosexuals not reproduce (Terry 1999).

Treating Homosexuality, Legitimating a Field

In the 1880s, sterilization for homosexuals began. Castration, clitoridectomies, and hysterectomies were used to decrease homosexual desire, and to prevent them from reproducing. By 1931, thirty states had laws legalizing the sterilization of "sexual perverts" (Terry 1999, p. 82). Perhaps the most lasting of the beliefs about the consequences of homosexuality, however, was simply that homosexuals could never be happy. Their sexual perversion, if not cured, would doom them to a life of despair, loneliness, and self-hatred, potentially leading to suicide. For others, the scarier risk was that contact with homosexuals could lead weak-willed and vulnerable heterosexuals to engage in homosexuality themselves, thus spreading the problem.

In arguing the distinction between congenital homosexuality (the illness) and immoral perversion (being a bad person), Krafft-Ebing and other psychiatrists maintained that only psychiatrists could truly determine the difference, and so it should be left to psychiatrists, not lawyers and judges, to determine whether a person should be sent to an asylum or prison (Oosterhuis 1997, 2000). Krafft-Ebing used both hypnosis and "psychic therapy," a form of talk therapy, to treat homosexuality (Oosterhuis 2000). By using biology (an inherited weak nervous system) to explain the cause of homosexuality, he helped, however, to free the profession from having to produce a cure, which it had been unable to do, at a crucial moment when psychiatry was coming under fire for not delivering on its promises of improved mental health for asylum patients. Freud also argued that only psychiatrists could treat homosexuality. He argued that homosexuality was a disruption of the Oedipal complex for men and the result of particularly acute penis envy for women, and therefore only psychoanalysts who understood these processes could help the homosexual resolve these psychological issues by clearing the blockages that stifled their innate heterosexuality.

Disseminating the Construction of Homosexuality

As the various psychiatrists and sexologists named and classified homosexuality (regardless of whether they saw it as a disease or normal human variation), they actually created a new sexuality that became available for people to take as a sexual identity. That is, as the scientific debates about homosexuality were conducted in the public arena, some people began to think of themselves not just as engaging in particular behavior but as a "type" of person with a sexuality that rendered them fundamentally different from other types of people. In urban areas, bars and other hangouts began catering to this "type" of person, further reinforcing homosexuality as an identity available for the taking (D'Emilio 1997). England saw, for example, as much as a 500 percent increase in the number of people arrested for homosexuality (Kardiner 1964). The number of people taking on this identity became so significant that after World War II it induced a sort of cultural panic. One psychoanalyst warned in 1954 that "we still have an alarming social situation in which perhaps 25 per cent of the males are removed from socially meaningful relations with women by homosexuality alone" (Kardiner 1964, p. 17).

Despite the large number of people identifying themselves as homosexual, however, few were entirely comfortable with this identity. Krafft-Ebing's case studies often included complaints of unhappiness from homosexuals or even horror at their own behavior: "After sexual intercourse . . . he always felt strengthened and refreshed, but morally depressed; because there was consciousness of having performed a perverse, indecent, and punishable act. He found it painful that his disgusting impulse was more powerful than his will" (Krafft-Ebing 1904, p. 284). Likewise, the homosexual patients that Freud wrote about felt similarly plagued by their homosexuality. As late as the 1960s, many self-identified homosexuals continued to seek treatment to be rid of their "sickness," in hopes of leading a normal (heterosexual) life.

Scientifically Normalizing Homosexuality

As we have seen, in regard to homosexuality there was some disagreement among scientists, especially between psychiatrists and sexologists, about the status of homosexuality as an illness and its need for treatment. It wasn't until 1973, though, that the American Psychiatric Association removed homosexuality as a psychiatric disorder from the second edition of its *Diagnostic and Statistical Manual,* the official listing of mental disorders in the United States. The process of scientific normalization began with Ellis and Hirschfeld, both of whom argued that homosexuality was a benign variation of human sexuality. Kinsey and his colleagues, however, were somewhat more successful in combating the notion that homosexuality was an illness. Kinsey reported that 37 percent of men had engaged in homosexual sexual activity to the point of orgasm at least once in their adult life (Kinsey, Pomeroy, and Martin 1948). As with masturbation, it became difficult to argue insanity or illness when faced with a research statistic that more than one-third of American men had engaged in such behavior. Kinsey also introduced the notion of a continuum of sexual preference, which challenged the categorization of just two kinds of people. By declaring that sexual preference actually had seven categories, and that only about 60 percent of American men were either exclusively heterosexual or exclusively homosexual in their behavior (with the rest being bisexual to some degree), Kinsey challenged the notion that there were stark differences between heterosexuals and homosexuals. Kinsey also showed that the homosexuals he studied were no more or less socially or psychologically well-adjusted than heterosexuals. Other researchers conducted similar studies on the psychological adjustment and functioning of nonclinical samples of homosexuals, also showing them to be as well-adjusted on all measures of mental health as heterosexuals (for example, Bell and Weinberg 1979; Hooker 1957; Weinberg and Williams 1974).

Sex Addiction

Defining Sex Addiction as Illness

It would be a mistake, of course, to think that the process of constructing sexual behavior as a social problem only happened in the past. Indeed, many new sexual problems have been created in recent years, notably sex addiction. The similarities between the constructions of both masturbation and homosexuality as diseases in the eigh-teenth and nineteenth centuries, and the construction of sex addiction as a disease in the 1980s, are remarkable. Most obvious, and perhaps attesting to the lasting influence of *Onania* and Tissot, is that compul-sive masturbation is considered the most common symptom of sex addiction (Carnes 2001). But other similarities are numerous. Like masturbation, the acceptance of sex addiction as a disease was sparked, in 1983, by a single publication, *The Sexual Addiction* (retitled *Out of the Shadows* in 1985). The author, Patrick Carnes, is neither a physi-cian nor a psychiatrist, but an addictions therapist who used the con-struction of sex addiction as a disease to help to establish a subfield of psychology called addictionology (Irvine 2005 [1991]). At a time when chemical treatment centers were struggling because increased competi-tion left them with too many empty beds (Peippo 2006), addictionolo-gists began arguing that behaviors could be just as addictive for some people as drugs or alcohol, and that out-of-control behaviors like gam-bling, eating, spending, and sex were illnesses that needed the same treatment as chemical dependency. This defined a whole new category of behaviors, and thus people, as addicts. Additionally, addictionolo-gists argued that many alcoholics and drug addicts actually had multi-ple addictions, so treating a person for alcoholism was insufficient if they were also, for example, a sex addict, and in fact, such a person would be more likely to relapse in their drinking if their underlying (sexual) addiction wasn't also treated (Carnes 2001).

Manifestations, Causes, and Consequences of Sex Addiction

Carnes (1997) defines sex addiction as "any sexually-related compul-sive behavior which interferes with normal living and causes severe stress on family, friends, loved ones, and one's work environment." No single behavior pattern defines sex addiction. Compulsive mastur-bation, pornography, prostitution, exhibitionism, voyeurism, indecent phone calls, child molestation, and rape can all be part of a sex addic-tion, together or alone, as long as the behavior has taken control of a person's life. "Even the healthiest forms of human sexual expression can turn into self-defeating behaviors" (IITAP 2001).

Carnes describes sex addiction, like Tissot described masturbation, as causing or being caused by a whole host of other ailments, including depression, eating disorders, alcohol and drug addiction, anxiety disorders, and sleep disorders. One of the common consequences of sex addiction is physical exhaustion (Carnes 2001), which Tissot also described as an effect of masturbation. Additionally, like Tissot, Carnes characterizes sex addiction as a serious, even "life-threatening" illness (1992, p. 10), with potentially devastating consequences: emotional instability, sexually transmitted infections, unwanted pregnancy, divorce, severe financial or legal problems, job loss, and physical injury. Rape, incest, and child molestation are seen as possible (though not inevitable) manifestations of the disease. Also, like eighteenth-century physicians concerned with masturbation and nineteenth-century psychiatrists writing on homosexuality, Carnes claims that sex addiction may lead to other paraphilias. He ranks the behaviors of sex addiction into three levels, with each successive level encompassing behaviors that are considered more deviant, harmful, and illegal. The first level, for example, includes use of prostitution and pornography, compulsive masturbation, and anonymous sex, while the second includes exhibitionism and voyeurism, and the third includes incest and rape. He argues that addicts' behaviors typically progress through the levels, because their behaviors need to become more deviant and more dangerous in order to produce the same level of satisfaction. Additionally, his Sexual Addiction Screening Test, used to diagnose the condition, includes sexual behaviors that are often considered deviant in our society, such as polyamory (openly having more than one ongoing intimate relationship) and sadomasochism, implying that sex addiction may be caused by (or cause) other "deviant" sexual behaviors.

Treating Sex Addiction, Legitimizing a Field

As with psychiatrists and homosexuality, Carnes and other addictionologists argue that some sex offenders are not bad people, but engage in illegal sexual behaviors because they literally can't help themselves—they are sexually addicted. Thus addictionologists like Carnes have been able to claim, just as Krafft-Ebing did, that they are uniquely qualified to determine whether a sexual offender needs treatment for addiction or legal punishment, and, if the former, to then provide that treatment. To incarcerate a sex-addicted sex offender without providing such treatment, the argument goes, is to eventually release dangerous predators who are unable to control their sexual behaviors, and therefore to sacrifice the safety of innocent children and adults. In 1996, Carnes created an official certification for sex addiction therapists (CSAT), which purportedly makes them more qualified to treat sex addicts than are other therapists and physicians. According to the Society for the Advancement of Sexual Health (SASH), in eleven years, nearly 500 therapists obtained such certification (personal communication, 2008). This has both legitimized and professionalized the field, and hence, like Krafft-Ebing and Freud with homosexuality, addictionologists have been somewhat successful at getting themselves recognized as uniquely capable of treating such an important problem.

Disseminating the Construction of Sex Addiction

The construction of sex addiction as a social problem circulated first in twelve-step recovery circles, and gained much of its popularity there. Indeed, the first book on sex addiction was published by a press specializing in chemical dependency, and was disseminated among addiction treatment facilities. The spread of the construction beyond these circles, however, was aided by the purposeful building of the sex addiction treatment field and by historical events.

Carnes, whose PhD is not in psychology but in counselor education and organizational development, created an institutional apparatus to legitimate the construction of sex addiction as a medical and social problem. Between 1987 and 2005, he started a number of organizations aimed at doing this. He began with the National Council on Sexual Addiction and Compulsivity (NCSAC), using it to promote and disseminate research on sex addiction in order to "promote acceptance of the diagnosis of sexual addiction and sexual compulsivity" (SASH 2012). Next, having determined that "the lack of research in the field was a major obstacle to its acceptance" (Schneider 2004, p. 3), Carnes became the founding editor for the academic journal *Sexual Addiction and Compulsivity*. In order to professionalize treatment providers and set standards in sex addiction therapy (which increased legitimation of the field), Carnes created the CSAT certification. He originally ran this certification program through the clinic where he worked, but in 2005 created the International Institute for Trauma and Addiction Professionals (IITAP) to administer the program. Additionally, Carnes became the founding chief executive officer of the American Foundation for Addiction Research, whose mission is to encourage and fund research on sex addiction. Carnes also wrote more than thirteen books on sex addiction, and started a publishing press dedicated to the topic as well as two websites that provide information about sex addiction. Each of these organizations serves to legitimize the others and thus, fundamentally, the concept of sex addiction. Several different agencies exist, and they often refer to, report on, or cite one another, giving the illusion of a wide range of different organizations and people all working on the same problem. In actuality, however, it is a very small community of like-minded people who are likely to share similar orientations to the concept of sex addiction, including the definition of the illness as well as its symptoms, diagnosis, and treatment.

Historical events also helped to increase the popularity of the construction of sex addiction as a social problem. In 1989, convicted serial killer Ted Bundy claimed in a television interview the night before his execution that he was addicted to pornography. It was difficult for the public to reconcile Bundy's good upbringing, good looks, high level of intelligence (he was in law school when he committed some of the murders), and appearance of total normality, with his violent and ghastly crimes. The notion that a disease turned Bundy into a serial killer was not only compelling, but also believable, and it frightened viewers: there was, as he had said, no protection against the effects of pornography addiction.

The second major event that brought sex addiction to the public's attention was the 1998 sex scandal involving President Bill Clinton and White House staffer Monica Lewinsky. As the scandal broke, both commentators and therapists started diagnosing the president with sex addiction, although none of them claimed to have actually treated Clinton or even spoken to him about his sexual behaviors or psychological health. Psychologist Jerome Levine (1998) even dubbed sex addiction "the Clinton syndrome" in his book of the same name. Although much of the press coverage noted that the existence of sexual addiction as an illness was debated among those in the mental health field, the reports nonetheless got people talking about sexual addiction, and the focus of the public discourse was on whether President Clinton had a sexual addiction, not whether sex addiction actually existed. As Carnes noted, "The controversy generated a gigantic leap in awareness. If we were thirty to forty years behind the public understanding of alcoholism, we suddenly were only ten to fifteen years behind now" (2001, p. xiii).

The result of this public acceptance is that thousands of people started to identify themselves or loved ones as sex addicts, and the afflicted began seeking help for their condition. In 2012, the SASH website listed 23 treatment centers, 540 therapists, and eight twelve-step recovery groups for sex addicts and their families (SASH 2012), and this, of course, does not include all such treatment providers. The construction of this category affects the way people view themselves and experience their sexuality. The sex addict feels every bit of the guilt and despair felt by the masturbator in the eighteenth century; indeed, suicide attempts are reportedly common among sex addicts (Carnes 1992). And it's no wonder, if they believe the claims: not only is this a serious, even life-threatening illness, but it can be dangerous for family members as well. Just as the masturbator feared not only personal consequences, but passing their insanity on to their children, sex addicts must fear the same, since "many sex addicts were abused as children simply by being in the presence of an adult sex addict" (Carnes 1992, p. 113). It isn't necessary that the sex addict actually have any sexual relations with the child to be abusive. Rather, by being overtly sexual or sexualizing other people in the child's presence (such as remarking on the size of a woman's breasts), the sex addict creates a sexually charged environment, which constitutes abuse because such an environment can, according to Carnes, cause long-term psychological damage (with the child, in turn, likely to become a sex addict).

Identifying as a sex addict affects the addict's view of self. Sex addicts often consider themselves, like alcoholics, to be always in the process of recovery but never cured, because without diligence and self-control, the sex addiction may resurface, especially in periods of emotional stress. As with masturbation and homosexuality, this is often a self-diagnosed illness, for which the afflicted seek treatment from professionals in hopes of a cure. In self-diagnosing, the "deviants" apply scientific discourse upon themselves, employing a type of power that they hand over to the professional, to whom they must confess their deepest secrets and transgressions. Treatment often includes, for example, keeping a journal of every masturbatory fantasy, dream, and thought, which subsequently is shared with a therapist or group.

Of course, as more pop icons such as David Duchovny and Tiger Woods enter treatment for sex addiction, some people question whether these men actually have an illness or just use it as an excuse for their behavior. At the same time that some people raise these doubts, however, the popularity of shows such as Dr. Drew's *Celebrity Sex Rehab,* and the repeated attention given to sex addiction by talk shows such as *Oprah* and in segments on shows like *48 Hours,* serve to reinforce that, even if some people use the diagnosis as an excuse, the illness itself is legitimate.

Scientifically Normalizing Sex Addiction

It is perhaps too early in the process to see much resistance to the construction of sex addiction by the scientific field. Despite the fact that early on there were some debates about the nature, cause, and correct name for the disorder, addictionologists have largely reached consensus on the matter. This is in part because Carnes and his model of sexual addiction have exercised tremendous power within the field: the public education, training and certification, research, and funding all filter through Carnes's organizations. Although his name is no longer represented on the lists of board members or directors for most of these organizations, many of the people who are listed either have been trained by Carnes or have coauthored with him.

Sex therapists, sexologists, and sociologists have spoken out against the construction of sex addiction, but that was primarily early in the construction process, and today most sexologists and sex therapists seem to have ceded the battle. Psychologists and psychiatrists, on the other hand, have never publicly challenged the construction with any concerted effort, but have resisted in one very important way: by denying it acceptance as a new diagnosis in the fifth edition of the *Diagnostic and Statistical Manual*. Despite persistent and dedicated effort on the part of the sex addiction advocates, the American Psychological Association continues to exclude sex addiction as a category in its manual of mental disorders. By maintaining chemical dependency and compulsive disorders as the official requirements for diagnoses of addiction, psychologists continue to express doubt about whether behaviors, including sex, can actually be addictive. Note that this is not the same, however, as denying that people may *feel* out of control of their sexual behaviors. Most psychologists would consider this as part of a compulsive disorder. Thus they do not necessarily deny the existence of the condition, but rather the way in which it has been explained and constructed by addictionologists. This is different than arguing, as Kinsey, Ellis, Hirschfeld, and others did with masturbation and homosexuality, that these sexual behaviors are normal variations, and that the distress felt because of these behaviors is due more to the lack of social acceptance of them than to anything inherently destructive in the behaviors themselves. If this chapter's perspective holds true, however, we would expect that in thirty or forty years the construction will be challenged sufficiently that even addictionologists will abandon the disease model.

Conclusion

Michel Foucault (1990 [1978]) argued that part of the move toward modernity has been the emergence of sexuality as a social, rather than personal, problem. The burgeoning fields of science claimed sexuality as a site of both study and control. This control, however, is different than the imposed will of the sovereign: it is a more democratic control, exercised against everyone, by everyone, so that people even exercise such control against themselves. One form that this control takes is through discourse: discourse shapes the ideas people have about sexuality, and thus ultimately affects not only their sexual behavior and identities, but even how they experience those sexual identities. When such discourse is grounded in the language and values of science, even without scientific "proof," it is particularly powerful, as science claims itself to be not only objective and dispassionate, but also the ultimate authority on such matters. Categories of sexual behavior have long been constructed as social problems, but whether we are speaking of masturbation in the eighteenth century or sex addiction at the end of the twentieth, the construction process remains very similar. Those seeking legitimation for their fields stake out areas of expertise by defining new sexual illnesses. They chart the psychological and physical manifestations of the illness, as well as its consequences, and then declare themselves the most qualified to treat the illness. The new construction disseminates through the culture, creating new sexual identities that previously did not exist. People begin to identify themselves as afflicted with the so-called illness, which serves to further reinforce the construction. Eventually, however, someone in the field uses the scientific discourse to resist the disease construct, and future generations ponder how anyone could ever have been so backward as to think the behavior was a problem, much less a disease. This does not mean, of course, that it ceases being a political issue: whether to include masturbation in sex education curricula is still debated, and gay and lesbian rights continue to be a pressing political issue, but they are now constructed as political or religious, rather than medical, issues.

The phenomena we have examined here—masturbation, homosexuality, and sex addiction—are not the only examples of this process. Sexual anorexia (the opposite of sex addiction), inhibited sexual desire disorder, erectile dysfunction, gender identity disorder (transgenderism), and children who perpetrate sexual abuse are all in varying stages of this process as well. While we cannot definitively claim that everything that has or will be considered a sexual disease or problem will necessarily go through exactly these same steps, the similarity nevertheless provides food for thought. Perhaps when you hear about these "diseases" in the news, you will consider who the "experts" are, and what they stand to gain from constructing them as social problems.

8

Murdered Mothers:
The Social Construction
of Troubling Statistics

Keith Roberts Johnson

The case of Laci Peterson, murdered during the late stages of pregnancy in 2003, was followed by extensive media coverage claiming that such homicides were common. Frightening headlines—such as "Why Pregnant Women Are Targeted" and "Many New or Expectant Mothers Die Violent Deaths" (Robinson 2005; St. George 2004)—depicted maternal homicides as part of a "terrifying phenomenon" that was apparently sweeping the country (*Good Morning America* 2007). "In various news reports, maternal homicide was touted as an epidemic among pregnant women, and research that concluded homicide was a leading cause of injury-related death was often cited" (Fontaine and Parmley 2007, p. 155). The *Journal of the American Medical Association* reported "the disturbing finding that a pregnant or recently pregnant woman is more likely to be a victim of homicide than to die of any other cause" (Horon and Cheng 2001, p. 1455). The *British Journal of Obstetrics and Gynecology* published an article titled "Violent Deaths: The Hidden Face of Maternal Mortality" (Granja, Zacarias, and Bergstrom 2002), while an *American Journal of Public Health* article was titled "Homicide: A Leading Cause of Injury Deaths Among Pregnant and Postpartum Women in the United States" (Chang, Saltzman, and Herndon 2005). The claims that pregnant women were at risk of homicide were successful in changing public policy. They led to passage of the "Laci and Connor's Bill" (officially titled the "Unborn Victims of Violence Act, H.R. 1997"). It was signed into law by President George W. Bush on April 1, 2004 (Fontaine and Parmley 2007).

Disturbing claims are not new; they are the stuff of social problem construction (Best 2008). What is new and surprising is the basing of such claims on articles in peer-reviewed medical journals. This chapter explores how an emerging profession of biostatisticians claimed to have discovered a troubling condition—the unrecognized deaths of young women related to pregnancy or childbirth. While statistics might appear to be dry, factual elements in social problem claims, they often play a key role in constructing social problems (Best 2001, 2004). When coupled with disturbing examples, numbers that seem to reveal that a problem is large and growing can become frightening. In addition, there may be a feedback loop wherein a perception of growing problem leads to greater awareness of that problem, leading to more cases being reported, and a concomitant further increase in the numbers. Thus, John Johnson (1995) found that media reports of child abuse increased tenfold during the period that laws were being considered and public attention was focused on the issue. In other words, the ability to craft troubling statistics can make claims-makers influential.

This chapter focuses on how studies of pregnancy-related deaths served the interests of the researchers. First, they laid claims that in some jurisdictions (hospitals, cities, and states) there were undiscovered women's deaths, or at least a higher number than were being reported elsewhere. Next they published articles in medical journals arguing that women's maternal deaths must be higher nationwide, judging from these local statistics. They successfully challenged official death counts and took control over the calculation of the death statistics related to pregnancy and childbirth to maintain the legitimacy of their claim, even as contrary evidence built up that women's maternal health was actually improving. Through their control over the statistics of maternal mortality, these professionals took a series of steps to change the statistics so that they appeared ever larger and more frightening. Their statistics on the dangers of childbirth shifted to the dangers of being pregnant, finally focusing on the frightening act of murder. Thus, I argue that the public concern about homicides of pregnant women was a byproduct of developments within a medical profession that sought to expand its influence in order to prove its continued value.

Statistics Support Claims of the Importance of Medical Professionals and Their Work

Studies of social problem construction have noted that medical authorities are not disinterested parties to the claims they make. Stephen Pfohl (1977) argued that the pediatric radiologists who identified the battered-child syndrome enhanced their profession's status in the process. Pawluch (1996) described how advances in the medical care of infants and children reduced once-serious illnesses in those populations and, in the process, threatened to eliminate the need for pediatric specialists; in response, pediatricians expanded their professional domain by assuming responsibility for a broader age-range of patients. Analysts of medicalization have pointed to the increased authority of medical professionals as they successfully define ever more phenomena as medical problems (Brown 1995; Conrad 2007).

The statistics of homicides of pregnant women come from a medical subspecialty—maternal mortality professionals (MMPs). Maternal mortality research has been a subspecialty within public health for decades. It began around the beginning of the twentieth century as an effort by obstetricians to identify and document the causes of maternal deaths (such as "childbirth fever"), and to recommend methods of reducing these dangers. That campaign succeeded. Mortality related to pregnancy and childbirth, once a significant problem in the United States, underwent a steep decline, from 850 deaths per 100,000 births in 1900 to 7.5 deaths per 100,000 births by 1980—a reduction of more than 99 percent (CDC 1999). In the face of this decline, most physicians who tracked maternal mortality through local medical societies found they lacked enough cases to continue their work, so that the value of the work itself was called into question (Buekens 2001; Pearse 1977) and many shifted their focus to other threats, principally infant mortality (Marmol, Scriggins, and Vollman 1969).

However, not all MMPs were physician volunteers. Resident biostatisticians at the regional and national levels who desired to make a career in this field needed to construct maternal mortality as an ongoing, significant problem, in sharp contrast to the view of the medical profession.[1] Although maternal mortality appeared to have declined in major part, MMPs mounted a challenge to the official statistics of the National Center for Health Statistics (NCHS). They claimed that there were more deaths from childbirth than officially recognized.

The controversy over maternal health statistics is not new; it reflects a history of competing claims about women's maternal health, who measures it, and the size of the problem that the measures reveal. In short, statistics of mothers' deaths vary, differences in interpretation and measurement parallel the interests of the professionals describing the problem, and instead of recognizing the range of variation in numbers, interested parties choose a single number selected to represent their vision of the problem. This is one way among many to socially construct a statistic.

The Construction of High Rates of Maternal Death

MMP studies at the hospital, local, and state levels often found elevated numbers of pregnant and postpartum women's deaths in comparison with official data. Arguing that maternal mortality was greater than found in national statistics, MMPs staked a claim that only they were able to discern and study this social problem of underreported maternal deaths (Smith et al. 1984). This claimsmaking was twofold; not only were maternal deaths a troubling condition, but they were also a hidden and terrible secret that only MMPs—as sympathetic experts—could locate and bring to public attention. As concerned biostatisticians, they claimed to have the expertise and motivation to uncover this hidden threat to vulnerable, pregnant women.

Their studies found higher (in some cases, much higher) death rates than the national rate (Atrash et al. n.d.). However, the number of maternal deaths had become so small that their statistics had very high error rates. Hospitals, cities, states, and even nations have come to have very low numbers of maternal deaths, so that small changes in these numbers can produce large changes in rates. For example, the 2005 reports of maternal mortality show that there was one death from that cause in Ireland, two in Denmark, and three in Sweden (WHO 2007, pp. 23–27). The World Health Organization acknowledged the statistical difficulties: "The [resulting] uncertainty bounds are extremely wide" (WHO 2002, p. 17).

In April 2010 in London, an announcement in the *Lancet,* a medical journal, that worldwide maternal deaths had declined to 342,900, caused controversy, especially since public health advocates continued to claim a much higher figure: "The number of women dying in childbirth worldwide has dropped dramatically, a British medical journal reports, adding that it was pressured to delay its findings. . . . A new, separate report . . . reached a very different conclusion . . . 500,000 deaths a year. The disagreement reveals the politics behind public health, where progress . . . can jeopardize funding" (Cheng 2010).[2]

In their articles, the MMPs consistently referred to the discrepancy between their statistics and official ones as the "underreporting" of the problem. But studying a large number of different settings (states, cities, hospitals, regions, and other sources of statistics) will find some with high death rates. Publishing cases with high death rates while ignoring the majority with low rates reflects a statistical bias—there is an inverse relation between the size of the reporting jurisdiction and the published maternal death ratio. In a review of those early studies, the US national maternal mortality rate (one study) is 9.1 deaths per 100,000 births, the rates in individual states (five studies) vary between 11.1 and 40.4, while city and hospital rates (five studies) vary between 21.9 and 51.6 (Atrash et al. n.d., p. 144, tab. 1). In short, studying smaller entities allows researchers to find and report cases with higher maternal deaths.

Another form of this bias is that a central city or county with specialized maternity hospitals or trauma centers attracts women with problem pregnancies from a wide area, thus distorting that hospital's maternal mortality rate (Ho et al. 2002, p. 1216). In one study, women who were transferred from one hospital to another (presumably to a facility specializing in problem pregnancies) were six times more likely to die than those not transferred (Panchal, Arria, and Labhsetwar 2001). Studies of single hospitals or cities, particularly those that specialize in maternal cases, often produce upwardly biased findings.

Publication of a series of such local studies with apparently higher maternal mortality rates in the 1980s and 1990s created a climate of scientific legitimacy for claims that maternal mortality was generally underreported (Atrash et al. n.d.). The title of a *Family Planning Perspectives* article repeats the claim: "U.S. Maternal Mortality Greatly Underreported, Collaborative Study Finds" (1988). The attention these findings received led to more studies, more reports of increased mortality, and a unifying of specialists studying maternal mortality, compared with generalist biostatisticians. MMPs affiliated with cities, hospitals, or regions with notably high maternal deaths were mobilized to conduct their own studies and report them as more evidence that supported the growing legitimacy of the claim that maternal mortality was being underreported. The MMPs and the "media" of professional journals were acting as a social movement through organizing and supplying peer-reviewed, professional research.

Expanding the Definitions of Maternal Death

MMPs next challenged generalist biostatisticians for control over the definition and measurement of all maternal mortality. As MMPs gradually assumed control over the measurement process, they would generate larger numbers that would be considered official. Citing the published studies as proof of underreported maternal deaths, several interest groups of the emerging MMPs joined together to promote new reporting standards that would capture more missing deaths on a national scale. These groups included the American College of Nurse-Midwives, the maternal mortality special interest groups in the American Medical Association and the American College of Obstetricians and Gynecologists, specialists from some state and local medical committees, and the Centers for Disease Control (CDC) (Krulewitch et al. 2001; Smith et al. 1984).

Their claims challenged the data collected by the National Center for Health Statistics. The CDC conducted a review of NCHS data, in part to standardize reporting but also to find evidence of national underreporting (Smith et al. 1984). The 2,690 case files of women who died while pregnant or shortly afterward during 1974 to 1976 had been sent by all US reporting areas to the NCHS. The NCHS classified 1,949 of these as maternal deaths. In its review, the CDC argued that 400 additional cases should be classified as maternal deaths. According to the CDC reviewers, cases where fatal conditions such as cancer, diabetes, heart problems, and the like, had been found to cause the mother's death by the NCHS should have been classified as cases of maternal mortality. They asserted that the state of being pregnant or postpartum could have exacerbated the women's fatal conditions (Smith et al. 1984). This review increased the number of maternal deaths by 20 percent. While the result was described as correcting underreporting, it actually relaxed standards defining maternal mortality (Zemach 1984).

Registries of maternal deaths are subject to an array of hidden biases, including incomplete reporting of deaths, but they are also subject to false positives—mistaken reports of maternal deaths. For example, Daniel Pallin and colleagues (2002, p. 1320) found that errors in registering pregnant or postpartum women's deaths (when they had not in fact died) were common, leading in major part to a false-positive rate of 19 percent. Yet while the review conducted by Jack Smith and colleagues (1984, p. 782) carefully studied the records of the 741 deaths not classified by the NCHS as maternal deaths, none of the 1,949 cases classified as maternal deaths were reviewed for false positives. The review was designed to locate additional maternal deaths, but not to identify any mistakes that might reduce the total. The conclusion of the Smith review that there was an underreporting of 20 percent of maternal deaths, therefore, is itself biased, even apart from differences in definitions.

Rita Zemach, head of the NCHS, responded to the claims of the Smith review in an editorial of the *American Journal of Public Health*. She advised that "part of the problem is the lack of consensus, and the changing definitions, as to what constitutes a pregnancy-related death," and cautioned against unrealistic expectations of the registry (Zemach 1984, pp. 757–758). However, the emergent MMPs were already conducting their own national research to bypass the NCHS.

In 1983 the MMPs, organized into the Maternal Mortality Collaborative, began a national study for the years 1980–1985 within the CDC. While the MMPs claimed that the number of maternal deaths they uncovered in this study was 37 percent greater than the number claimed by NCHS, their work changed the definition of maternal mortality to include still more cases (Rochat et al. 1988).

MMPs continually redefined what it meant to be pregnant and postpartum. The tight link between the perils of childbirth (shock, infection, hemorrhage, thrombosis, reaction to anesthesia, etc.) and the statistics of maternal mortality was steadily loosened. Eventually all women's deaths around the time of pregnancy or thereafter were classified as instances of maternal mortality (WHO 2002; Shadigian and Bauer 2005). Thus, a woman who dies in an auto crash months or years after having a pregnancy terminated becomes a case. This inclusive definition of maternal mortality facilitates statistical studies linking databases of pregnant women with registers of death certificates (Pallin et al. 2002). But the medical and social meaning of the resulting statistics has been lost. This change happened over years, as the definitions of pregnancy and mortality, and even the statistics measuring maternal mortality, underwent repeated changes.

The first change was to include some medical conditions, such as cancer or heart disease, that could be aggravated by pregnancy.

These cases were called "pregnancy-related maternal mortality" in the literature (Koonin et al. 1997; Nannini et al. 2002; WHO 2002). By setting aside the traditional consensus on causes of maternal mortality, MMPs opened their field to controversy about how far such definitions could reach. Their papers stated that only trained professionals (such as themselves) could determine from medical records whether a death had been accelerated or caused by pregnancy (Chang et al. 2003; Rochat et al. 1988; Smith et al. 1984). By 2000, maternal mortality was being calculated by three different statistics for three different levels of causes (WHO 2002). Because different researchers adopted different standards, studies appeared that were not comparable, making it hard to track changes over time. In a comparison of the new "indirect deaths" with the old "direct deaths" caused by the pregnancy itself, the former were found in Britain to be the greater number (CEMD 2001). Three different statistics measured different causes of death: maternal mortality (direct medical causes), pregnancy-related mortality (other medical causes that could have been affected by the pregnancy), and pregnancy-associated mortality (unrelated deaths, as from accidental injury) (Horon and Cheng 2001; WHO 2002). Each of these expansions was explained as an advance in eliminating underreporting and exposing the size of the apparently increasing problem.

As the definition of maternal mortality was being expanded, a second limitation of the traditional definition came under scrutiny. A diagnosis of maternal mortality had been limited to deaths within forty-two days of giving birth (Smith et al. 1984; WHO 2002). But once the possible causes had been expanded to include pregnancy-related conditions, deaths occurring much later could be assigned to a previous state of pregnancy. Initially, some MMPs used a time period of ninety days after pregnancy's end to include cases of maternal deaths (Shadigian and Bauer 2005). But that limitation soon expanded to one year, as established in the Maternal Mortality Unit of the CDC (Chang et al. 2003). By 2005, a review of the maternal mortality literature found that studies used time periods after pregnancy's end from forty-two days to eight years later (Shadigian and Bauer 2005). Obviously, the longer the timeframe adopted, the greater the number of deaths included. A review of different articles about maternal risk concluded that the varying definitions made comparisons impossible (Shadigian and Bauer 2005). In short, the MMPs had lost their consensus on their mandate; they were no longer monitoring maternal mortality, but newer, less-well-defined statistics of deaths variously associated with pregnancy and its aftermath.

Newly Constructed Statistics May Produce Even Larger Numbers

Biostatisticians have used the maternal mortality rate statistic of deaths per 100,000 live births because births and deaths are universally understood around the world (Buekens 2001; WHO 2007). But this ratio is only an approximation, for the number of births is not identical with the number of pregnancies. Pregnancies can end with a live birth but also through abortions (spontaneous or induced) and stillbirths. In the United States, the number of births and the number of pregnancies are known to be quite different. Arguably, one would have to consider the number of pregnancies to find the population of women at risk. In 1996, there were an estimated 6,240,000 pregnancies in the United States, compared to 3,891,000 births (US Bureau of the Census, 2002). One could include the number of spontaneous abortions (from medical records: 980,000) and induced abortions (1,370,000) as well as stillbirths to attain a total of pregnancies. A statistic of maternal mortality ignoring the number of pregnancies not leading to births increases the statistic by 62 percent in 1996 data. This statistic increases the apparent risk to pregnant or postpartum women, and makes them appear to be in greater danger than their nonpregnant age-mates. In the case of homicide, this flawed comparison has become the basis for claims that pregnant women are at a higher risk than women who aren't pregnant and appear to be "targeted" for murder.

There are additional problems with a statistic defining pregnancy over a lengthy time period, such as one year after its termination. In any mortality study the number of deaths counted comes from the population of women who had been pregnant or postpartum during the time period taken in the measure. Thus, a study of maternal mortality for the year 2000 with a one-year postpartum timeframe would include deaths in 2000 of women who became pregnant in 1998 whose pregnancies ended in 1999, as well as all women who were pregnant in 1999. Of course, all women pregnant in 2000 would also be included. The implications of a minor change like this in calculating a simple statistic are very great. The number of births (the denominator) is for one year, but the number of women at risk is derived over multiple years.

Large Numbers Support Claims to Take Action

Worldwide, an estimated 585,000 women died from complications of pregnancy in 1990 (WHO 1993). The 1990 WHO estimate was that 99.5 percent of those deaths (582,000) were in developing countries. One conclusion from this disparity is that the medical problems of maternal mortality have been essentially solved in the developed world (Shiffman 2000). The First Safe Motherhood Conference produced a Safe Motherhood Initiative to reduce maternal deaths in developing countries by 50 percent by the year 2000 (Mahler 1987; Shiffman 2000).

MMPs in the United States responded to this recommendation as though the difference between the United States and the third world did not exist, putting forward a demand in 1987 that the US maternal mortality rate be reduced from 7.5 per 100,000 live births to 3.3 by the year 2000, a reduction greater than 50 percent. This reduction was incorporated into the Healthy People 2000 federal initiative (US Department of Health and Human Services 2000). But the unmet needs of women in developing countries for health services, antibiotics, and prenatal care are enormous, and those needs define the changes required to reduce their high death rates. In contrast, in nations with modern health systems, little can be done to further reduce mortality: "maternal deaths in developed countries are now rare, and the factors that surround the death are often peculiar to the event, complex and are not generalizable" (Pattinson and Hall 2003, p. 232). While possibly more realistic, the recognition that there may be an irreducible minimum to the reduction of pregnant women's deaths stands in stark contrast to the claims of social movements, wherein all deaths are constructed as tragic and preventable. In short, MMP demands for a drastic reduction in US maternal deaths guaranteed that negative news would come from failure to achieve a goal that was out of reach.

When the year 2000 arrived, not only had the US maternal mortality rate failed to decline to its objective of 3.3 per 100,000 births, but it had actually increased from its 1980 level of 7.5 to 11 per 100,000 live births, an increase of about 50 percent (Christiansen 2006; WHO 2002). In contrast, the decrease for all industrialized countries over the period 1990–2005 was 23.6 percent (WHO 2007, p. 24), and with the exception of North America, all world areas reported declines in maternal mortality.

This result could be interpreted as an embarrassment for the US medical and public health fields. However, MMPs saw it from a quite different perspective. This high level of US maternal mortality was claimed as an *underreporting* of maternal deaths, just as underreporting had been claimed throughout the career of the MMPs. The reported rate of 11 deaths per 100,000 live births was increased to an estimate of 17 deaths per 100,000 live births in the United States to counter the claimed underreporting (WHO 2002). A still larger number was quoted by the CDC's director, 20 deaths per 100,000 live births (Marks 2002a). If this estimate were true, US maternal deaths had increased by 267 percent and would be double the total for all other industrialized countries combined.

The apparent increase in US maternal mortality is even more anomalous when we consider that other measures of US maternal health during pregnancy improved during this period, such as the percentage of women obtaining prenatal care, percentage of pregnant women not smoking, percentage gaining the ideal weight during their pregnancies, and proportion not suffering severe complications of pregnancy (Mahler 1987; Sondik 1999). The parallel statistic of US infant mortality was also reported to have met its Healthy People 2000 reduction goal over the 1990–2000 decade, while maternal mortality supposedly had increased (Sondik 1999).

The numbers reported by the MMPs make it appear that the progress of the past century in women's health has been reversed in the United States, with hundreds of unrecorded cases of dead mothers every year. According to the report "Deadly Delivery": "Disturbing as these figures are, they probably significantly understate the problem. There are no federal requirements to report maternal deaths and US authorities concede that the number of maternal deaths may be twice as high" (Amnesty International 2010, p. 16).

The "Deadly Delivery" report cites a total of 760 maternal deaths in the United States during 2006 (almost 20 per 100,000 births); if the actual number is up to "twice as high," then up to another 760 remain to be counted every year, redoubling the estimates. It is likely that the apparent increase is constructed by the MMPs through defining new cases, expanding definitions and time periods, expanding the numbers they do have by estimates of underreporting, and overstating numbers to create bad news. The expansion of the domain commanded by the MMPs is tracked by the expansion in the numbers of victims they construct and the statistics reporting them.

Professional Concern Turns to
Maternal Accidents and Homicide

The numbers of pregnant or postpartum women dying from medical causes may have declined markedly in the twentieth century, but women's deaths from accidents, suicide, and homicide did not (Forum on Child and Family Statistics 2005). These "injury deaths" attracted the notice of the MMPs as cases of maternal deaths that formerly were outside the medical model of childbirth risks. The expansion of MMP interest in a troublesome condition entered a new cycle. The foundation was laid to define deaths that were characteristic of young, healthy people to be an increasing problem for pregnant or postpartum women. When flawed statistics were used to measure injury deaths, the rates of death from these causes, like the statistic of maternal mortality, also appeared elevated among pregnant or postpartum women.

As when the career of the MMPs first began in staking claims of underreporting of women's childbirth deaths, a second flurry of papers were put forward claiming that there were more homicide deaths of pregnant or postpartum women than were revealed in national statistics. The titles of more recent MMP journal articles revealed this new focus: "Trauma: The Leading Cause of Maternal Death" (Fildes et al. 1992), "Hidden from View: Violent Deaths Among Pregnant Women in the District of Columbia, 1988–1996" (Krulewitch et al. 2001), and "Violent Deaths: The Hidden Face of Maternal Mortality" (Granja, Zacarias, and Bergstrom 2002). Even editorials in professional journals echoed this new orientation: "Study Uncovers 'Disturbing' Level of Pregnancy-Associated Homicide" (Ramsay 2001); "Have We Overlooked the Most Common Cause of Maternal Mortality in the United States?" (Alpert 2001). A review of the literature noted that "before the early 1990s, there was little research dedicated to homicide or suicide during or after pregnancy" and concluded that these injury deaths were "understudied" (Shadigian and Bauer 2005, p. 183).

Elaine Alpert summarizes this transition nicely: "Remarkable advances in the medical care of pregnant women have allowed pregnancy-related deaths to be reduced to the realm of rare . . . events. However, research has begun to elucidate a chilling association between pregnancy and intentional, lethal violence" (2001, p. 3). The discovery of this new threat escalates the basic narrative of women in peril in that these deaths are not just ignored (or at least underreported), they are carried out on purpose. Murder fits the needs of claimsmakers perfectly, for the deceased can be portrayed as innocent victims, and the cases defined as completely preventable. Although the numbers of such deaths may be small, they dramatize and mobilize support for viewing women's health as a social problem, and support claims for the need to reduce such deaths dramatically. The problem can be typified as the horrible death of a pregnant woman and her fetus (St. George 2004a, 2004b), while large numbers support claims that the social problem being typified is very great (Best 2001).

Homicide appears in journal articles as the substitute for the medical deaths that have been reduced over the twentieth century: "the 100-fold decrease we have seen in the nineteenth century medical complications is to be matched by a similar decrease in twenty-first century causes of fatality, most notably murder at the hands of intimates [the men in these women's lives]" (Alpert 2001, p. 3).

Maternal homicide studies, beginning with reports from single hospitals, cities, and states that highlight homicide deaths among pregnant or postpartum women, often asserted that such deaths were underreported and that the threat was unrecognized (Dannenberg et al. 1995; Dietz and Rochat 1998; Krulewitch, Roberts, and Thompson 2003). Based on these reports that established scientific legitimacy for the claim that murders of women were underreported, the MMPs took control of the statistics through a national database of pregnant or postpartum homicide cases set up in the CDC (Chang et al. 2003). They report: "Of all pregnancy-associated injury deaths (n = 1993), 617 (31.0%) women died as a result of homicide, ranking homicide as the second leading cause of total injury reported deaths . . . which represent 8.4% of the total of 7342 reported deaths" (Chang, Saltzman, and Herndon 2005, pp. 471–472). In this report a category accounting for only 8.4 percent of all deaths, by statistical sleight of hand, becomes a "leading cause of . . . deaths." This is accomplished by removing from view the medical deaths and only considering the "injury deaths." Thus we come full circle, as many MMPs turn away from their basic mandate, studying maternal mortality resulting from medical complications from childbirth, and substitute a more dramatic and frightening social problem that eventually leads to a moral panic.

Although the MMPs were able to conduct a major study of national maternal deaths from homicides, the study never addressed the basic question raised by their claim: Are pregnant women at greater risk of homicide than other women? It was enough to report that "awareness" of the problem had increased (Chang, Saltzman, and Herndon 2005, p. 471), as if the problem itself was increasing. A brief check of the *US Statistical Abstract* (2000) and the *Uniform Crime Reports* (FBI 2000, tab. 2.5) provides an answer to this question. For the year 1998, dividing the number of women of childbearing age murdered in the United States (1,966) by the total number of women of that age (60,108,000) shows that a woman's risk of death from homicide was 3.3 per 100,000. Calculating the comparable rate for pregnant or postpartum women is complicated because the CDC's data include all homicides within one year after giving birth, and a majority of those homicides occurred not when the woman was pregnant, but afterward. Even accepting the CDC's number of 70 deaths of pregnant or postpartum women a year (per 6,200,000 pregnant), the murder rate is 1.1 per 100,000, or one-third the rate for other women. Whether this difference is due to pregnant women actually being safer, or due to a massive, national underreporting of their deaths, depends on accepting the claims of the MMPs. The CDC's homicide database, in fact, was soon criticized by the MMPs for not locating adequate numbers of victims, and as being a case of alleged underreporting itself (Horon 2005).

Conclusion

The past century's reduction in maternal deaths by more than 99 percent is one of the greatest triumphs of modern medicine. But success in the twentieth century has led to a problem for the twenty-first-century professionals who have dedicated their careers to studying maternal mortality. As childbirth-related deaths declined, they justified their work by expanding the definition of maternal mortality and making dubious claims to support their new statistics. These biostatisticians have taken steps that undermine their profession's core competence in statistical skills and research in order to advance social problem claims. They first claimed that large numbers of deaths of pregnant and postpartum women were going unreported, then that the number of maternal deaths was increasing, despite evidence to the contrary. Finally, we have the basis for the moral panic, that murder was a particular risk facing pregnant women. The career of the profession follows a familiar path of expanding claimsmaking. It begins with locating sites where there are more deaths than usual, and advancing a claim that this finding is proof of official underreporting of the newly discovered problem. Once legitimized through published articles in medical journals, the maternal mortality professionals take control over the official statistics, and then follow a series of steps to construct ever larger numbers of deaths. Eventually they increase the official statistic by including estimates to counter the underreporting they claim to have found. As the number of women's deaths from childbirth continues to decline, new claims that include other causes of mothers' deaths have become a larger part of these professionals' work. It remains to be seen whether these new and expanding claims are sustainable, or if the profession will eventually lose its legitimacy as the social problem that supports the need for its existence is further reduced.

Afterword: The Moral Panic

Reports of homicides of pregnant or postpartum women have been widespread in the media. They most often focus on pregnant females while slighting the fact that the majority of homicides in the MMPs' research occur not during pregnancy, but during the year afterward (data recalculated from tables in Chang, Saltzman, and Herndon 2005). The MMPs are not separate from the media panic. Not only have they contributed to it, but they are also quoted as a source of legitimacy for the public's fears. They support a social problem definition of maternal mortality in media headlines: "Researchers Stunned by Scope of Slayings" (St. George 2004b). These claims that homicide is a major threat to pregnant women have been widely disseminated:

> Pregnant and recently pregnant women are more likely to be victims of homicide than to die of any other cause. (Family Violence Prevention Fund 2006)

> Homicide is the leading cause of death among pregnant or recently pregnant women. (Frye 2001)

> Several studies have found that pregnant women are more likely to die of homicide than of any natural cause. (Brown 2005)

In a further blending of fact and fiction, the Laci Peterson case led to a made-for-television movie, and to continued media attention to the investigation and trial of Scott Peterson:

> Scott Peterson's guilty verdict on Friday culminates nearly two years of sensational news coverage, one of the highest-rated TV movies and thousands of Internet postings. The world was gripped with the idea a man could kill not only the woman he married, but the child he conceived. Unfortunately, that scenario is not so rare. Murder is, in fact, the No. 1 cause of death among pregnant women. (Cook 2004)

Thus, homicide becomes an important but largely neglected problem, one that can be discerned and revealed only by skilled, determined, and highly motivated experts, the maternal mortality professionals. This leads to calls for further efforts to identify more unreported homicides:

> Additionally, other research has shown that a proportion of suicides, fatal overdoses and deaths that appear on the surface to be accidental may indeed be attributed to intimate partner violence. It can thus be inferred that domestic violence may well be the single most common cause of maternal mortality. (Alpert 2001, p. 3)

> Emphasis should be placed on making the diagnosis of pregnancy in women who are victims of fatal trauma and identifying the perpetrators of pregnancy-associated homicide. (Shadigian and Bauer 2005, p. 189)

As shown in the boundary expansion leading up to and including the CDC registry of women homicide victims (Chang, Saltzman, and Herndon 2005), the maternal mortality professionals have laid the foundation for shifting their focus from maternal mortality as a social problem of inadequate medical care to a more graphic problem of women as murder victims. However, this change in focus leads their profession away from public health concerns about prenatal care and safe delivery for new mothers. The clients of the MMPs, originally physicians and hospitals who adapted their practices to improve women's health, have changed and become diffuse. The statistics constructed by the MMPs have lost their focus and meaning. The MMPs have lost control of their core competency—monitoring the best single measure of women's health during pregnancy. In order to get back on track, the MMPs will need to undo a lot of the claims their members have made about hidden threats to pregnant or post-partum women, up to and including murder.

Notes

1. The replacement of physicians by biostatisticians over the years is also a replacement of male professionals by a predominantly female profession. A majority of all the authors of the MMP articles reported here appear to be female, as befitting a profession concerned with women's health. The implications of the women biostatisticians linking their work to the causes of feminists (domestic violence, women as victims, men as targeting their partners) is beyond the scope of this chapter. However, it has already been noted that ties between feminists and the MMPs have become close (Marks 2002b).

2. Maria Cheng's report is not entirely accurate in citing the United Nations as objecting to the smaller figure of mother's deaths. The medical journal's editor has not revealed the source of the pressure, and the larger number comes from an advocate's source, not the UN (Brainard 2010).

9

Prophets in the Wilderness: Predicting Financial Collapse

John Barnshaw

See, I am sending my messenger ahead of you, who will prepare your way; the voice of one crying out in the wilderness.
—Mark 1:2–3 (NRSV)

Since Malcom Spector and John Kitsuse (1973, p. 146) asserted there are "subjective elements" to the development of social problems, researchers have been eager to demonstrate how various troubling conditions come to be seen as social problems that individuals, groups, policymakers, and society should attempt to remedy. For example, Stephen Pfohl (1977, p. 318) demonstrated how the problem of child abuse was first identified during the nineteenth-century "house of refuge" movement, but it wasn't until nearly a century later, when pediatric radiologists took ownership over the issue and "discovered" child abuse, that social norms toward mistreating children began to change. Over the past four decades, there have been many more studies of how claims and claimsmakers draw attention to a troubling condition, policymakers decide to take action about the condition, and the issue is "successfully" constructed as a social problem in the sense that policymakers attempt to remedy the problem (for example, see Benson and Saguy 2005; Boyle, Songora, and Foss 2001; Jenkins 1998; Loseke 1992). Based upon this vast literature, one might conclude that nearly anything can become a social problem, provided there are claimsmakers willing to make claims about a troubling condition. However, at any given time, we can find many individuals and groups making claims, and yet most of these claims do not result in new social movements or in policymakers deciding to take up these troubling conditions. Thus it is reasonable to conclude that there exists a selection bias that leads researchers to choose to study successful claimsmaking activities that develop into new social movements or policy changes.

There are relatively few accounts in the social problems literature of people making claims about troubling conditions and policymakers failing to take action about these troubling conditions. A notable exception is research by Joel Best and Gerald Horiuchi (1985, p. 495), who found that urban legends such as the razor blade in the apple and other acts of Halloween sadism are examples of troubles being identified, but followed by little concern among the public and policymakers. Robert Stallings (1995) found that even when credible claimsmakers such as geologists made claims about the troubling condition of earthquakes, policymakers chose not to systematically address the threat of earthquake risk.

The lack of research on claimsmaking activities that do not lead to the successful outcome of a new social movement or policy change is an important issue for at least two reasons. First, by focusing only on claimsmaking activities that lead to social problems, researchers lack a comparison group for understanding why some claims are picked up by media, or draw the attention of policymakers, and why others do not prove similarly influential. Second, and perhaps more important, when claimsmakers do warn about pending troubling conditions, this allows policymakers to attempt to remedy a problem beforehand, which may be beneficial for society. However, when these warnings go unheeded, it raises the specter that additional remediation and claimsmaking will be necessary.

This chapter explores the claimsmaking activities of three financial experts who attempted to warn about the impending US financial collapse that led to the Great Recession. Within hours of the 2008 bankruptcy of investment bank Lehman Brothers, Merrill Lynch, once one of the five largest investment banks in the world, was acquired by Bank of America. The following day, American International Group, the world's largest insurer, was effectively nationalized by the Federal Reserve. By the end of the week, Federal Reserve chairman Ben Bernanke and Treasury secretary Henry Paulson would be on Capitol Hill requesting $700 billion to purchase "troubled assets" in what would become known as the Troubled Assets Relief Program (TARP), the largest federal intervention in the banking system since the Great Depression. The collapse of Lehman Brothers also sent the global financial system into freefall as credit began to freeze and trillions of dollars in shareholder value was wiped out. European banks wrote down a combined $1.6 trillion due to their exposure from the US financial sector (Wroughton 2009).

Given the severity and scale of the economic crisis and subsequent recession, how is it that some individuals were able to identify troubling conditions before the collapse of Lehman Brothers yet were unsuccessful in their attempts to draw attention to their claims, despite being accurate in their predictions. These "prophets in the wilderness" were economists and financial experts who attempted to warn executives, policymakers, and the public by making specific claims, only to be dismissed by the majority of economists, financial experts, and policymakers. Whether it was economist Robert Shiller, who believed that the housing market was overvalued, Nassim Taleb, who believed that investment banks such as Lehman Brothers were using inappropriate risk-modeling, or Kyle Bass, who sought to use his knowledge of the financial system to short (or sell off) securities, each of these individuals offered specific predictions that were ignored or dismissed at the time.

We begin our discussion of these unsuccessful claimsmakers, or "prophets in the wilderness," by discussing who these individuals were, what they observed about financial instability, and what they did with this information. From their experiences, we are able to observe five broad themes that help us understand how they made claims about the financial system. Following this discussion, the chapter returns to the issue of why their accurate predictions were not incorporated into the social problems process and did not result in policy or social changes.

Robert Shiller

Robert Shiller is a professor of economics at Yale University. He is coauthor of a series of indices that measure the value of home prices in at least ten metropolitan areas in the United States, commonly referred to as the Case-Shiller Indices. In addition to his research on home values, Shiller (1981, 1984, 2003) has also published numerous articles and books critiquing mainstream economic perspectives such as the efficient-market hypothesis. Shiller (2008) has also worked to develop an emerging paradigm in economics known as behavioral economics, which emphasizes the role that psychological processes play in shaping activity in economics and the financial system. Despite his sharp critiques of the mainstream approaches, his colleagues in economics have valued his knowledge and contributions to his field enough to elect him president of the Eastern Economic Association and vice president of the American Economic Association.

As the economy began to recover from the technology bubble and the subsequent shocks of the September 11, 2001, terrorist attacks, Shiller and his colleague Karl Case began to explore whether there was a speculative bubble in the housing market. In 2003, Case and Shiller looked at a variety of home prices in different metropolitan areas and concluded that although there were elements of a speculative bubble, most notably in areas on the coasts of the United States, there did not appear to be sufficient conditions to produce a substantial decline in national home prices. Shiller's prediction in 2003 about the lack of evidence to trigger a national slide in home prices is indicative of his not having a consistently negative outlook about the financial system. Rather, Case and Shiller's (2003) work used a variety of different data sources ranging from national home prices to sophisticated regression analyses of unemployment and housing starts, which they used to reach inferences that there did not appear to be evidence of a national housing bubble. Indeed, it is important to recognize that even an alternative claimsmaker, or "prophet in the wilderness," is fallible and might draw inferences that in retrospect are not accurate (in this case, Case and Shiller were ultimately wrong in their 2003 conclusions). However, what is important is their willingness to seek disconfirming evidence and explore alternative viewpoints based upon data.

As home prices continued to escalate, Shiller began to change his position on the likelihood that there might be a real estate bubble. In 2005, the second edition of his widely popular book *Irrational Exuberance* was released. Shiller used the opportunity to write a new preface stating that "people in much of the world are still overconfident that the stock market, and in many places the housing market, will do extremely well, and this overconfidence can lead to instability." Shiller then proceeded to predict that future rises in home prices could lead to "significant declines" in home prices and that these declines would, in turn, result in "a substantial increase in the rate of personal bankruptcies, which could lead to a secondary string of bankruptcies of financial institutions as well" (p. xv). Although

Shiller did not specifically mention Lehman Brothers, he did predict that home-mortgage defaults could trigger a greater instability in the financial system that could possibly lead to a worldwide recession. During this period, from 2002 to 2006, the conventional wisdom of economists, financial experts, and policymakers was that if there was any financial instability due to rising home-price values, it would likely be contained, and thus a worldwide recession would be highly unlikely. In June 2005, Shiller reiterated his concerns in an article in *Barron's,* stating that "the home-price bubble feels like the stock market mania in the fall of 1999" (Cassidy 2009, p. 19).

Nonetheless, it is conceivable that a few comments and some specific predictions linking previous financial instability with the possibility of future instability could be constructed as an attempt by Shiller to sell additional volumes of an already popular book. However, as interest rates began to rise, and adjustable-rate mortgages began to reset, Shiller and Case used their personas as respected claimsmakers to warn policymakers, the media and the public, and pretty much anyone who was in a position to do something, that their data now strongly indicated a substantial likelihood that home prices were in decline, which could cause great instability for the financial system. Perhaps the most profound and direct warning came in the form of an op-ed in the *Wall Street Journal* on August 30, 2006:

> Unfortunately, there is significant risk of a very bad period, with slow sales, slim commissions, falling prices, rising default and foreclosures, serious trouble in financial markets, and a possible recession sooner than most of us expected. Deterioration in that intangible housing market psychology is the most uncertain factor in the outlook today. Listen hard and watch out. (Case and Shiller 2006)

Despite the warnings, financial experts inside investment banks continued to securitize mortgages amid record profits, while policymakers continued to assert their belief that any problems in the residential mortgage market were contained (Bernanke 2006; Paulson 2008). Undeterred, Shiller (2008) took to writing another book in an effort to warn economists, financial experts, policymakers, and the public; he titled it *The Subprime Solution: How Today's Financial Crisis Happened, and What to Do About It.* Shiller's book was released one month before the bankruptcy of Lehman Brothers and the start of the global economic recession and consolidation of the remaining investment banks. Like *Irrational Exuberance* before it,

The Subprime Solution would go on to become an international best-seller, helped by the timing of its release coinciding with another downturn in the US economy, as Shiller's predictions had once again gone largely unheeded by his fellow economists, financial experts, and policymakers.

Nassim Taleb

One person who did listen to Robert Shiller, calling him "a visionary" and a man of "remarkable insights," was Nassim Taleb (2001, p. 35). Born in Amioun, Lebanon, and educated at the University of Pennsylvania and the University of Paris, Taleb is an author, financial expert, philosopher, and a professor of risk-engineering at the Polytechnic Institute of New York University. As a financial expert, Taleb has held a series of senior positions in a variety of major financial institutions, including seven of the ten largest investment banks. At investment banks, Taleb oversaw all four major types of derivatives—forwards, futures, options, and swaps (e.g., credit default swaps).

Nassim Taleb's first book, titled *Dynamic Hedging: Managing Vanilla and Exotic Options* and published in 1997, explored derivative trading strategies from the routine (so-called vanilla) to complex (so-called exotic). The book was a relatively popular finance book and established Taleb as a respected claimsmaker who had intimate knowledge and expertise of derivatives, one of the most complex areas in the entire US financial system. It was Taleb's views on exotic forms of finance, and particularly how firms assessed risk, that made him one of the most vocal critics in the industry.

In the late 1990s, as Value-at-Risk modeling began to gain greater acceptance as a viable tool for risk management, Taleb (a risk manager at the time) spoke out about this approach's problems. Value-at-Risk modeling attempts to predict future risks based upon historical conditions. Taleb knew that although historical data are often a good predictor of future behavior, even large quantities of prior observations do not ensure that future behavior will resemble that of the past. Therefore, since Value-at-Risk modeling is based upon prior observations, especially more recent observations, such modeling is largely unable to predict a rapidly changing future that has little correlation to the past. At a conference before many of the financial experts who relied upon Value-at-Risk, Taleb claimed that

Value-at-Risk "is the alibi bankers will give shareholders to show documented due diligence and will express that their blow-up came from truly unforeseeable circumstances and events with low probability—not from taking large risks that they did not understand" (1997a, pp. 2–3). Although acknowledged as a flaw by Value-at-Risk creator Philippe Jorion (1997), Taleb's claims were largely ignored by policymakers, regulators, and risk managers at investment banks because there was so little evidence to conclude that a massive negative outcome was likely to occur in the short term.

Over time, Taleb's vocal criticisms led him to be labeled as a "prophet of doom and boom." However, this moniker is an inaccurate assessment of his overall work, as it dismisses the claimsmaker rather than the claim (Appleyard 2008). In contrast to Shiller, who relied heavily upon longitudinal and short-term data to determine the extent to which something may be generalizable, Taleb often used data to determine the extent to which something may *not* be generalizable. Indeed, Taleb (2009) used data (20 million observations' worth) to demonstrate to economists and financial experts that Value-at-Risk modeling did not work, as it consistently underestimated risk. Throughout his many works, Taleb (1997b, 2001, 2007, 2009) actively searched for alternative approaches, but the lack of falsification from other perspectives often led him to his initial conclusions. This approach, while often seen by the public as culminating in negative scenarios, does not mean that Taleb is a prophet of doom, but rather a prophet crying out in the wilderness for a financial system to repent of its risky ways.

In an effort to help economists, financial experts, policymakers, and the public recognize the dangers of improperly assessing risk, Taleb wrote two books, *Fooled by Randomness* (2001), a treatise on the logical and methodological reasons why humans improperly assess risk, and *The Black Swan* (2007). "Black swan" is a reference to the Western European belief that all swans were white, until explorers visited Australia and found black swans. The "discovery" of black swans is illustrative of how holding to unassailable beliefs (e.g., swans are always white) that are consistently confirmed by empirical evidence can be problematic for two reasons. First, since black swans are *outliers,* their value lies beyond the realm of regular expectations. Second, black swans carry an *extreme impact,* as the mere presence of one black swan can challenge millions of observations over long periods to the contrary (all swans are white).

When taken together, an extreme event coupled with an extreme impact can have crisis-emanating consequences. Since Value-at-Risk modeling is based upon confidence intervals around likelihoods, rather than unlikelihoods, this model performs poorly in accounting for outliers. The second flaw is that even the most remote possibilities in the Value-at-Risk model, perhaps ones that could devastate a firm, or the broader financial system, are given near equal weight compared to other observations closer to the average. Yet inside academe and investment banks, academics and risk managers took solace in the simple historical fact that since the Great Depression, the US housing market had never dropped more than 5 percent in a single year (McDonald and Robinson 2009).

Thus, with little apparent downside, and little residential mortgage default volatility between 2002 and early 2006, requests to further expand and enhance borrowing continued in an effort to increase firm profitability, which it did, to record levels. But as borrowing became unsustainable at investment banks, Taleb's prediction that the Value-at-Risk model would provide bankers the "documented due diligence" they needed to prove that the collapse was the result of "truly unforeseeable circumstances and events with low probability—not from taking large risks that they did not understand" seemed to be confirmed by Lehman Brothers executives. Following the collapse of Lehman Brothers, the bank's chief executive officer, Richard "Dick" Fuld (2008, p. 1), in his only appearance before Congress, testified: "No one realized the extent and magnitude of these problems, nor how the deterioration of mortgages-backed assets would infect other types of assets and threaten our entire system." Yet Nassim Taleb had attempted to warn risk managers, the financial experts of the US system, and the public.

After the collapse of Lehman Brothers, Pablo Triana (2009a), a colleague of Nassim Taleb's, conducted a retrospective analysis of the available data from Lehman Brothers using Value-at-Risk modeling and found that, for the second quarter of 2008, there was a 95 percent certainty that maximum expected losses above the model would trigger on only three days and total no more than $100 million in losses. However, at the end of the quarter, Lehman Brothers reported a $2.8 billion loss, which was likely grossly undervalued, but nonetheless it marked the first quarterly loss since the firm had gone public in 1994 (Williams 2010). Triana's analysis led him to conclude that "only [Nassim] Taleb saw this coming, more than ten years ago. If only we had listened to him more attentively" (2009b, p. 2).

Unfortunately for Taleb, the timing of his comments did not come at a moment when a substantial number of experts were focused on the problem of Value-at-Risk modeling. In a euphoric economy, such warnings of improperly functioning models were discounted. Writing after the collapse of Lehman Brothers and amid a global economic recession, Taleb concluded that Value-at-Risk models lead to an increase of risk in society, and called for economists, financial experts, and policymakers to adopt stronger risk assessment approaches so as not to "put cigarettes in front of an addict—even if you give him a warning" (2009, p. xv).

Kyle Bass

J. Kyle Bass is a former investment banker for Bear Stearns and a managing partner of Hayman Advisors, a Dallas, Texas–based hedge fund (Faber 2009). After college, Bass began working at Bear Stearns, where he developed a penchant for conducting detailed research to better understand what exactly the firm was buying. This diligence earned him the distinction of becoming the youngest senior managing director in the history of Bear Stearns.

In 2006, Kyle Bass left Bear Stearns to start his own hedge fund, Hayman Capital Partners. As Bass began to investigate the home-mortgage origination boom, he soon wondered what happened to the worst home mortgages (Consumer News and Business Channel 2009). Soon, he discovered many highly speculative subprime loans originated by Quick Loan Funding CEO Daniel Sadek, who underwrote loans for pretty much anyone who was willing to purchase them (Gittelsohn and Campbell 2007).

Daniel Sadek immigrated to the United States from Lebanon at age eighteen, and soon earned a job pumping gas in Cypress, California, and shortly thereafter worked at a local Mercedes-Benz dealership selling cars to very wealthy individuals in Newport Beach, California (Gittelsohn and Campbell 2007). In 2001, Sadek realized that he was selling a great many cars to mortgage loan officers, and after seeing how little work a friend actually did to close his recently purchased home, Sadek paid $250 for a California Finance Lender license, posted a $25,000 bond, passed a background check, and established Quick Loan Funding (Faber 2009). Despite having only a third-grade education, Sadek soon had Quick Loan netting a million-dollar profit, and by 2005 the firm had more than 700 employees and was financing over $4 billion worth of loans (Mickadeit 2007).

Sadek spent his personal wealth on lavish trips to Las Vegas, luxury homes, exotic cars, and his personal dream, producing his own motion picture, *Redline,* a movie about wealthy financiers who have an interest in illegal street racing (Koltnow 2007). Sadek put up more than $26 million dollars of his own capital, including several of his own cars, one of which, a $575,000 Porsche Carrera GT, was purposely wrecked during a scene in *Redline* (Filipponio 2007). *Redline* failed at the box office, returning less than one-quarter the amount invested; critics panned the picture as "an idiotic action thriller, vanity project and testosterone-filled guilty pleasure whose sole purpose is to show off a fleet of million-dollar Ferraris and Lamborghinis belonging to fledgling movie mogul Daniel Sadek" (Lawson 2007, p. 1).

Kyle Bass was aware of Sadek's ambition to be a film producer and, after watching *Redline,* and its conspicuous consumption and wanton destruction of capital, decided that he should focus on who was purchasing Quick Loan Funding mortgages (Faber 2009). Bass began visiting with different Wall Street purchasers and asked them if they were worried about a decline in quality of mortgages available for origination. To his great surprise, the investment bank traders said, "No, we're not worried about the quality. We just package 'em up and sell 'em as fast as we can" (Faber 2009, p. 142). Indeed, Michael Francis, a former trader at Lehman Brothers, had looked at the possibility of improving the quality of underwriting, but concluded it was not feasible: "We would often have conversations around additional parameters that we should put on a program that frankly from a competitive standpoint, we just couldn't do it. It literally would have shut production down to zero" (Consumer News and Business Channel 2009, p. 3).

Bass also asked traders if they ever thought about what would happen when the investors from Europe, the Middle East, and Asia no longer wanted to purchase the then–highly lucrative mortgage-backed securities. One trader coldly answered Bass, "capital is ubiquitous today. It is free flowing and it will *never* stop" (Faber 2009, p. 142). The trader's use of "never" caught the attention of Bass because of the trader's tone of absolute certainty that the perpetual motion machine generating easy credit would continue indefinitely. Bass would later remark: "Every single crisis in financial market history has always been caused by free or easy credit. All the way back to the tulip bulbs in Holland. When you looked at the housing market, you'd find that people were borrowing 100 percent of the money for a home and speculating for free" (Faber 2009, p. 139).

With this new information, Bass and his colleagues soon focused on BBB-rated securities, commonly referred to as "junk" securities (i.e., junk bonds), because they are traditionally the lowest-rated security. However, before investing too seriously in a highly risky market, Bass wanted to make sure he wasn't missing anything. So, in August 2006, Bass flew to New York and sought disconfirming evidence from Michael Alix, chief risk officer for Bear Stearns. Bass gave a presentation to some of the very people he might soon take a position against, noting that his data indicated that home prices had risen more than 10 percent annually and were at unsustainable levels and predicting that defaults would rise and soon these home prices would come crashing down (Pittman 2007). Bass concluded his remarks by asking how Bear Stearns was going to manage this risk as a firm, but was quickly cut off by Alix, who told him to "worry about your risk management and we'll worry about ours" (Faber 2009, p. 149). As the stunned Bass was leaving the room, Alix put his arm around him and said, "That's a very compelling presentation you've got there. God, I hope you're wrong" (Faber 2009, p. 149; Pittman 2007, p. 1).

Bass still sought for more disconfirming evidence, convinced he had missed something in his analysis, and presented it to a prospective investor, who was so shaken by Bass's analysis that he arranged for Bass to meet with the Federal Reserve Board. Bass agreed, and at the end of his forty-minute presentation to the board, the Fed officials told him that "jobs are still growing and incomes are still growing; we don't see it the same way" (Faber 2009, p. 149). Bass later recalled how he could understand the Fed's response: "I mean, they're thinking, 'Who is this guy from Dallas telling me what's about to happen with our world?'" (Faber 2009, p. 149). However, the one thing that no economist, financial expert inside the investment banks, or policymaker at the Fed could ever answer for Bass was what would happen when the long-term relationship between median income and home price reached the critical point that was no longer sustainable.

This reality, coupled with his search for disconfirming evidence, led Bass and Hayman Capital to take out $110 million worth of credit default swaps and short positions, believing that an increase in subprime home-mortgage defaults would trigger a default in the securities (Pittman 2007). One of the securities Bass took a position against was in Nomura Holdings, which would eventually be the firm that purchased Lehman Brothers' Asian operations. This Nomura security (2006-HE2 M8), consisted of 37 percent of loans originated by Daniel Sadek's Quick Loan Funding, and when this as well as many of the other BBB-rated securities began to default, Bass and Hayman Advisors ended up making about $1.2 billion (Pittman 2007). In the end, Bass's due diligence had literally paid off as his timing of claims, warnings, and activities netted his firm over $1 billion, while his former employer Bear Stearns collapsed, signaling the beginning of the end for Lehman Brothers and the remaining investment banks in 2008, and the start of a broader global economic recession.

Other Prophets

Robert Shiller, Nassim Taleb, and Kyle Bass were not the only ones to make accurate financial predictions, or alternative claims, about the deteriorating conditions in the US financial system. Inside the investment bank Lehman Brothers, Larry McCarthy, managing director and global head of distressed debt trading, stated that there was substantial evidence to conclude that the subprime mortgage origination problems were not contained, and that this cascade would cause commercial banks to become unstable, which in turn would cause them to stop borrowing, resulting in a contraction of consumer borrowing and increased credit spreads (McDonald and Robinson 2009). Similarly, New York University professor Nouriel Roubini, nicknamed by the press as "Dr. Doom," predicted that the housing recession would set off a chain reaction that would ultimately lead to a deep and widespread recession (Mihm 2008). Hedge fund manager John Paulson, whose investment strategies mirrored those of Kyle Bass, but with greater effect and questionable legality, netted $20 billion for his investors and nearly $4 billion for himself, making this the largest short in Wall Street history (Lewis 2010). Billionaire hedge fund manager George Soros (2008) also predicted the collapse and concluded that the efficient-market hypothesis, the approach critiqued by Robert Shiller, could no longer be taken seriously outside academic circles, nor could the idea that financial markets are self-correcting and tend toward equilibrium.

Even policymakers such as North Dakota senator Byron Dorgan warned that the 1999 repeal of Glass-Steagall, a Depression-era piece of legislation designed to stop wild financial risk-taking, would result in casinolike prospecting through merging of banking with speculative activity in real estate and securities (Prins 2009). Similarly, the late senator Paul Wellstone noted:

> We seem determined to unlearn the lessons of history. Scores of banks failed in the Great Depression as a result of unsound banking practices, and their failure only deepened the crisis. Glass-Steagall was intended to protect our financial system by insulating commercial banking from other forms of risk. It was designed to prevent a handful of powerful financial conglomerates from holding the rest of the economy hostage. Glass-Steagall was one of several stabilizers designed to keep that from ever happening again, and until very recently it was very successful. (Prins 2009, p. 142)

On the economic policymaking end, members of the Federal Reserve Board of Governors such as Edward Gramlich were concerned about the predatory lending practices and a general lack of mortgage oversight in the subprime market, particularly among independent lenders such as Daniel Sadek's Quick Loan, which was not directly under federal supervision (Andrews 2007). In fact, Gramlich was so concerned about these practices that he met with Federal Reserve chairman Alan Greenspan personally to warn him. Yet despite these and many other warnings, the collapse of Lehman Brothers and the larger global economic crisis still occurred.

* * *

From this exploration of alternative claimsmakers, it should be clear that the collapse of investment banking and the global economic recession were not the result of completely unanticipated events that no one saw coming, but rather the result of economists, financial experts, and policymakers refusing to change course from the conventional wisdom or policies of the day. This devotion to the status quo led to the erroneous belief that the fundamentals of the financial system were strong. The remainder of this chapter explores how alternative claimsmakers, these "prophets in the wilderness" were able to arrive at accurate financial predictions and why their claims failed to result in policy or social changes. From their experiences, we are able to observe five broad themes that help us understand how they arrived at accurate claims and attempted to draw public attention about troubling conditions in the financial system.

Themes of the Prophets

First, none of these claimsmakers were "prophets of doom" or ideologues purposely looking for negative information only to have their predictions of instability and calamity verified. In sharp contrast to "prophets of doom"—people who intentionally attempt to create negative information about an asset or firm for profit-making purposes, all the alternative claimsmakers profiled in this chapter developed their negative outlooks or assertions of troubling conditions only *after* conducting their analyses. Second, all of these claimsmakers were respected and had some prior knowledge of and expertise with the extant problems and intricate workings of the complex financial system. Knowledge and access to information are important aspects of alternative claimsmaking, as they greatly enhance the likelihood that an individual can effectively evaluate assumptions or flaws in conventional wisdom. Over time, each of these alternative claimsmakers established themselves as respected members of their community and discussed their findings with those who held the opposing viewpoints.

Third, each conducted their own data analysis and did not rely solely upon "evidence" and analysis provided by others, and thus reached their conclusions independently rather than accepting conventional claims. Max Weber (1946) observed that in an increasingly rational-legal system focused on bureaucracy, individuals (particularly those in positions of authority) increasingly rely upon expert analysis as a means for decisionmaking. Thus the notion that economists, financial experts, and policymakers rely upon others to help make decisions should not come as a surprise. However, a key strategy to developing alternative claimsmaking is to avoid this rationalizing tendency and independently evaluate data based upon one's own analysis and begin to draw inferences.

Fourth, rather than reach a conclusion based solely upon data analysis, each of these alternative claimsmakers looked for disconfirming evidence. Philosopher Karl Popper (2002 [1963], p. 45) warned social scientists of the dangers of developing constructs and theories based solely upon verification, because the world is full of instances and anecdotes that can verify prior assumptions, and because instances of the "truth," once confirmed, appear manifest, allowing divergent viewpoints to be summarily dismissed. Instead, Popper argued that knowledge claims are best constructed when they are subject to falsification, meaning that these are claims that can be refuted based upon evidence rather than accepted based upon a phenomenon's presence. Too frequently during the euphoric financial days of 2002–2006, financial experts relied upon claims that supported their own suppositions and were unwilling to explore possible alternatives. Perhaps if these analysts had been more willing to falsify their suppositions or seek alternative explanations, the collapse of Lehman Brothers and the broader global economic crisis could have been avoided.

This lack of foresight or exploration of alternatives is best evidenced by the fifth, and perhaps most important, similarity among these prophets in the wilderness: each of these alternative claimsmakers attempted to warn someone who was in a position to resolve the identified problem. Since the collapse of Lehman Brothers and the start of the global economic recession, many individuals have appeared in media reports and the public to claim that they predicted the collapse of investment banking, or foresaw ominous trends in the financial system. However, upon more careful review, these individuals did very little, or nothing, to warn anyone who was in a position to resolve the identified problem prior to the collapse. Retrospectively, it may be much easier to see the increasing financial instability from 2006 to 2008, as we have ample evidence and a popular narrative, but each of the alternative claimsmakers profiled in this chapter attempted to warn others to change their ways in an effort to avoid catastrophe *before* the collapse of Lehman Brothers. Table 9.1 links these five themes of alternative claimsmaking into a coherent framework.

Why Did the Alternative Claimsmakers Fail?

Unfortunately, despite the ability of these claimsmakers to make accurate predictions about the US financial system, their attempts to warn those in a position to do something failed. Why did their predictions go unheeded and fail to produce policy or social changes? There are three broad reasons: a failure to properly articulate claims, a failure to foster and maintain public reaction, and a failure to properly attract policymaker attention.

A failure to properly articulate claims means that the troubling condition has failed to capture substantial media coverage or elicit a public reaction to the point that policymakers are willing to take up the issue to determine if new or existing policy should be reformed in light of the troubling condition. Donileen Loseke (2003) has previously

Table 9.1 Prophets in the Wilderness: Alternative Claimsmakers on Financial Collapse

Claimsmaker	Nonideological Because . . .	Respected Claimsmaker as . . .	Independent Analysis on . . .	Sought Disconfirming Evidence About . . .	Warned . . .
Robert Shiller	Initially optimistic about home prices	Author, professor	Historical home-price data	Home prices	Economists, financial experts, policymakers, media, public
Nassim Taleb	Consistently focused on Value-at-Risk modeling	Author, professor, stock trader	Value-at-Risk modeling	Value-at-Risk modeling	Financial experts, public
Kyle Bass	Focused on divergent viewpoints	Financial expert	Mortgage origination, securitization, derivatives	Mortgage origination, securitization, derivatives	Financial experts, policymakers

established conditions under which claims are likely to "spread," or successfully garner media attention and elicit a public reaction. Properly articulated claims are often constructed within a context of *difference with sameness,* meaning that a problem should seem new and different, but not to the point where the troubling condition is difficult to understand or boring. In this respect, the details of understanding risk associated with substantial home-price appreciation and the dangers stemming from the undervaluing of value-at-risk modeling may be too technical or "too boring" to garner widespread media attention or elicit a public reaction. Similarly, a troubling condition is more likely to gain a great deal of media attention when the condition is widespread and can affect a wide variety of people. For the most part, each of our alternative claimsmakers framed the troubling condition in terms of a specific risk and made a specific prediction, but did not emphasize the extent to which this risk could drastically affect the financial system and the public. This is not to say that our alternative claimsmakers did not understand the broader risk of their claims, for there is some evidence to conclude that they did; but for the most part, each chose to focus on specific risks.

In addition to a failure to properly articulate claims, each of our alternative claimsmakers largely failed to properly foster and maintain public reaction. Each of our prophets in the wilderness was able to attract some media coverage prior to the collapse of Lehman Brothers; however, the initial media coverage was not sustained, and largely failed to elicit a public reaction, or attract policymaker attention. This may have been partly due to the relative inability of the alternative claimsmakers to access resources essential for fostering and maintaining media attention and public reaction. Stephen Hilgartner and Charles Bosk (1988) have argued that media attention is a finite resource for which claimsmakers compete across time and space. Over time, for some social problems, such as abortion, crime, HIV/AIDS, public education, and many others, organizations have developed that allow for sustained claimsmaking activity about the particular troubling condition. In sharp contrast, all of our alternative claimsmakers were economists or financial experts and did not directly engage in the day-to-day process of constructing or advocating for a troubling condition. Thus, not having access to an established claimsmaking organization substantially limited their ability to gain access to scarce media attention in the public arena. This conclusion is similar to that of

Robert Stallings (1995), who found that claimsmakers asserting the troubling condition of earthquake threat were unable to foster and maintain media attention in the public arena because they did not have adequate resources to compete with and campaign alongside more established conditions such as child abuse, driving while intoxicated, or street crime.

Finally, alternative claimsmakers were unable to properly attract policymaker attention. Despite their attempts to warn someone in a position to do something about growing instability in the financial system, each of these claimsmakers was largely dismissed until after the collapse, when they were retroactively heralded as "heroes." These alternative claimsmakers and their claims went largely unheeded prior to the collapse of Lehman Brothers because there were powerful incentives for policymakers not to change course. Policymakers were reluctant to interfere with what appeared to be a normally functioning market mechanism so long as home prices were on the rise, minority homeownership was increasing, firms such as investment banks were making record profits, and a dominant deregulatory ideology had emerged. Taken together, we can see how properly articulating claims, properly fostering and maintaining public reaction, and properly attracting policymaker attention can greatly influence the likelihood of alternative claimsmakers gaining media coverage, eliciting a public reaction, and attracting policymakers' willingness to take on the troubling condition of financial instability. If we are to avoid future financial calamities (as well as technological), we must as a society work to better incorporate marginalized or alternative claimsmaking into our public arena.

Beyond better understanding future crises, "prophets in the wilderness" and unsuccessful claimsmakers constitute an important and historically neglected area of social problems theorizing. This lack of prior incorporation should give theorists pause as they strive to better understand the world of social problems. For example, one is left to wonder what is really known about claimsmaking activities if prior research has almost exclusively focused on successful claims and claimsmakers. What is really known about how claims are constructed? How do claims evolve over space and time? Why do some claims generate public attention? Why do policymakers decide to take up claims surrounding some troubling conditions but not others? These and many other questions lie at the most basic level of social problems construction. Kathleen Lowney asserted that failed "claims "can give us insight—perhaps even more insight than successful claims can—into the claimsmaking process" (2008, p. 349). This lack of prior incorporation cuts to the core of what constitutes an "expert." While a great deal has been learned in the decades since Spector and Kitsuse's assertion of "subjective elements," much remains to be learned about the construction of social problems.

Part 4

The Role of the Media

The media play a key role in constructing most social problems. Claimsmakers usually hope to reach a large audience, to convey their claims to the public, in hopes that some people who hear the claims may be moved to join their cause. Gaining media coverage offers a relatively quick, relatively inexpensive way to reach lots of people. In addition, having one's claims picked up by the media may help convince policymakers that they need to change social policies in order to address the claims. Thus, many claimsmakers work hard to gain media attention; they issue press releases, hold press conferences, organize what they hope will be newsworthy demonstrations, and generally work to get their claims covered in the media.

The changing media environment offers new opportunities for claimsmakers, but it also presents new challenges. As recently as a couple of decades ago, there were fewer media outlets. The proliferation of television channels and the rise of the Internet have greatly increased the media's capacity for and interest in covering claims. In a sense, claimsmakers compete with one another for media attention, but as the number of media outlets increases, there are more venues for coverage, making it easier to gain attention. In a world with twenty-four-hour news channels, many dozens of talk shows, and a seemingly endless number of Internet blogs, it is not that hard to find some media forum where one can promote a particular claim. On the other hand, all of those media outlets must compete with one another for the public's attention. The audience for claims is forced to choose among so many different forums that a claimsmaker who appears in a given forum—even, say, appearing on a top-rated cable news show—is lucky to reach even 1 percent of the population.

Constructionist analyses of social problems often examine claims that appear in the media, and many of the chapters in this book analyze claims as they are presented in media coverage. However, this part of the book presents three chapters that illustrate different aspects of claimsmaking in the new media environment.

In Chapter 10, Jennifer Dunn examines a discussion thread on the Internet dealing with the relative difficulty of having had an abortion, versus having given an infant up for adoption. Anti-abortion advocates often argue that some women experience deep regret and even psychological problems following an abortion, and insist that it is preferable to give birth and then arrange for adoption. But the women who participated in the discussion thread that Dunn analyzed experienced both—having an abortion as well as giving a child up for adoption—and their conversation suggests the complexities of comparing the effects of the two procedures: adoption is not necessarily a pain-free panacea for the problem of abortion. Of course, this is a narrow topic, and probably not of broad public interest, but that's the point. The Internet provides forums for even the most specialized claims.

In contrast to narrowly focused discussion threads, newspapers continue to present coverage of topics presumed to be of general interest. In Chapter 11, David Schweingruber and Michelle Horstmeier track newspaper stories about Internet addiction. Like other relatively new phenomena, it took a while for claims about Internet addiction to consolidate. In particular, the nature of what claimsmakers defined as the addicting content—was it pornography, or video games, or what?—shifted as Internet usage expanded. Studies such as this one are useful for reminding us that the same issue may be constructed, reconstructed, and then reconstructed yet again, as claimsmakers redefine the nature of the problem.

Finally, in Chapter 12, Brian Monahan and R. J. Maratea analyze a particular media outlet: Nancy Grace's cable television program, which focuses on popular cases of crime and victimization. Their analysis dissects the program's formula, showing how each episode uses a set of standard elements—including familiar segments, the host's values and ideology, and a rhetoric that invites viewers to see themselves as members of a like-minded, moral community. The specific cases examined may vary from one program to the next, and this year's cases may well have faded from memory by next year, but this program continues to construct the problem of crime within a consistent framework.

The contemporary media environment is far too complex to be completely surveyed in just three chapters, but these analyses hint at the various sorts of forums now available to claimsmakers who seek to bring their issues to public attention.

10

Abortion and Adoption: "Choosing Life" and the Problem of Regret

Jennifer L. Dunn

Recently, sociologists who study social movements have been interested in the emotions that are involved. Most activists try to get people to feel sympathetic toward the victims of whatever social problem the social movement is trying to change. So, activists talk a lot about the problem's victims, and many times, victims make up a large part of the initial group of people agitating for social change. In order to evoke sympathy, activists talk about victims who are greatly harmed and—this is important—who did not bring this harm upon themselves (because otherwise we might blame them for their own problems rather than change what the activists see as the cause of the harm). For example, some social movements teach us that rape victims are never at fault, no matter what they are wearing, or doing, or drinking, because rape victims do not cause rape, rapists do (or patriarchal cultures, or rape-conducive media, and so on). Others have explained that children are innocent victims of sexual abuse, whether by family members or the clergy, because they are too young to consent to sexual activity (Dunn 2010). Victims of Hurricane Katrina did not choose to stay in New Orleans and drown; rather, they had no way to leave. In short, social movement activists tell stories about victims that explain why the harm they experience is not their fault, so that we will feel sympathy toward victims and want to help them.

Currently, there is a growing social movement of "birth mothers" (or "first mothers" as they sometimes refer to themselves) who deeply regret placing their children with adoptive parents. These women argue that they did not relinquish their children of their own free will, or that they were not fully informed of the potential consequences of their choice, or that adoptive families reneged on their "open adoption" agreements after placement. Along with some adoptive parents and adopted children, they form a coalescing community of advocates for what they call "ethical adoption." (Participants in this movement belong to groups such as Ethica, Parents for Ethical Adoption Reform, and the First Mothers' Action Group.) Ethical adoption includes practices that would confer more rights on first mothers who agree to open adoption, such as giving them longer periods of time before their decision to relinquish a child becomes final.

This social movement often emphasizes the emotional harm that adoption causes *all* members of the adoption "triad" (adopted children and adoptive parents as well as birth mothers). In this chapter, I explore the responses of a small group of women to the rhetoric of the pro-life[1] movement, especially the injunction to "choose life" and place an unwanted child for adoption rather than opt to abort the pregnancy. I focus primarily on the arguments of women who have done *both* (that is, they have terminated one pregnancy, and agreed to adoption in a second case), but include the comments of some women who have done one or the other. The women whose voices appear here argue with considerable intensity that the distress of placing a child for adoption is far greater than that caused by terminating a pregnancy, contrary to the claims of the pro-life movement. They also discuss how they view "choice," and how it is constituted (or is not).

The data collection began after I read a blog post written by Kateri McCann (2009), an activist in the movement, a first mother, and author of the blog *Wet Feet,* who linked to a "guest" essay written by another first mother, Shaker Anonymous (2009). This essay was posted in early 2009 on *Shakesville,* a progressive feminist blog that typically covers a wide range of topics, and Shaker Anonymous wrote about her thoughts and experience of adoption and abortion. In addition to McCann's post and the eight comments she received, I reviewed the 245 comments, many of them quite lengthy, on the guest essay, which was titled "Breaking the Silence: On Living Pro-Lifers' Choice for Women." There are also quotes from earlier posts by McCann (2006a, 2006b, 2008) and from a blogger who directed McCann to the essay on *Shakesville* (Kellogg 2009). In the excerpts I have selected, women rhetorically and emotionally define themselves and the problem of regret, and they also typify the circumstances of their decisionmaking. My aim is to show what these women's online constructions of agency and victimization can tell us more generally about how people comprehend coercion, constraint, and choice in the context of social problems claimsmaking and identity work.[2] First, however, I provide some historical context for this online discussion that took place.

Ultrasound Legislation (and the Movie *Juno*)

While a great deal of the pro-life rhetoric surrounding abortion has emphasized harm done to "unborn children"—in keeping with the principle that the more victims a movement can highlight, the more potential sympathy it can generate (Best 1997; Loseke 2003)—pro-life activists have made a significant effort to construct women who have abortions as also damaged. The claim that women suffer after abortions is not new; debates about "post-abortion syndrome" began being reported in mainstream periodicals in the late 1980s (e.g., Painter 1989). The notion that viewing ultrasound images of the fetus could induce women to change their minds about having an abortion, and thus prevent the depression and other consequences that pro-life advocates claim follow abortion, is more recent. It follows upon the increasingly routine use and sophistication of ultrasound monitoring in pregnancy.

In the second paragraph of her essay, Shaker Anonymous told readers that her post had been "stewing since [she] heard about the recent rash of pre-abortion ultrasound legislation." At the time she wrote, mandatory pre-abortion ultrasound legislation was being proposed in eleven states (sixteen states already had some kind of legislation in place), with some requiring that a woman considering an abortion view an ultrasound first, or that her physician provide her with a photograph from the ultrasound. *USA Today* reported on the topic, quoting anti-abortion Nebraska state senator Tony Fulton, who said: "Many times these are young mothers who are in vulnerable situations. And they are about to make a very grave choice. This is about informed consent" (*USA Today* 2009). While Senator Fulton did not specify the gravity of the consequences for "vulnerable young mothers," in an article the following day at RH Reality Check, a "new media" website devoted to countering the "reckless rhetoric" of opponents of reproductive rights, Kathleen Reeves (2009) chided Fulton and other "arrogant" legislators, concluding that while "there's no doubt that, as a woman, it's hard to predict how you'll feel after an abortion," a mandatory ultrasound "sheds no light on the decision and adds nothing to the emotional process."

Speaking for the pro-life campaign, in an editorial in the online pro-life news "clearinghouse" Lifenews.com, Steven Ertelt wrote about the Kansas ultrasound legislation, billed by its sponsor, Republican representative Lance Kinzer, as the "Women's Right to Know and See" proposal. Ertelt (2009c) quoted Kinzer as saying that the legislation "promotes a woman's physical and psychological health" as well as "protecting fetal life." He also quoted a Kansans for Life legislative director, Kathy Ostrowski, who told Ertelt, "Abortion is irreversible, with results that can produce a long-lasting, negative impact." This is clearly a reference to maternal as well as fetal harm.

This rhetoric also underlies two related campaigns in the pro-life movement: the claim that abortions cause depression and the claim that many women regret the decision to terminate their pregnancies. Ertelt (2006), for example, cited (without providing references) a 2004 study in the United States and a 2006 study in New Zealand under the headline: "Abortions Cause Severe Depression for Women, New Study Shows." The list of long-term consequences, according to Ertelt, includes major depression, anxiety disorders, and alcohol and drug abuse. In 2009, just prior to Anonymous's post, Ertelt's headline read: "Post-Abortion Counselor Confirms Abortions Cause Women Mental Health Issues"; and he went on to note, "one doctor who counsels women after abortion says the proof is in the actual experiences of women who regret their choice. . . . To deal with the psychological pain of an abortion they grieve, [Dr.] Mintle says women often turn to drugs or alcohol" (Ertelt 2009a).

A week later, Ertelt headlined: "Women Who Regret Their Abortions Will Speak Out" (at a then upcoming rally). According to Ertelt (2009b), the pro-life movement "has a rich history of focusing not just on the death of an unborn child in an abortion but on the pain and regret millions of women [feel] following an abortion" and the rally would allow women "harmed by abortion" to prevent future abortions by "sharing their own stories of regret, grief, and physical, spiritual and psychological scars."

Importantly, the pro-life movement advocates adoption as the solution for women with unwanted pregnancies. Another writer for Lifenews.com, Ken Conner, wrote in 2007:

Adoption is truly a win/win/win situation. With adoption, the child "wins" because he or she is not only given the chance to live, but to live in a home with loving parents who can provide for his or her needs. Adoption is also a win for those couples who choose to adopt because they have the benefit of a precious new life to nurture. Finally, adoption is a win for the birth mother because she benefits from knowing that she has made the mature and beautiful choice of giving life to a child, providing for that child by finding a safe and happy home, and selflessly sharing that new life with others. When adoptions are done right they are occasions for joy all around. (Conner 2007)

This rhetoric and counter-rhetoric constitute the historical context for why Shaker Anonymous (2009) began by saying, "While I am touched that so many men in such various states are so deeply worried about women possibly being all sad from having an abortion, I wish to point out to these compassionately bleeding hearts that the alternatives are not exactly without their own emotional consequences." She went on to say that she had endured both experiences, and that "if we're going to have a seemingly neverending discussion about the sorrow and remorse caused by abortion, then it is about goddamn time we hear from birth mothers too."

This brings me to another bit of context for the discourse I examine in this chapter: the movie *Juno* and the discussion it generated among critics of the "you can just place your baby for adoption" rhetoric. In early 2008, this movie (about a pregnant teenager who decides to carry her baby to term and place it for adoption) was in theaters and generating discussion on various women's blogs. Included was a post titled "Juno, or Why Adoption Isn't Cute," by Cecily Kellogg (2009), a pro-choice feminist and author of the blog *Uppercase Woman,* who links to many women in the ethical adoption movement. Kellogg began with the caveat that she had trepidation about going to see an adoption "comedy" because "in the last four years that I've been reading blogs by women who were going through the adoption process, the one thing that has been clear to me is that *it is not fucking funny*" (Kellogg 2009). Then she explained how the movie was a "damned sly anti-choice statement . . . because the whole movie makes the process of adoption look so easy and simple. Ug." Kellogg then linked to a post by McCann (whom I mentioned earlier and quote several times later) in which the latter described her post-adoption pain. Kellogg (2009) quoted this excerpt from McCann's post (2006b):

"The anesthetic had worn off, and I was raw, naked, freshly separated. My body unleashed the primal force of loss so that I could not speak, I could not make a sound. I could not sob. I could not think. The hall of mirrors collapsed in shards stained with the blood of my psyche. Within a month I was suicidal."

A day later, McCann thanked Kellogg, and responded to people who had commented on Kellogg's post. She wrote about the "primal wounds" of adoption, averred that she was not anti-adoption but that adoption was a "necessary institution with draconian and inhumane processes that should be updated and reformed." She pointed out that while people are "resilient" and adoption often "works": "A child cannot be adopted without also having been relinquished. And every person in the triad is entitled to grieve what has been lost" (McCann 2008). Many commenters agreed. Jesspond said: "Oooh, the myths make me crazy. Fairy-tale adoptions with everyone smiley and happy all the time. . . . But *every* story has some pain" (Jesspond on McCann 2008). Jody wrote:

> I'm just astounded, and I guess I shouldn't be but I am, that the editors of the same sections of the paper that often run the stories about 1960s-era birth moms and their pain about that process, cluelessly ran positive reviews of a movie that basically re-iterates the fairy tale told to those birth moms. . . . Because isn't that what *Juno* is? The fantasy birth mom that "gets on with her beautiful life" so that the adoptive parents never have to give her a moment's conflicted thought? It makes you wonder whether anyone has ever heard a single thing any birth mother has ever written about her experience." (Jody on McCann 2008)

About a month later, McCann was interviewed in the *Chicago Tribune* for an article about first mothers' feelings toward *Juno*. McCann told reporter Nara Schoenberg of "the tears, the nightmares, the spiraling depression," and of how "her experience has led her to utterly reject *Juno*'s suggestion that adoption is a shortcut to a happy ending." "The reality is," McCann told Schoenberg, "you're kind of debilitated by this loss for the rest of your life in the same way as if you lost a child to death" (Schoenberg 2008, p. 1).

These examples show that there are "rhetorics of regret" in at least two social movements—the pro-life movement and the ethical adoption movement. In each setting, activists describe the emotional pain women experience as a result of an action they have taken, and the long-term consequences that result. The negative emotion of regret is linked to the decision to have an abortion, on the one hand, but also to deciding to place a child for adoption (the very solution pro-life activists propose to alleviate regret) on the other. In what follows, I examine the narratives of women who claimed to have made both of these decisions, as well as the stories and reflections of women who said that they had considered both paths. I also share some discussion by women whose mothers placed them for adoption, and even that of a few adoptive mothers who took the rhetoric of regret quite seriously as they pondered their own decisions to adopt.

In all cases, I try to show not only that women framed regret differently when they compared abortion to adoption, but also that they linked regret to "choice" in very dissimilar ways, because the decisions they talk about regretting are the ones they claim they did not freely choose. Their divergent images and narratives help us to understand more about the logic of claimsmaking in social movements, which must always contend with issues of harm and choice and emotions (Dunn 2010; Goodwin, Jasper, and Polletta 2001; Loseke 2003). As I noted at the start of this chapter, activists need to convince us that there are victims, and evoke our sympathy in part by showing us the innocence of these victims. I begin by looking relatively briefly at how first mothers constructed these particular harms, and then I show some of their oppositional framings of choice, especially their *lack* of choice.

"There Is No Such Thing As 'Over' with This": Contrasting Images of Pain and Suffering

In Shaker Anonymous's initial post, in the section where she insisted that we "hear from birthmothers too," she also said:

> I have given a baby up for adoption, and I have had an abortion, and while anecdotes are not evidence, I can assert that abortions may or may not cause depression—it certainly did not in me, apart from briefly mourning the path not taken—but adoption? That is an entirely different matter. . . . Believe me when I say that of the two choices, it was adoption that nearly destroyed me—and it never ends. The only comparison I have is the death of a loved one. The pain retreats, maybe fades, but it comes right back if I poke at it. . . . There is no such thing as "over" with this. (Shaker Anonymous 2009)

McCann (2009) commented: "Also having experienced an abortion and an adoption, I can echo this point." Of the abortion she had when she was sixteen, McCann said: "While it was certainly harrowing, it was finite. I'm sorry that it had to happen, but I have no qualms over the decision I made. It was the right one. End of story." She then added:

> Adoption, as I've written . . .is more of a chronic condition than a trauma that heals eventually. I am fortunate that I am in a period where this monster is sleeping. But when E [the daughter McCann placed for adoption at birth, when McCann was a young coed] surfaces again the pain will be just as intense as it has ever been. The body doesn't forget, and she was part of my body. And there is the other issue of her reaction to my decision, and the lifelong consequences she will experience. This is a loss that keeps on losing. (McCann 2009)

In both of these excerpts, the authors compared their emotional state following an abortion to their emotional state following an adoption. For abortion, Shaker Anonymous described it as one in which she was "briefly mourning" and McCann found the experience "harrowing" but nonetheless "finite." Placing a child for adoption, on the other hand, involves grief that is not brief (never "over" and "it never ends") and, as McCann implied, that is not finite (a "chronic condition rather than a trauma that heals eventually").

Both women also emphasized the depth of their adoption pain in these conjoined posts. Here is the story that dandelionfield, responding to Shaker Anonymous, told about placing her firstborn daughter for adoption:

> I'm a birth mother. My story of pain after adoption sounds similar to yours. A decade of struggling to get out of bed, of numbness, of depression, of grieving. The only thing that even began to help me heal was having another child, and that only because of the overwhelming distraction. But even that: I was shocked to find that I could look at my second daughter and feel grief because she wasn't my first daughter. It was (is) my first daughter I wanted. Could I go back, I would give up everything to change my decision. A decision I made based on oddly romanticized writing about the "chance" birthmothers give their babies, the "sacrifice" they make for love. . . . Now I have two daughters and am working toward my MA. I love my daughters, but neither of them fills the place in my heart that my first daughter left. And no one, no one, can give me back that decade during which I was a walking zombie and engaged in self-

destructive behaviour and longed to die as a result of grief and self blame. I have no doubt that an abortion would have brought its own regrets and its own emotional baggage. But would that compare to what I went through? I *know* it would not. (Dandelionfield on Shaker Anonymous 2009)

Wasabi commented on McCann's post:

I give a huge ditto to this post and the original that spawned it. I also have experienced adoption and abortion. For me the abortion came after the adoptions and I never looked back. Maybe those first couple of months if I got too drunk I felt bad but that was with a life-time of abortion=murder conditioning to overcome. I never felt more certain about any choice I made and it's not something that keeps me up at night at all. The adoptions are the sleeping monster indeed. (Wasabi on McCann 2009)

Wasabi was responding to a commenter whose colleague's pregnant daughter was considering adoption, who "really believes that her daughter would just be able to move on like nothing happened." Wasabi said, "I'm quite sure that's what she thinks. I know it's what my mom thought. She has found it very inconvenient over the years to have to face that she was horribly wrong and wrong to pressure me to this path" (Wasabi on McCann 2009).

In Wasabi's comments, we can observe another theme, one more explicitly related to choice. Wasabi framed herself as having felt "pressure" from her mother, to make a decision that was "horribly wrong," but on the other hand, she "never felt more certain about any choice" than the one she made to terminate a pregnancy. This is a sharp distinction, and one that is important, because our cultural logic of victimization instructs us that women who make free choices are different than women who are coerced. The former are agents, but the latter are not, and only the latter are (or can be) constructed as victims (Dunn 2010). Victims are people who did not *choose* the harm that befalls them, and if they are made to seem as if they did, we tend to feel less sympathy for them (and they are more likely to blame themselves). The "feeling rules" (Hochschild 1979) for sympathy are pretty much the same as the feeling rules for victimization, and researchers have documented the importance of having "sympathetic victims" for social movement claims (Clark 1997; Dunn 2010; Loseke 2003). With this in mind, I turn now to a closer look at women's constructions of "choice" in this discussion.

Ignorance, Betrayal, and Coercion

There are a number of ways in which we commonly understand "free will" to be compromised. If we do not have all the facts, we cannot provide "informed consent," making "ignorance" or "naivety" culturally available and understandable reasons for making a regretful choice. Or, people may consent, assuming or believing things that turn out to be untrue: that is, because others lie to them or betray them. Last, people who are pressured, coerced, or forced to do something clearly have not done so willingly or given their consent. All of these are reasons women give to explain why "choosing life" was not, in fact, a choice. Earlier, I showed pro-life activists using a "vocabulary of victimization"—the language of ignorance, betrayal, and coercion—to construct images of women who would change their minds about aborting if they saw ultrasound pictures and were educated about the negative consequences of abortion. Here, I turn to the same kind of rhetoric in the story Shaker Anonymous told and in the responses to her story.

Ignorance

Shaker Anonymous (2009) discussed ignorance of the emotional consequences of placing a child for adoption: "I've googled over the years about the psychological effects of giving up a baby, and what little I found is astonishing." McCann (2009) quoted her, noting: "It's a huge problem that the only information about the consequences of placing a child for adoption are mostly anecdotal." Here is how Shaker Anonymous described her experience:

> What I didn't realize at the time—because not one person in my whole life had ever seen fit to mention the possibility, including the pre-adoption counselors—was that I'd spend so long hovering on the edge of suicide, desperately trying to find some way to deal with an all-consuming pain I had no idea even existed. . . . I don't know what the post-adoption counseling is like now, but in my day, it was through the adoption agencies or religion. In my case, the adoption agency was Catholic, lots and lots of Catholicism, so no help there; I was also extremely upset that they provided psychiatric, drug-assisted help, but [they did] not mention that it was possible you'd have need for it until after it was too late. This is the kind of thing you *really* need to know before you make the decision, if only to brace yourself. (Shaker Anonymous 2009)

dandelionfield echoed Shaker Anonymous in part of her response to this post when she said:

> And I too have been shaking my head at the pro-life hypocrisy: it was one of their birth crisis centers which first asked me "wouldn't it feel good to give someone a gift like a baby?["] (My baby is not a gift, I thought, not a thing to be given away . . .). Not one of these pro-life people talk about the mental health of a mother who has lost her baby because she had no money. (dandelionfield on Shaker Anonymous 2009)

In 2006, in a blog post called "The Myth of the Happy Birthmother," McCann wrote:

> The happy birthmother fantasy is like an anesthetic. Adoption's epidural. When it wears off, everyone has accepted your happy ending and moved on. Here you are, this hole getting bigger every year, having told everyone repeatedly that everything was great and you are happy and relieved and feeling very wise. . . . I believed it: I treated birthmother grief as a puzzle I could outsmart. Relinquishment without the consequences of loss. (McCann 2006a)

Years later, McCann posted this about the movie *Juno:*

> It's vintage adoption mythology straight from the "baby scoop era"[3] that's been refashioned for a new generation. If there was any kind of counterpoint in mainstream culture it wouldn't be such a big deal. For most people, *Juno* just confirms everything they already thought about relinquishment—that the pain is negligible and most often for the best. . . . Mythology like *Juno* perpetuates our silence. As long as we are silent, people will think it's okay to solicit the babies of young, vulnerable women for people they know to adopt. (McCann 2008)

In this excerpt, McCann framed ignorance of the consequences of adoption in terms of "mythology," made worse by being the only narrative available. This creates an unwitting complicity between the adoption industry and adoptive parents, and McCann's image of pregnant potential birthmothers as "young, vulnerable women" suggests a population not fully capable of informed consent, as naive as she was when she made her deeply regretted choice. Like McCann, dandelionfield spoke of the "oddly romanticized writing" about adoption upon which she had based her decision, and LilyRose conjoined ignorance with betrayal when she said:

> You know, I knew I couldn't be a "good parent." And I thought it
> would be worthwhile to do something nice for my baby and for his
> adoptive parents (I was pretty naive)—and for my trouble I was left
> emotionally crippled for life. How would you feel, if you threw a $10
> [bill] in the Salvation Army kettle at Christmas—and the attendant
> Santa broke both your legs? (LilyRose on Shaker Anonymous 2009)

Like many social movements (Dunn 2010; Plummer 1995), ethical
adoption activism centers upon the contrasting of myth and truth. For
adoption, a process long shrouded in secrecy and only recently coming to be more "open" (a term that has many meanings and that is
highly contested), this is one area where there is an emphasis on
questions of choice and consent.

Betrayal

The issues of deliberate misrepresentation and lying that such activists
construct are at the heart of another problem that birth mothers talk
about: betrayal. One woman (Megpie71 on Shaker Anonymous 2009),
responding to Shaker Anonymous, described her mother's experience
after relinquishing her first child during what was likely the baby
scoop era: "[My mother] signed the 'consent to adoption' form thinking it was a consent to have the name of the child's father on the
child's birth certificate; she was lied to about when her son was adopted; she had the entire process misrepresented to her—she didn't give
that child away, she had it taken." Here is a similar story, written by
OuyangDan, which raises multiple concerns:

> I had a friend who under some strange circumstances gave birth
> after not realizing she was pregnant (which is a long story). She
> was rushed to the emergency room for stomach pain, and just a
> couple of hours later, her Catholic mother was talking her through
> signing adoption papers. She had no choice, no agency, only a
> mother who was concerned that if anyone found out they would be
> a huge embarrassment. So my friend, still half doped by the drugs
> they had given her, signed what she believed was a semi-open
> adoption for the baby she delivered. Still reeling from the realiza-
> tion of what happened, she believed that she would be able to know
> this child somehow, receive pictures and updates. . . . The [organi-
> zation] her mother contacted told her a few months later that she
> had in fact signed a closed adoption, and I can't believe for the life
> of me that someone still on drugs in a hospital can be expected to
> make permanent, legal decisions. . . . She was shut out faster than a
> blink. (OuyangDan on Shaker Anonymous 2009)

Coercion

When women talked about being forced or coerced into placing their children for adoption, this was the least ambiguous and clearest oppositional framing of "choice." In the preceding story, the birthmother "had no choice, no agency," and this theme recurred throughout. Here is another narrative, this one from a woman who was able to compare her own experiences of adoption and abortion:

> Anonymous, I want to thank you for writing this, even though I cried while reading it. I have been in your shoes, and I know the pain you're talking about, I've known it for the last 36 years (my daughter was born in April of 1972, when I was 18, and my mother forced me to give her up for adoption). . . . I've also had 2 abortions (pregnancy happens to me even when I'm using birth control like the pill or an IUD), and I don't grieve over the abortions like I grieve over having lost my daughter. Anyone who thinks it's easy to carry a child in their body for 9 months and then hand it over to strangers without another thought has another think coming. This is something that you live with for the rest of your life, and no matter how you try, no matter how much counseling you eventually get, you *don't* "get over it." You learn to carry on as best you can, but sometimes it's a very hollow life (and yes, I had another child, my son is 33, and I love him very much, but having him doesn't help the loss I feel when I think of my daughter). (Vesta44 on Shaker Anonymous 2009)

Although Vesta44 expected that her mother would have forced her into having an abortion had there still been time, she wrote that two later abortions (presumably by choice) were not a source of similar grief and loss.

Another interesting way that women compared adoption and abortion in the context of choice had to do with the consequences for the children they placed (in stark contrast to the "It's a Child Not a Choice" bumper stickers one often sees). For example, AnonMom posted:

> No support has helped ease the pain of the loss to adoption. The abortion? I mourned it for a week or so. Yes, I know *some* women who pro-lifers drag around, testify that they mourn that loss all of their lives and look at children and wonder what theirs might have looked like. But let me tell you this: dead is dead and you may have regrets—even guilt and shame. But when you lose a child to adoption you have the regret, guilt and shame *plus* you wonder if your child is being well cared for. After an abortion, you do not die inside when you read about abused adopted kids! You do not wonder if an

aborted fetus wonders about you, feels loved, or feels abandoned
despite being well cared for. . . . You do not have to live knowing
that those you trusted: social workers, your parents, clergy . . . who
talked you into this "choice" as "best" for you and your child
because it would give him "advantages" you couldn't—and then
have to learn that is [*sic*] adopters died or divorced, didn't want him.
(AnonMom on Shaker Anonymous 2009)

AnonMom acknowledged grief, guilt, regret, and shame for choosing
abortion, but cast it as short-lived and terminal as opposed to having
"never gotten over it." Like others, she implicitly constructed betrayal by "those you trusted" and a process replete with deliberately hidden consequences. Similarly, July4th1969 (on Shaker Anonymous
2009) said, "Abortion is much easier to live with for me than knowing that an adoptee has to also face lifelong issues of grief, self-worth
and self-destructive behaviors."

For some women adoption was their only choice because abortion
was not (especially in an era or subculture when unwed mothers, and
teenaged mothers, were shamed and stigmatized). The final few stories that I want to share used this kind of explanation, one that delin-
eates social forces that act to hinder agency. One woman, meshorer,
put it like this:

Thank you so much for telling our story. I gave birth in 1968 when
not only were there no resources for "unwed mothers" but not even
the recognition that such resources were critically needed. We bad
girls just went off to a "home for unwed mothers," quietly gave
birth and were expected to merrily live our secretly soiled lives.
Abortions were still illegal then but were clandestinely available to
those with the money and right connections. I had neither.
(meshorer on Shaker Anonymous 2009)

Some wrote of their own mothers:

Thanks, Anonymous. I wish my mother had had a choice.
Relinquishing me in the 1960s took something strong and good out
of her that I don't think will ever be replaced. When I had to
choose, I chose abortion. I've never regretted that. (PixieCorpse on
Shaker Anonymous 2009)

It took years before Mum was ready to accept that she really hadn't
had a choice. It was the 1960s in Australia, she was a good
Christadelphian girl, she wasn't married, and she was pregnant. She

wouldn't be able to support a child on her own. . . . So she took the only other option available, in that place at that time. She relinquished her child for adoption. (Megpie71 on Shaker Anonymous 2009)

Some adoptive mothers mulled over the issue of how much choice the birthmothers of their children really had. One woman, carol_h, talked about the birthmother of the son she had adopted from Korea twenty-four years previously. She said, "We know that she was an 18-year-old high school student when he was born," and continued:

The papers that came with him say that she went to the hospital, had him, asked that he be adopted into a good family, and left. I try to image her pain and loss and cannot. I have never forgotten that the joy we had in our baby came at the expense of another woman. . . . I have always been strongly pro-choice and being an adoptive parent did not change that. . . . I do not know if abortion was an option for her and I don't know if she would have been better off with an abortion. Only she knows that. (carol_h on Shaker Anonymous 2009)

The last story I want to include is that of Angelive09, who considered adoption, but decided against it. Her story, of choosing not to relinquish her baby, of choosing to have an abortion, and of choosing to have two more children, is different from the stories of the first mothers and the "choose life" advocates. Here is what she wrote:

Thank you so much for bringing up this topic. I myself have struggled with issues similar, I got pregnant when I was 19 and was sure I was not ready to be a mother. Initially, I wanted to have an abortion but it was not an option for me. I was living in a very small, christian, conservative, South Georgia community and an abortion was not available unless you drove to Jacksonville or Atlanta. I spoke with an adoption agency the entire time with the intention of giving my baby up for adoption when born. But, when the baby was born, I just couldn't do it, I had fallen in love with this infant for better or worse and she was mine. . . . There was no way I could've given her up, I feel it would've completely destroyed me. I am vehemently pro choice and I am thankful that I had the choice to have her, I chose to keep her and she is loved! That being said, I have also had an abortion, at that time my boyfriend was seriously addicted to methamphetamines and I did not want to bring a newborn baby into that kind of life. Eventually, I did get married and 4 years later I chose to have 2 more children. I do not have any regrets about having the abortion because I knew I could never go through with adoption. (Angelive09 on Shaker Anonymous 2009)

This narrative is interesting because of the multiple situations and constructions of choice that Angelive09 described. She began by saying that the first time she was pregnant, abortion was not a choice, given her social and geographical location—implying that had it been possible, she would have ended the pregnancy. She then explained that the adoption she considered was not a choice either, because she was not emotionally able to "give up" the infant she had fallen in love with, despite being a teenage mother. She then chose to terminate an unwanted pregnancy when she was able to do so, and chose to have two additional children after getting married. So, despite being unable to choose abortion for her first pregnancy, Andelive09 portrays herself as an agent from that point forward. And, as one might expect from the stories I have shared thus far, her agency is accompanied by a singular lack of regret: "I chose to have all three of my children and thank god that I have had a choice in the matter!" (Angelive09 on Shaker Anonymous 2009).

This woman—"vehemently pro choice" and a person who claimed to have chosen not to place her child, to have an abortion, and to keep subsequent children—epitomizes a broad definition of choice that acknowledges structural, cultural, and situational constraints. Angelive09 nonetheless professes agency, but not regret. In contrast, we can return to the previous posts and comments and think a bit about how they fit within the structural, cultural, historical, and political forces that were operating during the time they were told.

Conclusion: Choice, Claims, and Consequences

My intention in this examination of a discourse—an online conversation in which images of issues and rhetoric and vocabularies of victimization converge—has been to provide some details of what some women actually say about their experiences, as opposed to what is said by social movement activists making claims on their behalf. Because the stories I have excerpted here are "victim narratives" (Davis 2005), they are replete with documentation of harm, much of it emotional (grief, loss, betrayal, and regret). They are also cries to be heard and pleas for sympathy, in common with all the stories of the wounded, unjustly treated, and deserving that typify victims in social movements such as the growing call for adoption reform.

Thus, as in the narratives of survivors of child sexual abuse, battered women, survivors of rape, and survivors of clergy abuse, victims portray the pain as devastating and undeserved (Davis 2005; Dunn 2010; Loseke 2001). These narratives tell stories about women and their children who are terribly harmed, and innocent. In the case of women who regret "giving up" their babies, their innocence resides in their naivety, in being misinformed (sometimes cast as deliberate), their betrayal, and explicit pressure, coercion, or force. "Informed consent" is absent from their tales and, because of this, so too is choice as we ordinarily understand it. First mothers are not responsible for the harm done to them, and believing this we can feel sympathy for them consistent with our cultural code of agency (Dunn 2010).

So far, then, we have another example of a vocabulary of victimization, in keeping with a cultural repertoire with rather clear "rules" (closely aligned) for what constitutes victimization and for who deserves sympathy. What gives this case some interest beyond its affirmation that these rules can extend into realms that are not yet criminalized is this: first, we normally associate "regret" with choice, and second, the discourse itself centers explicitly on choice, rather than implicitly—as in most victim narratives and social movement claimsmaking. What does a person regret? We regret the things that we could have done differently; the choices we made that turned out to be wrong. To be or feel "sorry," to be "apologetic" or "repentant," to feel "remorse"—these are all meanings and synonyms for regret that signify accountability. These are not the only synonyms: others are "sadness" and "disappointment," which also appear in the discourse. But mostly the women who regret placing children are very clear that what they thought was a choice or what people presented to them as a choice was not really *their* choice, and not a choice they would have made if they had known better.

Further, it is ironic that this is specifically a discourse of choice: Shaker Anonymous subtitled her blog post as "Living Pro-Lifers' Choice for Women," and the discussion therein is mostly about being "pro-choice" and how the availability of adoption as an option is a dangerous diversionary tactic from a movement that would restrict choice. The women deconstruct the rhetoric of the pro-life movement to argue that "choosing life" is either a choice with terrible consequences, far worse than abortion (the right to choose), or a choice that women have been forced into prior to the legalization of abortion, and will be forced into again if the pro-life movement should prevail.

Finally, both "sides" use the rhetoric of regret and link it to choice, but in fairly different ways. That a word like "regret" can be so variously understood suggests that rhetoric in social problems claimsmaking has near infinite linguistic possibilities. That women can simultaneously deconstruct the rhetoric of choice and construct themselves as victims— while arguing their agency in other matters and putting both victimization and agency to political purpose—suggests that we have at least a few new avenues of social problems claimsmaking to explore, as well as interesting new places in which to find them.

Notes

1. For the sake of simplicity, I have chosen not to put "scare quotes" around the terms I use to describe the pro-life and pro-choice movements, thus avoiding the need to continually point out that the terms that members of these movements use socially construct abortion and reproductive choice.

2. The Internet is increasingly providing social movement scholars with a rich source of claims to analyze; this is because one of the very first things a new social movement does is create a website, and prior to that, movements often seem to get their start from like-minded bloggers who begin to link to each others' blogs and point each other toward others making similar claims.

3. "Baby scoop era" is a term used by many activists and others in the adoption reform movement to refer to the years between 1945 and 1972, when a large majority of middle-class white women who became pregnant out of wedlock chose or were forced to give up their infants to adoptive families; these families were able to simply "scoop" up those babies in abundance (Fessler 2006; Solinger 2000).

11

The Evolution of Internet Addiction

David Schweingruber
and Michelle Horstmeier

The Internet can be a source of personal problems. Adults engrossed in chat rooms ignore their spouses and families. Students neglect their schoolwork to play online games. Employees engage in "cyber-slacking" when they are supposed to be working. Household savings are depleted by gambling, stock trading, auctions, and pornography consumption.

What public issue, if any, can encompass these disparate personal problems? Or, as a practical matter, what phenomenon could an expert claim expertise in that would allow him or her to give (and sell) advice about all these problems? What framework could a reporter use to report on all these incidents? What cultural vocabulary could the participants—victims and perpetrators—in these events use to make sense of them?

One answer that emerged in the mid-1990s—as the Internet was rapidly expanding into homes and schools—was "Internet addiction" (or "Internet addiction disorder"). Internet addiction drew from an existing cultural narrative about addiction to substances and behaviors and proved flexible enough to encompass new troubling conditions that emerged from the Internet during subsequent years.

Although it is easy to talk about social problems as though they are stable categories that do not change over time, all social problems have histories. The boundaries for social problems—exactly what is considered part of the problem—can shift. For example, while the category of rape is many centuries old, in recent decades feminists argued that the meaning of rape needed to be expanded to encompass marital rape and date rape. Claims about Internet addiction are interesting because they reveal how rapidly the domain of a particular social problem can shift.

This chapter draws upon sixteen years of newspaper coverage to analyze the creation of Internet addiction as a social problem. In particular, it shows how the category has evolved as technology has developed and become more familiar and more integrated into social life. We constructed our sample using a Lexis-Nexis search of US newspapers for the term "Internet addiction" between 1995 (when the term was coined) and 2010. This produced 676 results. We narrowed the sample by eliminating duplicates and articles with only incidental mentions of "Internet addiction." The 238 articles we kept in the sample included someone—either the writer or a subject in the story—using the concept of Internet addiction to make claims about troubling conditions related to problematic Internet overuse. We read the articles in this sample, focusing on their claims and the rhetorical techniques used to make them. We also recorded which Internet activities were claimed to be problematic in each article.

The Creation of Internet Addiction

Internet addiction began as a joke. In 1995, New York psychiatrist Ivan Goldberg made a post on PsyCom.net in which he purported to describe "Internet addiction disorder" and its diagnostic criteria (Goldberg 1995; see also Federwisch 1997). The post was intended to read like an entry in the *Diagnostic and Statistical Manual of Mental Disorders* and at least some journalists didn't get the joke—for years Goldberg's criteria showed up in newspaper stories that contained no mention of the fact that they had been intended as parody. It's a distinction that's easy to miss. While later examples of Internet addiction humor tend to be more obvious (e.g., a tongue-in-cheek "Webaholics" site lists signs that you're an addict, including: "You get a tattoo saying, 'This body best viewed with Netscape 2.0 or higher'"), Goldberg's parody included such symptoms as "a need for markedly increased amounts of time on Internet to achieve satisfaction" and "markedly diminished effect with continued use of the same amount of time on Internet." A line about "involuntary typing movements of the fingers" is Goldberg's best material. Goldberg also created an "Internet addiction support group"—also a joke—and became one of the first go-to sources for journalists looking for experts on this new malady. However, Goldberg's stardom was soon supplanted by someone who took Internet addiction more seriously.

"I was looking at a lot of jokes about people addicted to the internet, and one night one of my girlfriends called me crying," Kimberly Young told the *Chicago Sun-Times.* "She said 'My husband is addicted to America Online. He just won't get off line'" (Jackson 1997). This inspired Young, then an assistant professor of psychology at the University of Pittsburgh at Bradford, to begin her research into what she initially called "pathological Internet use." Young founded the online Center for Internet Addiction Recovery in 1995 and presented her first academic report on the topic at a 1996 meeting of the American Psychological Association. Another paper presented to the association in 1997 was widely reported in the media. Young published *Caught in the Net* in 1998 and has since written additional books on cyber-sex, cyber-affairs, online gaming addiction, and Internet addiction among Catholics, and has edited an academic handbook on the topic. She quickly became—and remains—the most important spokesperson for the purported disorder.

The birth of Internet addiction was probably inevitable—both as joke and psychological construct. Addiction was already widely used to make sense of a variety of personal problems, including dependencies on chemical substances (alcohol and other drugs), but also various compulsions (overeating, sex addiction) and even social processes (codependency). The concept of addiction was also subject to criticism and mockery.

Addiction is one way of framing the problem of people misusing time, energy, and other resources. This, of course, is an age-old problem. People engage in activities—often engrossing ones—that, by community standards, are wasteful and compete with favored activities, such as planting or harvesting crops, performing religious rituals, and so on. This wastefulness is often framed from a moral or religious perspective (see, for examples, the biblical book of Proverbs: "He who gathers crops in summer is a prudent son, but he who sleeps during harvest is a disgraceful son" [Proverbs 10:5]; "Those who work their land will have abundant food, but those who chase fantasies have no sense" [Proverbs 12:11]).

The modern idea of addiction is an example of *medicalization,* the tendency to frame troubling conditions as medical problems. However, "addiction" was not originally a medical term; rather, the concept of addiction itself became medicalized. The English word is derived from a Roman legal term that "refers to the judicial action of legally sentencing a person to be a bond slave"; the English meaning involves "a similar state of servitude, not to a slave-master but to a 'habit or pursuit'" (Alexander 2008, p. 28). Prior to the nineteenth century, addiction could be both positive and negative, but the definition was "simultaneously narrowed, moralized, and medicalized" (p. 30), largely due to the influence of the temperance movement, so that it came to refer to the compulsion to take a drug. Thus, the late-twentieth-century expansion of "addiction" by the "recovery movement" to encompass "behaviors" and "processes" like "money, food (too much or too little), sex, 'putting oneself down,' the Internet, people, gambling, . . . exercise, [and] 'loving too much'" (Lowney 1999, p. 106) can be understood as a "reassertion of the traditional definition" (Alexander 2008, p. 35) of addiction. However, this expansion of the concept remains controversial, both within the medical profession and by cultural commentators who see addiction as a way of avoiding moral responsibility.

The development of "process addiction" represents an instance of *domain expansion* (Best 1999, 2008), whereby new claims about troubling conditions piggyback on more established ones. The *master frame* (Snow and Benford 1992) of addiction offered a cultural resource for claimsmakers who were framing new troubling conditions like Internet addiction, and this cultural resource proved flexible enough to accommodate a series of new Internet activities.

Establishing Media Conventions for Internet Addiction

Defining deviance requires defining "normal" behavior (Becker 1963). Early articles on Internet addiction presumed that a very low level of Internet use was normal. A 1997 article contrasts "most of America's 20 million 'netizens' [who] surf the World Wide Web only once a week or so" with "perhaps as many [who] have become so addicted to the Internet that it's wrecking their lives" (Hendrick 1997). Of one problematic Internet user, it was said that "not a day goes by that he doesn't check his e-mail" (McLeod 1995). And the chief technical officer of an Internet service provider was "surprised to find that one user spent 120 hours on line at home one month—the equivalent of four hours a day in front of the computer" (McLeod 1995). A *Dallas Morning News* story, citing Young's study, claimed that "avid computer users who were not viewed as addicts" averaged just eight hours of Internet use a week" (Watts 1997).

With this expected low level of use (by today's standards), activities like checking e-mail daily could be given as signs of excessive use. Checking e-mail is, in fact, the only specific Internet activity mentioned in Young's "Internet Addiction Test" ("How often do you check your e-mail before something else that you need to do?") (Young 1998, p. 31). One "recovering computer addict," the main character of a story on "lonely computer addicts," "went from sending e-mail, to surfing Web sites about Latin America, to learning how to program a Web page for work" (Henderson 1996).

Internet addiction at this point was largely about social interaction. Chat rooms and online multiplayer games were the most mentioned Internet activities in stories about addiction (see Figure 11.1). The Internet allowed people to make new—often intense—friendships with people online, to the detriment of "real world" friendships. Today, what were intended to be descriptions of problematic Internet use sometime sound like advertisements for the Internet's beneficial effects. Said Young of chat rooms: "Many times, chat rooms allow individuals the opportunity to meet certain unmet real-life needs such as social support, a sense of belonging in a group, or bringing out hidden parts of one's personality" (Stanley 1997).

A key part of a social problems claim is a *typifying example,* a dramatic case that illustrates the troubling condition (Best 2008). The early typifying examples for Internet addiction came in two main types: (1) an adult (usually a woman) finds that online social interactions are more engrossing than her spouse, causing her to neglect her marital and family duties and leading to marital strife; or (2) a high school or college student neglects their schoolwork and "real world" friendships for Internet activities.

One of the most dramatic early typifying examples was that of Sandra Hacker, an Ohio woman who was charged with child endangerment for allegedly spending up to twelve consecutive hours online while her three children fended for themselves. Accounts of the incident played up how Internet addiction had distorted Hacker's housekeeping performance: police "found broken glass, other debris and human feces on the walls of a playroom of her apartment" (Reuters 1997) but "the computer area was clean—completely immaculate" (Weeks 1997).

Figure 11.1 Frequency of Mention of Selected Activities in Newspaper Articles About Internet Addiction, 1995–2010

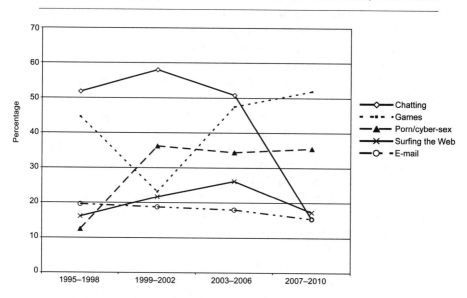

These two types of examples remained a mainstay of coverage of Internet addiction, with a few modifications. While wives (often without full-time employment outside the home) were featured more often in early stories, husbands addicted to pornography or to massively multiplayer online role-playing games (MMORPGs) also became common figures in the articles. Although most typifying examples focused on school or family life, some involved the workplace, with trouble caused for either the employers (e.g., "cyberslacking," legal issues involving pornography) or the employees (e.g., being fired). Additionally, several deaths attributed to Internet addiction became used as typifying examples:

- In 1996, a South Carolina man was charged "with strangling a Baltimore housewife during a sexual encounter they arranged while corresponding in an Internet chat room. The woman's death ended a graphic E-mail relationship they had carried on for seven weeks before she left her family to turn her 'virtual' relationship into the real thing" (Watts 1997).

- In 1999, "a twelve-year-old Missouri boy . . . shot his mother, and then himself, after she took away his computer. In his suicide note, the boy lamented his mother had taken away his whole world" (Morrison 1999).
- In 2006, twenty-one-year-old Shawn Wooley, described as an addict of the online game EverQuest, shot himself in front of his computer. His mother blamed the game (Bean 2006).
- In September 2007, "a thirty-year-old man in southern China dropped dead in an Internet cafe, apparently from exhaustion, after playing an Internet video game for three days" (Watson 2007).
- By 2008, ten Koreans had "died from blood clots from remaining seated for long periods in internet cafes" (Dumenco 2008); or in a slightly different version, ten Koreans had died "because gamers would go excessive hours without food or sleep" (Stuart 2008).
- In 2010, a Korean husband and wife obsessed with online role-playing games were charged with negligent homicide after their three-month-old daughter died (Sang-Hun 2010).

The latter four cases illustrate two trends in how Internet addiction is presented in the media: (1) the typical addict has now become a young male gamer (not a lonely housewife), and (2) typifying examples are frequently imported from China and Korea.

Addictive Internet Activities

Many features of stories about Internet addiction have remained constant during the sixteen years covered by this study, including the reliance on psychological experts as claimsmakers and the use of dramatic typifying stories. However, the activities that engross users have changed. Figures 11.1 and 11.2 show the changing pattern of Internet use. For simplification, the sixteen years are combined into four four-year periods: 1995–1998 (56 news articles), 1999–2002 (69 news articles), 2003–2006 (61 news articles), and 2007–2010 (52 news articles). The two graphs indicate the percentages of stories in each period that include various activities as examples of Internet addiction by claimsmakers. Some stories don't mention any specific activities. Some focus on one of them. Some mention as many as eight. Figure 11.1 details five activities that are mentioned in articles during all four periods: chatting (which includes chat rooms, Internet relay chat, AOL Instant Messenger, and similar technologies), games (which, when specified, usually refer to interactive games), porn/cyber-sex (including online pornography, sexually focused interactions, and unspecified references to online sexual addiction), surfing the Web (used to code references to "surfing" and also the viewing of news, information retrieval, and other such activities), and e-mail. Figure 11.2 details four activities that don't appear in the articles until the second or third periods: social networks, gambling, auctions/shopping, and stock trading.

Early reporting on Internet addiction focused on social interaction (as opposed to the solitary viewing of pornography or surfing the Web). Chatting and games dominate coverage during the first period. Chatting is the most mentioned activity in the first (51.8 percent), second (58.0 percent), and third periods (50.8 percent). As pornography and cyber-sex become more frequently mentioned as addictions for males, chatting often comes to be described as a typically female addiction. During the final period, mentions of chatting decline sharply (15.4 percent). Claims about pornography rise from the first (12.5 percent) to second (36.2 per-

Figure 11.2 Frequency of Mention of Selected Activities in Newspaper Articles About Internet Addiction, 1999–2010

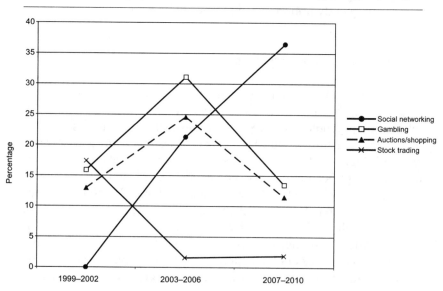

cent) periods, with addicted husbands becoming a common typifying example. Pornography remains one of the most mentioned activities in the third (34.4 percent) and fourth (35.5 percent) periods.

Claims about games decrease through the first (44.6 percent) and second (23.2 percent) periods, but increase during the third period (47.5 percent) and then become the most mentioned addictive Internet activity during the final period (51.9 percent). The uptick in interest corresponded to the introduction of World of Warcraft and the most recent version of EverQuest, the two most mentioned games. Both are MMORPGs and are said to be addictive by design—EverQuest is nicknamed "EverCrack." Claims about games also show up more frequently during the final period because of increased coverage of Internet addiction in Korea and China. Not only are games the most mentioned online activity, but they are also the most frequent topic of stories about Internet addiction that mention only one activity. In the third and fourth periods (2003–2010), twenty-nine stories focus on one addictive activity; twenty of these are about gaming.

By comparison, surfing the Web (16.1, 21.7, 26.2, and 17.3 percent during the four periods) and e-mail (19.6, 18.8, 18.0, and 15.4 percent) aren't viewed as standalone addictive activities. They tend to be mentioned in stories about multiple activities that keep people engrossed online. By the fourth period, mentions of chatting have decreased substantially to the level of surfing and e-mail. We suspect that the widespread engagement in these activities by many people in their daily lives has made it more difficult to view them, in themselves, as troubling conditions. (Mentions of e-mail sometimes appear because e-mail is listed in Young's assessment of Internet addiction; otherwise its frequency would be even lower.)

Turning to Figure 11.2, almost all claims about stock trading being addictive occur during the second period (17.4 percent), which corresponds to the height and burst of the dot.com bubble. Claims about auctions/shopping are usually about eBay. These appear in the second period (13.0 percent) and peak in the third (24.6 percent), but then drop to the level of chatting, e-mail, and surfing the Web by the fourth period (11.5 percent). We suspect that shopping, even by auction, has become a routinized Internet activity. Claims about gambling appear in the second period (15.9 percent), peak in the third (31.1 percent), but then fall off in the fourth (13.5 percent).

Almost all claims about social networks being addictive are about Myspace or Facebook. These appear in the third period (21.3 percent) and become as frequent as pornography in the fourth (36.5 percent). It remains to be seen whether routinization will make social networking less significant in claims of Internet addiction in the future.

Claims about other online activities being addictive are also found in these newspaper stories. Bulletin boards and news groups are mentioned in 16.1 percent of stories during the first period, but disappear as those technologies become less important. Writing and reading blogs and use of Twitter (during the final two years) also receive some mentions. Fantasy football is called "the leading Internet-driven workplace diversion" and "the new porn" in one story (Vataj 2005), but failed to gain any traction as a social problem.

Changing Coverage

Newspaper coverage during the last four years of our sample suggests several trends. First, reporting reflects the continuing development of new engrossing technologies—texting, Twitter, iPad apps, and so on—many of which are accessed through handheld devices. These technologies compete for attention with cell phones, gaming consoles, and other electronic devices. The concept of "technology addiction" is beginning to appear, suggesting further domain expansion of "addiction."

Second, much of the more current reporting reflects a more sophisticated approach to the topic than in the earlier years when the Internet was rapidly expanding into homes and schools but many people still had limited experience with it. Coverage typically notes that potentially addictive technologies are usually beneficial and also hard to escape. Overuse is placed alongside other issues raised by new technology, including how it shapes the way people attend to and interact with the "real world." These stories are sometimes found in college newspapers, often as part of a tongue-in-cheek confession of addiction, as a way to reflect upon the role of technology in the lives of college students.

Third, Internet addiction has become an international phenomenon, particularly in South Korea and China. While the scientific status of Internet addiction is still the subject of debate in the United States, where the first dedicated treatment center (located in Washington state, not just online, as earlier centers were) was not opened until 2009, these two nations have multiple government-run treatment centers and boot camps. In South Korea, Internet addiction has become a widely accepted medical problem. Korean and US commentators attribute this to Korea's strong embrace of the Internet. "Korea has been most aggressive in embracing the Internet," Koh Young-sam, head of the government-run Internet Addiction Counseling Center, told the *New York Times*. "Now we have to lead in dealing with its consequences" (Fackler 2007). In China, the government "has launched a campaign against what the Communist Youth League called a 'grave social problem that threatens the nation'" (Cha 2007). To critics, the Chinese government's embrace of Internet addiction "dovetails a bit too nicely with China's broader effort to control what its citizens can see on the Internet" (Cha 2007). In Korea, though, Internet addiction is typified as a problem of online gaming.

While China and South Korea have adopted the concept of Internet addiction from the United States, US claimsmakers have begun to take their typifying examples from these nations. When psychiatrist Jerold Block wrote an editorial in the *American Journal of Psychiatry* calling for Internet addiction to be added to the *Diagnostic and Statistical Manual*, his evidence came from South Korea, specifically ten "game-related deaths in Internet cafes" (Stuart 2008). To these claimsmakers, Internet-awash South Korea represents "the future."

Incomplete Institutionalization

Joel Best (1999) describes an "iron quadrangle" of actors needed to institutionalize a social problem: media, experts, activists, and government. Newspaper reporting on Internet addiction shows little evidence that the US government (unlike the Chinese or South Korean governments) or (nonexpert) activists have been much involved in the problem of Internet addiction. The reporters who wrote the stories in our sample drew upon a group of experts (as well as a number of confessed addicts and others affected by the problem) for most of their information. The most prominent experts promoting Internet addiction have been psychologists in the business of treating the disorder. These include Kimberly Young, founder of the online Center for Internet Addiction Recovery; Maressa Hecht Orzack, founder of the Computer Addiction Service at McLean Hospital in Belmont, Massachusetts; and David Greenfield, founder of the Center for Internet and Technology Addiction in West Hartford, Connecticut. All three are frequently quoted in Internet addiction stories. Mentions of

Young's center, information from its website, and items from her assessments frequently show up in news stories, perhaps because mentions of the center show up prominently during Web searches for "Internet addiction." Another group of counselors who appear frequently in these stories are university campus counselors. Stories on Internet addiction in campus papers frequently include quotes from counselors and from student addicts to provide a local angle on the issue. These experts frequently act as advocates for institutionalizing the term "Internet addiction," but Internet addiction doesn't seem to have gained organized (nonexpert) advocates, as have other Internet problems such as pedophilia.

The gold standard for institutionalizing a mental disorder is inclusion in the American Psychiatric Association's *Diagnostic and Statistical Manual of Mental Disorders*. As many articles on the controversy over the status of Internet addiction mention, the malady is not listed in the *Diagnostic and Statistical Manual*. In fact, the last major revision (DSM-IV) was published in 1994, shortly before the creation of Internet addiction. DSM-5 is scheduled to appear in 2013. The draft of DSM-5 does include a new category called "behavioral addictions," but gambling will be the only disorder included. Internet addiction will be relegated to the manual's appendix, "with a goal of encouraging additional study" (American Psychiatric Association 2010). Inclusion of a disorder in the *Diagnostic and Statistical Manual* is significant because insurance companies typically won't cover treatment for unincluded disorders.

Advocates for including Internet addiction in the *Diagnostic and Statistical Manual* muster three rhetorical strategies in arguing that problematic Internet use is addictive. The first strategy is simple analogy to other forms of addiction. Young and others derived their assessments of Internet addiction from other behavioral addictions and found people who were addicted by those standards. The second strategy is to focus on the seriousness of the troubling condition itself. "Marriages are being disrupted, kids are getting into trouble, people are committing illegal acts, people are spending too much money. As someone who treats patients, I see it," David Greenfield, founder of the Center for Internet and Technology Addiction, is quoted as telling a reporter (Donn 1999). By implication, those who deny that the Internet is addictive are downplaying its serious consequences. The third strategy refers to brain chemistry. Internet addiction (or its gaming and pornography variants) are said to release the same chemicals (variously reported as dopamine or endorphins) as do drug addictions. Mentions of brain chemistry first appeared in 2001 in our sample of articles and became more prominent throughout the decade.

Opponents of the concept of Internet addiction reject the analogy to addiction as unscientific and instead rely on comparisons with other behaviors. "People no more suffer an addiction to the Internet than someone . . . who reads books all the time suffers from 'book addiction disorder,'" psychologist John Grohol, a frequent critic of Internet addiction, was quoted saying in response to early claims (Stanley 1997); "television addiction" is another frequent foil. However, opponents of the concept of Internet addiction don't deny that problematic use of the Internet can be a psychological problem; they simply disagree about how the problem should be conceptualized. Perhaps Internet addiction is a symptom of another disorder, like depression, or would be better described as an "impulse control disorder" or some other formulation. In any case, they call for more research. Thus, while troubling Internet use has not (yet) been institutionalized as "Internet addiction," it has been incompletely institutionalized as belonging in the realm of psychology, where it is the subject of a *frame dispute* (Best 2010). (For a sociological critique of Internet addiction, see Johnson 2009).

In addition, the concept of Internet addiction has entered the culture in another significant way. It has become a commonly understood expression for overuse of the Internet—whether serious overuse resulting in broken marriages and suspension from college, or as a lightheartedly (and often first-person) description of someone's reliance on Facebook, texting, Tweeting, iPad apps, or any other new technology. While the future of "Internet addiction" as a scientific concept for framing problematic Internet use is unclear, its use as a familiar cultural resource is well established.

12

Breaking News on *Nancy Grace:* Violent Crime in the Media

Brian A. Monahan and R. J. Maratea

Crime is arguably the biggest social problem in the United States. This is not to say that it is inherently more important than other social problems or that it is somehow more deserving of our attention and outrage. Rather, the point is that no other social problem in modern history has consistently drawn as much concern, public consternation, and political response as has crime. Countless social problems come and go with surprising alacrity, but there remains a constant sense that crime is "out of control" and "about to get worse." From an early age and throughout our life course, we are told to be afraid of crime and adopt a near constant state of vigilance, lest we become its next victim.

The media are by any measure a key cog in the production and perpetuation of these crime concerns. Crime and criminals—along with the individual and institutional attempts to control them—have long been staple features of popular entertainment, and the growth of cable and satellite television in recent decades has brought with it a wave of "reality" and fictional programs that focus extensively on criminality (Fishman and Cavender 1998). At the same time, crime continues to be one of the most prominent substantive topics in the mainstream press, with crime stories littered throughout the daily headlines of print, television, and online news sources. As Steven Chermak noted, covering crime "capitalizes on the public's fascination with gore and entertainment" (1994, p. 105).

The deluge of crime-related content in the press and in popular culture yields a number of patterned messages about crime, many of which run counter to established empirical realities of crime. For instance, while crime rates in the United States began a long-term decline in the early 1990s, the amount of violent crime depicted in news and entertainment media was actually increasing. Barry Glassner (1999) found that the number of murder stories on nightly network news broadcasts rose by 600 percent between 1990 and 1998, despite the fact that murder rates actually declined by 20 percent during that time. Similarly, Danielle Soulliere (2003) analyzed a selection of popular crime programs and found a significant overrepresentation of violent crime: 66 percent of criminal incidents on the analyzed episodes were murder or attempted murder, which vastly outpaced murder's share (less than 1 percent) of the crimes recorded in the 1999 *Uniform Crime Report.*

While the reasons for the gap between perception and reality in crime coverage are many, it is, for the most part, a matter of headlines and plotlines. The entertainment ethos that has long been a hallmark of popular culture has increasingly come to inform modern news work (Monahan 2010). Media attention in both the news and entertainment realms is commonly reserved for those occurrences that offer the most novelty and shock value (Lundman 2003). Coverage favors sensational events that feature salacious details and that can be depicted via a steady stream of alarming examples and shocking numbers (Best 1999; Orcutt and Turner 1993). Consequently, the vast majority of crime coverage grossly exaggerates the nature and extent of the problem (Killingbeck 2001).

The implication of all of this is that the extensive coverage of crime in the media, rather than providing much needed insight into the complexities of crime's causes and remedies, fuels a narrow, deeply flawed understanding of crime, criminals, and criminal justice. Indeed, numerous studies have found that the average citizen's working knowledge of crime and criminal justice derives primarily from the crime messages they receive from news and entertainment media (Romer, Jamieson, and Aday 2003). Despite the well-publicized drop in crime rates, a recent study found that 67 percent of Americans continue to perceive that crime is rising while a mere 17 percent believe that it is decreasing (Jones 2010). This virtually endless cycle of misleading crime messages in the media, when coupled with the tremendous public reliance on the media for making sense of crime-related issues, requires that we pay close attention to how the media portray crime, as this is a crucial component in the creation and communication of our shared understanding of crime and criminals.

In this chapter, we focus on *Nancy Grace,* a highly popular cable news crime program. Since its inception in 2005, this program has become a primary influence on how the public, the press, and political leaders identify "the crimes that matter." We argue that the representation of crime on *Nancy Grace* offers needed insights into how crime is constructed in news and entertainment media and in other public arenas where crime concerns and policies are shaped and implemented.

We conducted a content analysis of thirty original episodes of *Nancy Grace* that were broadcast between June 28, 2010, and July 28, 2011. The original project design called for a sample of episodes aired from June 28, 2010, through the end of that calendar year. When it became apparent to us that the Casey Anthony trial would be a watershed moment for this program, the sampling frame was extended to accommodate coverage of the trial. Transcripts for all thirty analyzed episodes were retrieved through Lexis-Nexis, while full episode video was procured for eleven of these episodes. The analysis focused primarily on the transcribed content, with video utilized to better contextualize transcribed content and identify on-screen elements of the presentation not evident on transcriptions. Data analysis was conducted using a "tracking discourse" approach. This manner of content analysis hinges on the examination of "numerous documents in order to become familiar with formats and emphases, while suggesting topics and themes" that emerge or remain consistent over time (Altheide 1996, p. 70). Using this approach allowed us to identify the principles of selection, prominent framings, and production devices used in the patterned constructions of crime, criminals, and criminal justice on *Nancy Grace.*

Nancy Grace: The Person and the Program

> Our Founding Fathers wanted courthouses to be big enough for the whole community to come in and watch justice unfold. I think that's what our whole show is all about. (Nancy Grace, quoted in Johnson 2006)

Nancy Grace is a former prosecuting attorney who has used the experience and stature derived from her career in the legal realm as the basis for a transition to the role of media legal analyst. Grace routinely notes that her passion for the law is a result of personal trauma, claiming that the murder of her fiancé spurred her toward law school and shaped her staunch ideological pursuit of "victim justice." Grace's first full-time foray into television legal commentary came in 1996, when she was hired to cohost Court TV's *Cochran and Grace* (with Johnny Cochran, famed defense attorney from the O.J. Simpson trial). That program was short-lived, but Grace quickly became a mainstay at Court TV as a host for various sensationalized legal analysis programs (e.g., *Trial Heat* and *Closing Arguments*) and as a resident legal expert whose commentary was widely sought, not only on Court TV programs but also in national cable and broadcast news coverage. Along the way, Grace further solidified her status as a legal expert by writing books and articles and becoming an increasingly vocal advocate for victims' rights.

By the mid-2000s, Grace had become perhaps the best-known legal analyst in US media. But her efforts also made her an immensely polarizing figure; she draws fierce support from adherents favoring her victim-centric approach and elicits outrage from opponents who see her approach to crime coverage as little more than an attention-seeking gimmick. Nonetheless, the increased notoriety resulted in a 2005 move from Court TV (by then renamed truTV) to CNN's Headline News Network, where she was hired to host a one-hour program in primetime. That program—titled *Nancy Grace* (and the data source for the present analysis)—was initially billed as a "nightly celebrity news and current affairs show" but, fueled by Grace's ideology and the ratings success that accompanied its coverage of crime (relative to other featured topics), the show was reworked to make it a vehicle for "all crime, all the time" content.

By the end of 2005, *Nancy Grace* was clearly Headline News Network's flagship program. Airing nightly for one hour in primetime (8–9 P.M. Eastern standard time, followed by a subsequent airing later in the evening), Monday through Friday, the program drew surprisingly robust ratings, given that it was a narrowly focused crime program with a polarizing host that aired on a marginal cable news channel. Ratings for *Nancy Grace* received regular boosts from a number of high-profile crime cases (which, not coincidentally, Grace had helped bring to prominence), including the trial of pop icon Michael Jackson, the disappearance of Jennifer Wilbanks (a.k.a. "The Runaway Bride"), the Natalee Holloway saga (which was a centerpiece of Grace's coverage for several years), the Duke lacrosse scandal, John Mark Karr's self-implication in the disappearance of JonBenet Ramsey, the death of Anna Nicole Smith, and a litany of celebrity misdeeds, missing kids, and murdered moms. Viewership steadily increased as *Nancy Grace* became a go-to source for breaking crime news. The high-water mark for viewership to date occurred on July 5, 2011, when the verdict was announced in the Casey Anthony trial (a case that Grace was the first national host to report on and that she covered more than did any other network or program): more than 5 million viewers tuned in to Grace's live broadcast that afternoon, which represented the highest viewership for any network covering the trial and made it the most watched program in the history of Headline News Network (De Moraes 2011).

The success of *Nancy Grace* is attributable to many factors, but the show's unwavering focus on the crimes of the day is vital to its appeal and makes it markedly different from most other news programs. Few news shows are able to enjoy such a narrow substantive focus; the majority of news programming is designed to have a broad appeal in hopes of attracting a wide audience whose members will be interested in some, but not necessarily all, of the content. Consider, for example, the morning programs on the broadcast networks (e.g., ABC, CBS, and NBC). Crime is a staple feature in their respective content cycles, but it is just one of many topics to which they are expected to attend. As a result, there is limited time to devote to issues of crime and deviance, and the issues that do receive coverage must be attended to in a way that fits the general-interest ethos of these programs (e.g., offering relatively brief crime segments, limiting the use of potentially disturbing depictions or videos, quickly and concisely putting the details in order, and so on). *Nancy Grace* does not face similar constraints. Its content selection and presentation reflect an underlying assumption that audience members have an interest in crime and criminal justice, and no apparent efforts are made to identify or capitalize on any other substantive interests those audience members may have.

When a criminal incident or court case is featured on *Nancy Grace,* it is extensively dissected during the course of the hour-long program. Grace and the revolving collection of experts (e.g., lawyers, psychiatrists, advocates, former victims, and a host of specialists) who are invited into each evening's broadcast pore over the details of the case and offer an array of observations, questions, and sweeping generalizations about the events, issues, and principal figures involved. The presentation style is notably fast-paced, with each guest allotted a brief moment to raise a question or make a statement before they recede to the background, their place temporarily taken by another expert or guest. For her part, Nancy Grace serves as a sort of "ringmaster" for the proceedings. Though she does routinely provide lengthy remarks to open and close the broadcasts, her primary role is to direct the conversation by calling forth individual experts for comment, incorporating viewer comments into the on-air presentation, offering occasional summaries of key details, and editorializing about the ongoing discussion.

Analysis

Researchers have repeatedly shown that exposure to crime coverage (particularly coverage that overemphasizes violent and random crimes) affects individuals' fear of crime, promotes punitive attitudes regarding crime, and directs attention to certain types of crime, often to the exclusion of more common criminal incidents or other pertinent social issues. Our analysis reveals that *Nancy Grace* furthers many of these familiar patterns in crime coverage, while also adding new elements to the mediated representation of crime. In the remainder of this chapter, we outline the ways that *Nancy Grace* contributes to the construction of crime as a social problem by outlining how crime is packaged and presented on *Nancy Grace;* illustrating how Grace uses this image of crime to promote notions of "justice," which she then employs as a malleable rhetorical device to announce her own moral authority and promote a narrowly punitive understanding of crime and criminal justice processes; and demonstrating how Grace effectively cultivates a "community of concern" around her image of crime, which affords her a wide base of populist support that enhances her status as an advocate for truth and justice.

"Bombshell Tonight": Images of Crime on Nancy Grace

> *Grace:* Breaking news tonight, live, Alabama. A young Russellville dad heads to work, leaving his two little boys, Angel and Christian, ages 5 and 6, at home, safe and sound with the baby-sitter. But when Daddy gets home from work, Angel and Christian [are] gone. Amber Alert issued for the two little boys. And what about the baby-sitter? Was she overpowered, beaten, kidnapped, attacked,

left tied to a staircase or the kitchen chair? No, the baby-sitter is the kidnapper! Bombshell tonight. As we go to air, little Angel and Christian found alive.

Nancy Grace specializes in violent crime, packaging it as an urgent and indiscriminate threat that is directly relevant to audience members. All of the featured criminal events in the thirty episodes analyzed for this study were violent in nature. Not all violent crime, however, appears to be eligible for inclusion; the vast majority of the violent crimes selected for attention involved a narrow range of criminal events (abductions and disappearances, abuse, and murder) carried out primarily against young children, teens, or women. Children are the most common victims in cases featured on *Nancy Grace,* and these cases include both boy and girl victims. The few cases centered on teen or adult victims in our sample featured only female victims, with coverage of the disappearance of Susan Powell, a young mother in Utah, in the spring of 2011, being typical of how these cases are presented:

> *Grace:* Breaking news tonight. Live to Utah and the mystery surrounding the disappearance of a gorgeous young stock broker, mother of two, 28-year-old Susan Powell, last seen when Daddy suddenly announces at midnight Sunday night he's taking boys ages 4 and 2 camping in the snow. They get back home. He says Mommy's gone, vanished. Bombshell tonight. In the last hours, skeletal remains discovered in the Utah desert. Is it the body of mother of two, Susan Powell?

The patterned representation of crime on *Nancy Grace* suggests that violent crime is common, random, committed by people from all walks of life, and disproportionately targets a rather narrow subset of the population (i.e., white children and women, typically from middle-class or affluent families). Of course, formal measures of crime (e.g., the FBI's *Uniform Crime Reports* and victimization surveys) consistently tell us that this image of crime is patently false: violent crime is much less common than nonviolent crime and, when it does occur, is overwhelmingly more likely to produce victims who are young, urban, African American males.

The image of crime on *Nancy Grace* is not accidental. There is little to suggest that the program's producers attempt to accurately reflect crime as an empirical category; instead, the goal appears to be to select cases that are most likely to be entertaining, compelling, and, above all, compatible with Grace's ideological notions of the crimes that matter most. The narrow version of crime on *Nancy Grace* is cultivated to increase the perception among targeted viewers (adults between the ages of twenty-five and fifty-four) that crime is a problem that is salient to their lives. Focusing exclusively on violent crimes against "upstanding citizens" and "innocent victims" (who happen to be demographically similar to targeted viewers or their friends and loved ones) enhances the likelihood that audience members will find the protagonists and their exploits relatable and emotionally resonant, thereby making them more likely to tune in regularly. The extensive coverage of crimes against children makes more sense amid this brand of "media logic" (Altheide and Snow 1979), as child victims are particularly amenable to framing as angelic victims undeserving of what has befallen them at the hands of their evil, irredeemable assailants. This polemic contrast was perfectly articulated during Grace's coverage of Casey Anthony, the "tot mom" who "gets a sexy tattoo in the days after Caylee goes missing, and then has a pizza party at the tattoo parlor" while "Caylee's skull, her empty eye sockets, her little teeth, matted clumps of light brown hair embedded in weeds and vines, little Caylee's disassembled bones lay in a virtual trash heap."

In Pursuit of "Justice": Combating Crime on Nancy Grace

Crimes are selected for attention on *Nancy Grace* precisely because they can be vividly and unambiguously cast as indicators of moral failings and broad threats to social order, thus providing the necessary contextual license for the punitive rhetoric espoused by Grace and other on-air commenters. Crime can be framed as both a source and a manifestation of injustice, which is crucial to the rhetoric Grace uses to promote her personal ideology of crime. Indeed, justice is a central theme in how crime is presented here. For Grace and her adherents, each crime selected for attention represents a particularly egregious form of "injustice," signaling to the audience that there is a perceived imbalance in the moral order that demands both legal and populist redress to return to a state of "justice."

Grace's inflammatory, morally charged demeanor allows her to categorically identify for her audience when offenders are guilty and deserving of swift justice. Guilt, then, is determined when Nancy Grace identifies a blameworthy party. Justice is only achieved when the punishment inflicted by the criminal justice system meets her expectations of an appropriate response. This is nowhere more evident than in Grace's coverage of the Casey Anthony trial in the summer of 2011. When the "not guilty" verdict was announced on July 5, Grace immediately called forth the "innocence versus evil" frame that had characterized her coverage of this case (and so many other cases involving child victims) and used it to articulate her contention that justice had not been achieved:

> *Grace:* Tonight, a verdict has been rendered in the case of tot mom. Not guilty. The devil is dancing tonight, but I believe that since June 16, 2008, there's a little angel in heaven named Caylee. And God bless her. I hope she knows nothing of our goings-on here at the Orlando courthouse. I hope that Little Caylee somewhere is happy tonight.

The use of justice as a malleable rhetorical tool is further evident in the coverage of the disappearance of Abbi Obermiller, a seventeen-year-old girl from Ohio who had been missing for twenty-one days (in June 2010) when the case was first featured on *Nancy Grace.* Grace's initial framing of this case presented Obermiller's disappearance as an abduction, with her boyfriend, Robert Young, implicated as the abductor:

> *Grace:* She [Obermiller] goes missing from her grandmother's house in the range of just six hours. She was texting back and forth with the boyfriend. . . . Well, what's mysterious about it to me, sergeant, maybe we differ, is that he is texting her a location to go to and then she is never seen again. To me, that's a little mysterious. I also find it mysterious that the boyfriend won't take a polygraph. Why won't he take a polygraph, sergeant?
> *Sgt. Jim Fulton* (Norwalk [Ohio] Police): Well, in my opinion, guilty people don't take polygraphs.
> *Grace:* Well, you're preaching to the choir, sergeant. Preaching to the choir.

Here we had what Grace presented as an open-and-shut case: a young high school student goes missing and police call her boyfriend a person of interest after identifying text messages exchanged between the two shortly before her disappearance. Although it was noted that Obermiller had apparently left her grandparent's home voluntarily, Grace and her guest used the string of text messages that suggested an arranged meeting, together with Young's unwillingness to submit to a polygraph exam, as clear-cut evidence of his guilt in the kidnapping and possible murder of the "gorgeous, 17-year-old coed, honor student, number one in her class, volleyball star." The framing of Young as a devious offender held strong, even as a pair of defense attorneys who were invited to join the discussion of the case as invited experts attempted to counter that frame:

> *Grace:* Let's unleash the lawyers.
> *Randy Kessler* (defense attorney): My advice is that [Young] is at a fork in the road. And he can do one of two things. If he knows anything, come clean, it won't be as hard on him. If he's done something terrible, he needs to lawyer up, clam up, and see what kind of deal he can come up with.
> *Grace:* What about it, Manuelian?
> John Manuelian (defense attorney): I absolutely agree. He should not take that polygraph test. His lawyer should advise him to keep his mouth shut.
> *Grace* (interrupting): Yes, you two, if it was your daughter you wouldn't be saying that.
> *Manuelian:* You're right. I have a daughter. But, I'm speaking from the perspective as an attorney.

The problem, however, was that Obermiller had not been kidnapped; she had run away from home following repeated arguments with her parents relating to her strained relationship with them. Her intent was to remain hidden until she turned eighteen, after which she and Young could then elope and get married. Even as this information came to light after Obermiller was found by police hiding in the attic insulation of Young's apartment building, Grace steadfastly continued to assign criminal culpability to Young:

> *Grace:* I'll tell you who should be in police custody: the boyfriend and, you know, frankly, this little girl for putting her parents through pure hell, dragging them across the floor of hell all this time, found hiding in insulation, hiding down in the pink or yellow insulation in the fetal position in the attic of her boyfriend's apartment. All I have to say is, news flash, praise the Lord. There is a God. Abbi has been found, she is safe, and now she is in a whole heap of trouble. I don't want our viewers to really get the wrong impression of her. She's number one in her class, straight-A student, volleyball star. Her dream before she got hooked up with 20-year-old Robert Young was to become a researcher in oncology and help find the cure for cancer. I know people bandy that about almost as a joke

> now, but that was her dream, that has been her dream for a long
> time. And the loving parents that she had. And then she hooked up
> with this, there he is, Bobby Young.

The offender frame was affirmed by various experts invited into the
coverage, such as Pat Brown, a criminal profiler and author: "this poor
girl has hooked up with a guy who seems like an extremely controlling
and creepy dude to me, and might be psychopathic since he's willing to
blatantly lie to the police. 'I didn't text her,' when clearly he did."

This case underscores the core crime messages of *Nancy Grace*
in a number of ways. It forcefully demonstrates that violent crime is a
problem everywhere, even in the presumably safer confines of subur-
ban life in Middle America. It reinforces the program's underlying
"society in decline" narrative by conveying to audiences that crime is
rampant and that even our most valued, cherished, and innocent
members of society are being victimized on a daily basis by the most
heinous acts imaginable. Crime is presented as a spectacle to be
gawked at, remarked upon, and outraged by. This makes great sense
from a pragmatic standpoint: those charged with producing five one-
hour programs about crime per week need crimes that are captivating
in their own right, even before the show's producers apply frames and
craft narratives. However, it is also important from a symbolic standpoint, as the constructed images of crime on *Nancy Grace* provide a
context in which Grace and other featured on-air commentators can
express their moral indignation at the state of society, criticize the
inadequate responses by the justice system, and propose the solutions
that would achieve justice.

The fast-paced nature of *Nancy Grace* generally precludes Grace
and her guests, who are mostly victims' family members, law enforcement officials, lawyers, and show correspondents, from engaging in
explicit policy debates or discussions that meaningfully contextualize
the legislative process and the challenges of regulating crime. Instead,
what is offered is a series of generalized statements about crime being
bad and out of control followed by populist appeals about the need to
"do something." This narrow view of the crime problem means that
Grace and the production staff rarely attempt to look beyond the confines of their own show for a solution. Crime is first positioned as a
threat to the moral order; then, once the details of a given case have
been explained, Grace and her correspondents proceed to debate what
needs to be done for justice to be achieved. This not only portrays their

interpretations of events as objective reflections of truth and justice—often while cases are still ongoing—but also casts Grace specifically, and mass media more generally, as essential components in the justice process. Media actors, in effect, become instruments of repair (Altheide 1992); they function as righteous figures who inform audiences about what crime looks like, where it is happening, and how society should respond in order to recalibrate the moral order.

When Grace misinterprets a case by jumping to conclusions or offers a flawed analysis of available information (as in the Obermiller case), it is simply ignored or brushed aside (it should be noted that very few of the experts invited into the discussion appear willing to counter Grace's assessments or otherwise cross her). Grace is constantly presented as an impassioned advocate whose professional expertise and personal experiences render her uniquely qualified to navigate viewers safely through a world of heinous crime and steadfastly pursue justice for them and those like them. The malleability of the "justice" concept is key to Grace's status as a moral authority on crime and criminal justice; its meanings are readily modified to meet the needs of Grace, the show, and her audience, as was the case when Abbi Obermiller's true actions were revealed and dissected on the June 30, 2010, broadcast:

> *Grace:* Back to you Ellie [Ellie Jostad, chief editorial producer of *Nancy Grace*]. What is the boyfriend charged with? Bobbie Young.
> *Jostad:* Right. Well, Bobbie Young is charged with obstruction of official business, interference of custody, contributing to the unruliness of a minor, and falsification.
> *Grace:* That might land him six months. Unleash the lawyers. Jim Elliot, what about it? What can you really expect? What kind of jail time can he do?
> *James Elliot Jr.* (city attorney): Doesn't sound like anything terribly serious to me, Nancy.
> *Grace:* Jail time, jail time, jail time, Jim.
> *Elliot:* Yes.
> *Grace:* What am I looking at? What can I get? Six months, a year maybe?
> *Elliot:* Six months. I would think six months.
> *Grace:* Well, unfortunately, I'm going to have to agree with you. I wish it was a little bit more. What about it, Penny?
> *Penny Douglass Furr* (defense attorney): I don't think they should get any jail time. I think they're just teenagers who took off together.
> *Grace:* I didn't ask you what you thought. I asked you what really he's going to get.

Douglass Furr: If anything, he'll get probation.
Grace: Yes, I know she will with her stellar record. Randy Zelin, what
   about it? What is he looking at?
Randy Zelin (defense attorney): Look, he's looking at jail time.
Grace: Can we keep him in the can a couple of nights to scare him?

This exchange is telling because of the noticeable shift in how the
crimes and proposed punishment are being framed. Even as Grace
eases away from framing Young as a criminal offender, she and her
legal correspondents still describe him as a deviant (e.g., an overly
controlling "bad guy") and suggest that he is still deserving of at least
a few days in jail "to scare him."

Interactions between Grace and the invited experts demonstrate
how fiercely Grace maintains her role as the sole authority in these proceedings. The above exchange with a defense attorney sees her invali-
date what the attorney says by tersely noting, "I didn't ask you what you
thought." This is common practice throughout the analyzed episodes, as
seen in the April 29, 2011, broadcast during a debate regarding the
moral and legal implications of pictures of Casey Anthony socializing
with friends while her young daughter was missing:

Grace: And you know that not every piece of evidence has to show she
   committed the murder. In circumstantial evidence cases, Alex
   Sanchez [a defense attorney, whom Grace was inviting to join the
   conversation], the pieces fit together like a puzzle. When you put
   the first piece, you don't necessarily see the landscape. It's only
   when you get all the evidence you see the murder. That's what circumstantial evidence is, Alex.
Sanchez: Yes, but you know, Nancy, I'll tell you the truth. I'm surprised
   that any seasoned prosecutor, and you included, would want to
   have this evidence come before the jury because you know that
   you're setting up a major appeals issue.
Grace: No, I don't know that!
Sanchez: And the purpose of this evidence is simply to . . .
Grace: Hey, Sanchez! [speaking loudly in an attempt to drown out the
   voice of Sanchez]
Sanchez: encourage the jury . . .
Grace: Just stop just a moment! [shouting more loudly]
Sanchez: to engage in speculation . . .
Grace: Don't tell me . . .
Sanchez: and that's unfair. You know that.
Grace: what I know. What I know is that these photos are relevant to
   her frame of mind. That's what I know!
Sanchez: Right, but you're forcing . . .

Grace: And take a listen to Nejame. Nejame? [attempting to redirect the
   conversation to another attorney on that day's panel]
Sanchez: Because you're forcing . . .
Grace: Sorry, I keep for some reason hearing irritating buzz. Oh, it's
   Sanchez still in my ear! Nejame, tell him why it's relevant.

A Community of Concern:
Rallying Around Crime and Justice on *Nancy Grace*

Whether preaching for "jail time, jail time, jail time" or belittling
legal correspondents who disagree with her, Nancy Grace positions
herself as the unquestioned leading moral authority in these proceedings. By extension, her loyal viewers are situated as pseudo-partners
in the fight against "injustice." Audience members are repeatedly told
that they are vital to the broader efforts to identify and thwart the
types of crimes and criminals featured on this show.

The format and content of the show, coupled with Grace's presentation style, serve to infuse the coverage with a sense of kinship between
Grace and her audience. Certainly, the way crime is framed on the show
(i.e., simplistic, decontextualized portrayals of violent crime that depict
morally decrepit offenders preying on the innocent and vulnerable
among us) makes it easier for targeted audiences to identify and align
with Grace's moralizing sentiments and punitive rhetoric. Still, there
are numerous production elements in *Nancy Grace* that suggest active
efforts to cultivate solidarity between Grace and her audience. This is
accomplished through the subtle use of inclusive language, frequent
attempts to incorporate viewers into the presentation, and the use of
personalizing agents and "feeling moments."

During each episode, Grace reinforces the audience's role in her
efforts by reminding them that she does what she does *for them* and
that she could not do it as well *without them* (i.e., their viewership
and support). This is often done subtly, through the use of verbal cues
that personalize her efforts to the audience (e.g., "we," "my friends,"
"dear"). Grace's on-air exchanges with callers (there are usually three
or more of these per episode) reflect the efforts to affirm and demonstrate this connection:

Grace: To P.J. in Louisiana. Hi, P.J.
Caller: Hi, Nancy.
Grace: Hi, dear, what's your question?
Caller: First of all, thanks for everything that you're doing for everyone.
Grace: Thank you.

While Grace routinely expresses outrage and contempt for the featured crimes and criminals—and indignation at the lawyers who dare to disagree with her—her interactions with viewers are typically very pleasant, like two friends making amiable conversation. Often, Grace invokes individual audience members in a way that goes well beyond mere pleasantries to suggest a deeper, more meaningful connection with her audience:

> *Grace:* Thank you to Leonor in El Paso, for the beautiful, framed cross-stitch of my parents. It was so beautiful I gave it to my mother as a Mother's Day gift. I just don't know how you did it. It was just gorgeous. And I want to thank you. It's hanging in my parents' home tonight.

Attempts to forge these connections—or at least to create the perception that they exist—are found throughout the episodes, with viewers routinely making it clear that they care about Grace as a person. This is evident in the following pair of on-air exchanges with callers:

> *Grace:* We are taking your calls. Out to Sarah in Pennsylvania. Hi, Sarah.
> *Caller:* Hi, Nancy. Love to you and your family.

> *Grace:* To Elaine in Illinois. Hi, Elaine. What's your question, dear?
> *Caller:* Hi, Nancy. How are you feeling?
> *Grace:* I'm good.
> *Caller:* Oh, good. I'm still hoping you got my letter about the poem with Zahra Baker. I know you're very busy and popular, so I don't know if you ever got to that one.
> *Grace:* Well, busy, yes. Popular, don't know so much about that. A lot of defense attorneys don't like me too much. But I will go on a search for your letter, Elaine in Illinois. Now, what is your question, dear?

These communications are not always initiated by viewers, as Grace regularly reaches out to her audience members in personal ways, such as by extending birthday wishes:

> *Grace:* And happy 23rd birthday to Brittany, a nursing student, loves her family, her faith in god, time with friends, traveling, shopping. She's beautiful on the inside and the outside. Her dad is a Methodist minister. Happy birthday, Brittany.

And by celebrating birth announcements:

> *Grace:* And congratulations to San Francisco defense lawyer Daniel
> Horowitz and his beautiful wife, Valerie, welcoming their new
> baby girl, Chloe. What a beauty. Welcome to the world, baby
> Chloe.

And commemoration of various life milestones achieved by loyal
viewers and friends:

> *Grace:* And happy anniversary to Georgia friends Richard and Helen
> Kite, 62 years together. You are an inspiration to all of us.

Another oft-used device that helps to bring a familial element to
the show is Grace's willingness to incorporate stories of her children
and anecdotal tales that reflect the universal challenges of parenting.
References to her children serve to underscore the danger posed by
the kinds of crimes featured on the show (e.g., child abduction). The
fact that Grace—the moral authority on crime and a well-connected
legal expert—is fearful of such things reinforces to the viewers that
they ought to be frightened as well. This can be seen in an exchange
with a caller on the April 29, 2011, broadcast, during the discussion
about Casey Anthony's actions while Casey's daughter was missing:

> *Caller:* Hello, Nancy. My question tonight is, how many of those de-
> fense attorneys have children of their own and would know that
> they wouldn't be doing what she was doing? If that would have
> been one of my kids missing, I'd have been all over the country
> looking for them, not in a bar looking for them.
> *Grace:* You know, Beverly, I remember I had taken the children to the
> beach and we were in one of those little souvenir shops. Actually,
> it was kind of big. It was long. And I had my eye on both of them
> and they wanted, like, little key chains. And I reached up to get
> them, I got them off, I turned around. I had Lucy but not John
> David. Do you know how fast a baby can get stolen? And the front
> door was way far away from me. I cannot even imagine if one of
> them went missing and then I go out and work as a shot girl—like
> the old cigarette girls—that they would walk around bars in a short
> skirt with cigarettes on a tray that went around their neck. You
> know, she had that with shots. That's what she was doing during
> her investigation.

Grace draws on her role as a mother to young children as a basis for
articulating her moral outrage and forging an emotional bond with

viewers. Her children are invoked often enough to suggest that any references to them are not accidental. In fact, they should be understood as an important component of the rhetorical toolkit that Grace draws from to frame the crime problem on the show. This is evident in Grace's coverage of the Casey Anthony verdict on July 5, 2011. When arguing that Caylee Anthony's death remained an "injustice," Grace used a seemingly innocuous story about her children to underscore the extent to which innocence had been violated with the death of Caylee (and not countered due to the acquittal of Casey):

> *Grace:* There is no justice until someone is accountable for how this girl was treated, for how this girl is trying to rest in peace tonight, but can't because whoever had her—and obviously most people here believe it was Casey Anthony—took her and just tossed her away. You know, something very poignant to me, the swampy land, the swamp where Caylee's body was thrown away like trash. Liz [producer on *Nancy Grace*], I'd like to see some pictures of Caylee, please [images of Caylee appear on screen]. The other day . . . Lucy was going to ballet and John David and I were going along to watch. And we had to step across this little walkway, and it was muddy. And they didn't feel like putting their shoes on yet. So I carried one across the mud, then I went back and got the other one and carried them across. . . . I didn't want their little feet to touch a rock or to get all muddy and messed up. And I was thinking about throwing Caylee's body out there in that swamp.

The most explicit efforts to cultivate this community of concern occur in the final minutes of each episode, where Grace extends thanks to viewers while also showing pictures of children and pets sent in by viewers, presenting glowing testimonials and well-wishes for valued viewers. In fact, nearly every episode includes the host offering a solemn tribute to a fallen US soldier at the close of the show:

> *Grace:* Let's stop and remember Army Specialist Matthew Boule, 22, Dracut, Massachusetts, killed [in] Iraq. Awarded Bronze Star, Purple Heart, Army Achievement. Wanted to enlist since age 4 when he dressed in camouflage. Lost his life 72 hours after proposing to his girlfriend. Loved paint ball, soccer, street hockey, his niece and best friend, Britney. Dreamed of flying Blackhawk helicopters. Leaves behind parents Sue and Leo. Brothers Michael and Christopher. Sister, Wendy. Fiancee, Kat. Matthew Boule, American hero.

All of this is delivered with soft, welcoming language that is incongruous with virtually every other element of the program. For the better part of fifty-eight minutes, Grace acts like a carnival barker commanding her audience to step right up and see the sordid and grisly truths of violent crime in our society. However, in these closing moments she makes the program more about her audience than it is about crime. With this, Grace reminds viewers that she is not some distant television personality; she is a trusted friend who fights the good fight to keep them and their loved ones safe. Each episode comes to an end with a warm and reassuring refrain:

> *Grace:* Thanks to our guests but especially to you for being with us. See you tomorrow night. Until then, we are looking. Keep the faith, friend. Goodnight.

Conclusion

Crime enjoys unrivaled prominence as a social concern. The perpetuation of our collective concerns about crime is attributable in large part to its unwavering presence in news and entertainment media. The torrent of coverage produces a vast array of patterned messages about crime, criminals, and the criminal justice system. The problem, of course, is that a great many of these messages are errant—if not downright false—and thus contribute to a flawed understanding of crime that promotes punitive solutions and ever more expansive social control policies.

In this chapter, we have shown how the construction of the crime problem on *Nancy Grace* furthers several common patterns in media representations of crime, including an overemphasis on violent crime and a disproportionate focus on female and child victims. At the same time, we have attempted to demonstrate that *Nancy Grace* represents a unique repackaging of the crime problem for modern life. As an hour-long, prime-time cable news program that focuses exclusively on real-life heinous crimes and legal dramas as they unfold, it is unlike any other media production. Crime is fashioned into a compelling bundle of captivating visuals, sordid details, moral indignation, and collective outrage—fused together by a narrative that reflects and reinforces shared notions of morality and justice—giving it an urgency and sense of collective import that viewers find appealing. The effort that Grace and her staff devote to creating an emotional connection with viewers heightens its appeal and promotes a sense of cohesiveness around the show's core messages that is rarely found outside of human interest stories and "soft news" programming.

Though this chapter has not focused on the media effects of its messages, it is clear that *Nancy Grace* has emerged as a prominent vehicle through which popular crime concerns are packaged and presented. Its ratings have steadily increased since its inception, and it continues to enjoy solid footing in the media landscape (remarkable given the fierce competition for prime-time viewers and the high rates of turnover in cable news programming). Moreover, the record viewership during the verdict phase of the Casey Anthony trial suggests that Grace has emerged as a go-to source of crime news and knowledge. Grace's critics view these developments with disdain, seeing this program as little more than the latest example of the "dangerous nexus between the agenda-setting function of the media and the commodification of criminal trials and investigations" (Fox, Van Sickel, and Steiger 2007, p. 203). Grace's supporters, on the other hand, point to these developments as affirmation that their "crusader of justice" for the twenty-first century has arrived, and she is ready to "fight the good fight."

Part 5

Policy Outcomes

Successful claimsmaking campaigns lead to new social policies; people who have the power to change policies—policymakers—decide to respond to the social problem by passing laws, establishing regulations, or simply doing things differently. Policymaking involves another stage of social construction, in which the claims that originated with activists or experts must be reworked to fit the needs of the policymaking institution. For instance, it is one thing for claimsmakers to call for a new law, which they may imagine is a simple matter of articulating a general principle. Legislators who actually try to craft a law must take into account a variety of legal and technical concerns, as well as the interests of other parties who may not share all of the claimsmakers' concerns and priorities, to say nothing of the likely responses of the courts that will determine whether the new law is constitutional.

In constructing policies, policymakers have to make choices, choices that may, in retrospect, seem less wise than they might have appeared when the policy was first established. This means that policies often inspire new claims—policy outcome claims—about the effectiveness of the policies. Various critics argue that policies are flawed: some warn that policies are insufficient, that they don't do enough to deal with the problem; others insist that policies are excessive, that they go too far and in the process create new problems; while still others claim that policies are misguided, that an entirely different approach is needed. Evaluating how well a policy works,

and deciding whether it needs to be modified and what the appropriate changes might be, can inspire heated reactions, and even new
claimsmaking campaigns.

The three chapters in this part of the book all deal with policy outcomes. In Chapter 13, Rachel Bacon offers an example of a sequence
of policymaking followed by policy outcome claims that the policy
was flawed. When the federal government first sought to regulate fat
in foods by requiring that food manufacturers include labels with
nutritional information on their products' packaging, it chose to concentrate on saturated fat, and to require that food labels specify the
amount of saturated fat a serving of the food contained. The policymakers who established these regulations were guided by the medical
research of the time, and there had been a well-publicized campaign
by experts to draw attention to the dangers of saturated fat. These initial regulations ignored trans fat, and it was only years later, after
research began to suggest that trans fat was actually more harmful
than saturated fat, that experts and officials revised the regulations to
require nutritional labels to include information about trans fat. In
short, new research findings led to claims that the initial food labels
had overlooked a key health threat, and needed further modification to
take the risks of trans fat into account.

Some policies may be subjects of debate while they are being considered and may remain controversial after they are enacted, with claims
and counterclaims about whether a policy represents a step forward or
actually makes things worse. In Chapter 14, Jenine Harris examines one
such state-level controversy: the debate that followed the 2008 passage
of the Smoke-Free Illinois Act. This law prohibited smoking in nearly
all public places and workplaces, including casinos. In the three years
following the passage of the new law, many claimsmakers—legislators,
business owners, lobbyists, residents, and researchers—continued to
debate the law's merits and consequences. Since casinos are major
employers and tax-revenue generators, many people were concerned
that customers would flee Illinois to neighboring states, where smoking
was still allowed in gambling establishments. Tax revenue fell after the
law went into effect, but claimsmakers debated whether it was the anti-
smoking policy that caused the decline.

The effects of some policies extend beyond a single country, and
policy outcome claims may vary from one nation to another. In
Chapter 15, Lynn Letukas considers the massive relief effort mounted
by the United States, European countries, and other nations around

the world to aid the countries harmed by the Indian Ocean tsunami of 2004. The US press interpreted this disaster relief policy favorably, but Letukas shows that reactions varied in the nations receiving the aid: India argued that it was self-reliant, and that aid efforts directed to it were excessive; Indonesia warned that it needed more aid than it was receiving, that aid was insufficient; and Thailand insisted that the aid being directed to it was misguided, that it needed different sorts of support from the West. Thus the same policy was constructed in very different ways in different countries.

Arguments about policy outcomes are important, because many claimsmaking campaigns begin as critiques of existing social policies. In fact, reexamining many of the chapters in this book will reveal that many claims challenge the policies currently in place.

13

In the Shadow of Saturated Fat: The Struggle to Get Trans Fats Noticed

Rachel J. Bacon

Trans fat, also called partially hydrogenated fat, has been a part of the American diet for over a century. As an ingredient in products like Crisco and margarines, use of partially hydrogenated fats increased dramatically after World War II put stress on the nation's supply of butter (American Heart Association 2010). The hydrogenation technique used to create trans fat also greatly improved the shelf life of packaged foods. Food companies took advantage of the economic benefits of these partially hydrogenated fats by replacing their products' animal-based saturated fats, known to spoil quickly, with the much more stable, and cheaper to produce, trans fat (Rogers 2011).

Both saturated fat (which our bodies already produce naturally) and trans fat (usually contrived artificially) have been linked to increasing a person's cholesterol levels. While cholesterol is a necessary nutrient for proper body functions, having too much of it in your blood can increase the risk of coronary heart disease, which may lead to a heart attack or other cardiovascular problems. Saturated fat and trans fat are not equal in how they influence cholesterol levels, however. Mehmet Oz, of the popular daytime television show *Dr. Oz,* recently wrote in *Time* magazine that trans fat is "the only fat that is universally accepted as bad" and "new research is finding that some saturated fats (like those found in coconut oil) may actually be good for you" (2011, p. 50). The accepted reason for this difference is that the chemical structure of trans fat somehow causes it not only to increase bad cholesterol (low-density lipoprotein [LDL]), but also to decrease good cholesterol (high-density lipoprotein [HDL]), while saturated fat has not been found to decrease good cholesterol (Mensink and Katan 1990).

Today, health-conscious consumers who are interested in limiting their intake of saturated fat and trans fat can find the individual amounts of each fat listed on a packaged food product's nutrition label. However, putting trans fat on nutrition labels didn't become required by the Food and Drug Administration (FDA) until 2006, while saturated fat labeling became required in 1993. Why, if trans fat is considered worse than saturated fat, was saturated fat labeled earlier than trans fat?

Most previous scholarship regarding trans fat labeling spends no more than a few paragraphs exploring how concern with saturated fat contributed to the story. Many authors who mention the labeling focus on the resulting policy and public reaction after the trans fat labeling legislation was passed in 2003. Topics covered in these papers include proposed revisions for trans fat labeling (Brandt 2011), case studies of how individual cities and states have further banned trans fats in restaurants (Tan 2009; Wochos 2007), consumer responses to media coverage of the legislation, as well as public knowledge concerning trans fat before and after the bill was implemented (Jasti and Kovacs 2010; Kozup, Burton, and Creyer 2006; Lin and Yen 2010; Niederdeppe and Frosch 2009; Wise and Brewer 2010), and how corporations directly or indirectly influenced the labeling process (Freudenberg, Bradley, and Serrano 2007; Freudenberg and Galea 2008). One notable exception is a recent dissertation (Schleifer 2010) from which this chapter borrows both theoretical and substantive material to build a social constructionist case for how trans fat became a social problem.

This chapter analyzes the claims, counterclaims, and respective platforms and frameworks used by the anti–saturated fat and trans fat campaigns to illustrate how advocates found themselves in a position of opportunity to have saturated fat recognized as a problem before trans fat gained similar recognition. The anti–saturated fat campaign benefited from unequivocal scientific support and prominent science-based claimsmakers, as well as vast media exposure, and this focus on saturated fat interfered with the anti–trans fat campaign's ability to compete for public attention until the saturated fat problem was effectively "solved" through legislation. Therefore, this chapter concentrates on what happened before the trans fat labeling legislation was passed in 2003. It also takes a constructionist approach in identifying the factors that allowed for saturated fat labeling to become successful, and that acted to hinder trans fat labeling.

The Anti–Saturated Fat Campaign

Saturated fat's story began in the late 1940s as scientific research about its health effects began to accumulate. Its relationship with increased cholesterol levels came to the forefront of the public's attention in the 1960s, when coronary heart disease was being described as the nation's number one killer (*Time* 1961). Concern about how much saturated fat was present in restaurant cooking oils, butter, and manufactured foods continued to increase and then boomed in the 1980s when consumers were shocked to discover that even some tropical oils, such as coconut and palm oil, were also high in saturated fat (Rogers 2011). During the late 1980s, the anti–saturated fat campaign really picked up speed. Activists' claimsmaking put enough pressure on policymakers that saturated fat content was required to be listed on nutrition labels under the Nutrition Labeling and Education Act of 1990. The framework of the campaign against saturated fat in the public and political domains played an integral role in how trans fat labeling was approached during the 1990s.

Experts as Claimsmakers

The anti–saturated fat campaign's first advantage over the anti–trans fat campaign came in the form of its early promotion through the media by a well-known expert, Ancel Keys. As a medical expert, Keys was able to use his status to legitimize his claims concerning saturated fat's contributions to poor health. "Experts rank among the most influential claimsmakers because they are thought to have special knowledge that qualifies them to interpret social problems" (Best 2008, p. 98). Keys became a celebrated expert: he helped to publicize that saturated fat was harmful and warranted national concern.

Keys, a well-respected physiologist from Minnesota, was known for designing the K-rations that were used by soldiers during World War II. In the years after the war, he founded the Laboratory of Physiological Hygiene at the University of Minnesota, became chairman of the

International Society of Cardiology, and worked as a consultant to the World Health Organization and the Food and Agriculture Organization (Schleifer 2010). His contributions and connections allowed him to accumulate monetary support from the US Public Health Service, the American Heart Association, the International Society of Cardiology, and six foreign governments to fund studies that brought him in contact with diets from around the world. In his travels, Keys took notice of how people who managed to survive on very small food portions in war-torn countries somehow had better cardiovascular health than comparatively well-fed Americans (*Time* 1961).

In 1947, he began working on a fifteen-year study that evaluated how different factors, such as lifestyle and diet, affected the overall health of 286 middle-aged Minnesota businessmen. By the time the study was nearing its end, twenty-seven of the subjects had suffered from heart attacks, eighteen of whom had also had high cholesterol. This led Keys to speculate about how diet contributed to heart disease. His ambitious Seven Countries Study, published in 1958, examined diets from around the globe, and revealed what appeared to be a relationship between diets high in saturated fat intake and an increased risk for heart attacks. During the study, Keys became particularly fascinated with what he considered a definite connection between the low-fat Mediterranean diet and a significantly lower rate of cardiovascular disease. Inspired by his findings, Keys and his wife wrote a best-selling cookbook in 1959 called *"Eat Well, Live Well,"* which was full of heart-healthy recipes based on his research (*Time* 1961).

In 1961, Keys appeared on the cover of *Time* magazine for an article titled "Medicine: The Fat of the Land." The cover story highlighted the concern felt by the American public about high cholesterol by using a frightening statistic: "the nation's No. 1 killer: coronary artery disease . . . accounts for more than half of all heart fatalities and kills 500,000 Americans a year—twice the toll from all varieties of cancer, five times the deaths from automobile accidents" (*Time* 1961, p. 48). The article gave background information about Keys's previous accomplishments in working with the military and even mentioned the success of his cookbook. It also presented Keys as an influential contributor to new research on cholesterol by outlining the results of his Minnesota businessmen and Seven Countries studies.

During his interview for *Time,* Keys condemned Americans' food habits by claiming that a high-fat diet was a root cause of high cholesterol levels and, therefore, coronary artery disease. Keys declared:

"The only sure way to control blood cholesterol effectively . . . is to reduce fat calories in the average U.S. diet by more than one-third (from 40 percent to 15 percent of total calories), and take an even sterner cut (from 17 percent to 4 percent of total calories) in saturated fats" (Time 1961, p. 48). Keys strongly endorsed a diet similar to the one he had adopted for himself, in which foods high in saturated fat were reduced as much as possible or replaced with healthier alternatives. The combination of Keys's scientific influence and the popularity of the diet endorsed in his cookbook helped to familiarize the public with the potential dangers of saturated fat and legitimize any subsequent actions taken by other groups to combat what was considered a growing problem.

Activists Respond to Consumer Frustration

In response to a growing interest among consumers in maintaining a healthy diet, food manufacturers began making claims on their products' packaging that highlighted supposed health benefits, such as "low fat" claims. Since there was no set FDA standard for what allowed a company to make these claims, they could easily be exaggerated to the point of misleading consumers into buying a product that didn't deliver on its promises. Before the Nutrition Labeling and Education Act of 1990 was passed, nutrition labels were only required on products that made health claims, and since these claims weren't very well regulated, many health-conscious consumers were becoming frustrated that they could not trust labels to help them make good food choices (Prevention Institute 2002).

There were two major activist groups, the Center for Science in the Public Interest (CSPI) and the National Heart Savers Association, that took advantage of public opinion regarding labels and took it upon themselves to present saturated fat as a problem within that context. In order to prove that the threat of saturated fat was serious enough to require legislation, they mounted public campaigns that actively sponsored consumer education regarding saturated fat's risks and criticized companies that used saturated fat instead of "healthier" alternatives. Their claims were spread through various forms of popular media to the point where their stance could not be ignored by policymakers.

The CSPI was founded in the early 1970s by microbiologist Michael Jacobson, and two other scientists, to educate the public about various health risks and push for regulations to protect consumers. The CSPI pursued a number of projects simultaneously, such as limiting sodium nitrite in cured meats, advocating for sodium labeling, and standardizing the definition for what was considered an organic food (CSPI 2011a, 2011b). It also began to distribute a collection of news articles related to these projects in their *Nutrition Action Newsletter.* In the 1980s, the CSPI focused on the saturated fat problem by launching their "Saturated Fat Attack" campaign. They identified saturated fat as the most dangerous contemporary health threat to Americans by publishing articles in their newsletter and in books such as their 1986 *Fast Food Guide.* These resources criticized restaurants that used cooking oils made from saturated fat while praising those that had switched to vegetable oils, which were often partially hydrogenated and contained trans fat (Schleifer 2010).

Another activist who became involved with promoting saturated fat labeling was Nebraska millionaire Philip Sokolof. He became personally invested in spreading the news about the potential health risks of saturated fat after he suffered a near-fatal heart attack in 1966. He told his story in a 1991 *Time* magazine article titled "A Crusader from the Heartland: Philip Sokolof" (Jaroff 1991). In the article, Sokolof described how he had founded the National Heart Savers Association using his own money and conducted cholesterol tests for 200,000 people across the United States to gather his own statistics about the problem. Starting in 1988, Sokolof began placing advertisements in newspapers that warned people about the "poisoning of America." The ads featured pictures of popular brand names and restaurants that were accused of including large amounts of saturated fat–laden palm oil, coconut oil, and beef tallow in their products. These ads were everywhere, informing people about the presence of saturated fat in foods that had once been considered healthy (Jaroff 1991).

Success: The Nutrition Labeling and Education Act of 1990

The pressure placed on food manufacturers and the FDA to respond to the outcry against saturated fat ultimately contributed to the passage of the Nutrition Labeling and Education Act of 1990. Hailed as a success, the bill required food manufacturers to include labeling that showed the amounts of certain nutrients, such as total fat, saturated fat, and cholesterol, contained in their food products, and further required the use of labels like "low fat" be limited according to standards set by the FDA.

Standards were issued for saturated fat that would help consumers determine the healthfulness of their food through the use of a standardized daily value. Working from the recommendations of government health advisers, the FDA established that consumers should consume no more than twenty grams of saturated fat per day (McClellan 2003). A product could claim that it was "low in saturated fat" only if it contained less than "one gram of saturated fat per serving and also only if less than 15 percent of its calorie content came from fat." However, the saturated fat content was not required to be listed "if the food contained less than half a gram of total fat per serving and if no claims were made about fat or cholesterol content" (US Food and Drug Administration 1995). The level of success experienced by the anti–saturated fat campaign created a popular frame for how standards and labels for other nutrients, such as trans fat, should be structured.

The Anti–Trans Fat Campaign

The story of how trans fat became recognized as a social problem is more complicated than that of saturated fat. Although preliminary research investigating trans fat emerged around the same time that saturated fat was attracting attention, none of it was promoted by a prominent scientist or covered in widely circulated popular magazines. Instead, the first claims against trans fat were made by relatively obscure researchers who lacked the funding or political influence to compete with the claims that became so well-established by the anti–saturated fat campaign. Additionally, the idea that trans fat was unhealthy was seen as a threat to the beneficiaries of the anti–saturated fat campaign's efforts to replace saturated fat with trans fat alternatives; consequently, much of the early trans fat research was attacked in order to defend saturated fat's position as a primary public health threat.

After the 1990 labeling act "solved" the saturated fat problem and the intensity of public concern about it began to wane, new research about trans fat was pioneered by more prominent institutions that proved difficult for advocates and policymakers to ignore. Compared to the anti–saturated fat campaign, however, the anti–trans fat campaign pursued a much less dynamic form of claimsmaking that did not include much media coverage. The public's lack of familiarity with the specific differences between the health effects of saturated and trans fat led to considerable disagreement among policy-makers about how nutrition labeling should be applied to trans fat. Trans fat needed to be repackaged in a way that differentiated it from saturated fat so it could be addressed on its own terms. Ultimately, changes in the political arena helped to revitalize the forward momentum of slow insider policymaking to create an opportunity for trans fat labeling by 2003.

Early Trans Fat Research

In 1957, about the same time that Ancel Keys was working on his many fat-related projects, Fred Kummerow, a professor from the University of Illinois who mostly conducted animal studies, began research regarding the presence of trans fat in animals and humans. Kummerow became interested in learning what the possible health effects of trans fat consumption might be, and even though the monetary support available to him did not allow for a large-scale study of trans fat, he managed to publish about seventy articles containing information about trans fat over the length of his career (Schleifer 2010). Another scientist, Mary Enig from the University of Maryland, published a study in 1978 about a possible connection between trans fat and cancer rates in the *Journal of the Federation of American Societies for Experimental Biology.* Her paper did not discuss the relationship between trans fat and cholesterol, but it did manage to raise a few eyebrows among beneficiaries of the anti–saturated fat campaign (Schleifer 2010). Neither Kummerow's nor Enig's publications received attention in any major media outlets, and they did not have the capacity to concretely define the effects of trans fat on heart health; however, consumers who were particularly health-savvy heard rumors about trans fat's uncertain health effects and became suspicious about products containing partially hydrogenated fats.

Bullying from the Anti–Saturated Fat Campaign

As the anti–saturated fat campaign began to gain ground, groups interested in replacing saturated fats with what they thought could be healthy alternatives were quick to attack and discredit Kummerow's and Enig's findings. Food manufacturers, fast food restaurants, and margarine companies—which had already begun to see the commercial benefits of switching to the more publicly accepted partially hydrogenated vegetable oils—were understandably averse to having rumors about trans fat force them to change their formulas again. Chief among the critics of trans fat research were Thomas Applewhite from Kraft and J. Edward Hunter from Proctor and Gamble, both of whom were also representatives from the Institute of Shortenings and Edible Oils (Schleifer 2010). Enig explained in an interview for *Gourmet* magazine that she had been visited by "angry men" from the institute shortly after publishing her article in 1978 (Teicholz 2004). Both Applewhite and Hunter attempted to discredit the claims made by Kummerow and Enig by criticizing technical aspects of how their studies were designed (Schleifer 2010).

Activists were also concerned about how the emerging evidence against strongly endorsed saturated fat alternatives could affect their campaign. In 1988, an article was published in the CSPI's newsletter titled "The Truth About Trans: Hydrogenated Oils Aren't Guilty As Charged." The article attempted to calm any fears about consuming margarine or partially hydrogenated oils that may have arisen among consumers because of the early trans fat research: "Despite the rumors, there is little good evidence that trans fats cause any more harm than other fats" (Blume 1988, p. 8). The article stressed that many of the trans fat animal studies had produced contradictory results, while the few human studies that had actually found a relationship between trans fat and high cholesterol were poorly designed. Mary Enig's 1978 study was also accused of being flawed, and a few scientists were quoted criticizing Enig's conclusions. While the article did admit that trans fat could possibly increase cholesterol levels, it asserted that current studies proved trans fat did not increase cholesterol levels more than did saturated fat and, therefore, that consumers were still better off replacing butter with alternatives such as margarine (Blume 1988).

Groundbreaking Research from Overseas

So far, the results of studies assessing the relative harms from trans fat and saturated fat were mixed. This made it difficult for trans fat to be viewed as anything other than vaguely and uncertainly related to increased cholesterol levels. Only particularly knowledgeable readers could pick up on the extent of trans fat's possible dangers. After the 1990 labeling bill was passed, effectively solving the saturated fat problem in the eyes of activists and the public, more concrete evidence for trans fat's negative health impact started to appear in respected journals that reported on studies from around the world and in the United States. The most influential report was published in 1990 by Dutch researchers R. P. Mensink and Martijn Katan in the *New England Journal of Medicine*. It was this article that first advanced the now widely accepted idea that trans fat is actually worse for cardiovascular health than saturated fat. In their article, Mensink and Katan claimed that trans fat not only increased bad (LDL) cholesterol, but also decreased good (HDL) cholesterol as well. Saturated fat, on the other hand, had not been found to decrease HDL cholesterol levels, but only to increase LDL levels. The 1990 Dutch study was mentioned in several popular US news journals, although at that time there was no organized activist group that was ready to step forward and take advantage of the short-lived publicity (Schleifer 2010).

The US companies that used partially hydrogenated vegetable oils were concerned about how these new findings might affect their business and were unwilling to react based on the results of only one study. In hopes of proving the Dutch researchers wrong, several groups, such as the Institute of Shortening and Edible Oils and the United Soybean Board, banded together to form the Trans Fat Coalition and fund a similar study conducted by the US Department of Agriculture. The study was designed similarly to the Dutch study, except that the amount of trans fat used was more in line with the amounts found in US food products. When the study was completed in 1994, the researchers were surprised to find that the conclusion was the same: trans fat increased bad cholesterol levels while also decreasing good cholesterol levels (Schleifer 2010).

Walter Willett's Scary Statistic

Also working on trans fat research in the 1990s was Walter Willett, chair of the Department of Nutrition at the Harvard School for Public Health. He, along with some of his colleagues, published a number of articles concerning trans fat in the *Lancet* and the *New England Journal of Medicine*. Willett's first major paper about trans fat was published in the *Lancet* in 1993. In it, Willett presented new findings from a comprehensive nursing health study that had evaluated the diets of over 166,000 women and identified trans fat as a primary factor in higher rates of coronary artery disease in women (Cohen 2006).

In 1994, Willett and Albert Ascherio summarized some of the recent discoveries in trans fat research in the *American Journal of*

Public Health. In the article, Willett and Ascherio not only acted as scientists, but took on the role of policy advocates as well. After presenting information about trans fat from the scientific community, they outlined a few possible options for dealing with the trans fat problem, such as having companies voluntarily switch to alternative ingredients, or adding trans fat content to nutrition labels. Most important, they presented an estimate of how many people could be adversely affected by consuming trans fat: "more than 30,000 deaths per year may be due to consumption of partially hydrogenated vegetable fat. Furthermore, the number of attributable cases of nonfatal coronary heart disease will be even larger" (Willett and Ascherio 1994, p. 723). While Willett and other scientists contributed a great deal to setting the stage for the anti–trans fat campaign, they did not move into primary leadership positions for advocating trans fat labeling.

Advocates Address Trans Fat

The addition of new research from Harvard and Europe contributed a great deal of credible information to the anti–trans fat movement, but since no activist group had come forward to present trans fat as a problem, there was a significant lack in leadership to organize the information and attract policymakers' attention. Philip Sokolof's National Heart Savers Association had already disbanded after his efforts to institute saturated fat labeling and replace beef tallow in popular restaurants had succeeded. It was the CSPI, convinced by the accumulating research and Willett's statistics, that took up the mantle and decided to promote trans fat labeling. But the CSPI was also busy pursuing causes other than trans fat, so it was unable to concentrate the entirety of its resources to support the proposed law in the way that a personally driven activist like Sokolof could. With fewer resources and allies available to sustain a dynamic and attention-grabbing campaign against trans fat, the CSPI opted for a more private, insider form of claimsmaking that targeted the FDA and policymakers, but failed to draw enough public attention to trans fat's health risks.

In 1994, the CSPI submitted a petition to the FDA proposing an amendment to the 1990 labeling act. It claimed that the FDA had failed to educate Americans about the presence of all the unhealthy fats in their food because the amount of trans fat was lost within the "total fat" category on nutrition labels. It also cited information from the Dutch and Harvard studies to help support its position. The CSPI proposed that the amount of trans fat present in a food product should therefore be added to the amount of saturated fat present in the product (US Food and Drug Administration 2003). This would have required that the two fats be combined into one line so that a product with two grams of saturated fat and two grams of trans fat would be listed as having four grams of saturated fat; the logic being that adding the two fats together would allow consumers, who were largely unfamiliar with trans fat, to still be able to make a healthy decision.

The FDA's response to the petition was mixed. It did not argue that trans fat was not bad for consumers' health, but it did not take the petition to the next stage of legislation either. While the FDA acknowledged that the current information on trans fat was enough to warrant further attention, it was reluctant to group trans fat and saturated fat together without clear evidence that could confirm trans fat as having the exact same effect on cholesterol that saturated fat did.

Proposals, Comments, and Revisions

As more research about trans fat continued to pile up, the CSPI revised its petition and sent a new version to the FDA in 1998 that proposed two options for inserting trans fat labeling. The first option followed the 1994 petition by suggesting that trans fat and saturated fat be added together, but with an asterisk at the bottom that would list the grams of trans fat separately. The second option suggested that the two fats would be included under a line called "saturated fat + trans fat" whenever trans fat was present (US Food and Drug Administration 2003). The problem with both options was that the CSPI was still assuming that the effects of trans fat and saturated were equal, even though the evidence now suggested they were not.

In 1999, the FDA published a proposed rule, similar to the first option suggested by the CSPI, that would be open for public discussion via comments sent to the FDA (US Food and Drug Administration 2003). Since trans fat had yet to garner any significant media coverage, the majority of the general public who were aware of the proposal were those who had become informed through the CSPI's influence. Therefore, comments made to the FDA from consumers were overwhelmingly in favor of combining the amounts of trans fat and saturated fat onto a single line rather than labeling them as two separate lines. There were, however, many food manufacturing companies that had worked to reduce the saturated fat levels in their products to meet consumer expectations and were unwilling to accept the idea that those levels would suddenly increase due to the addition of a fat unfamiliar to most of the public. Some of these companies brought forward competing scientific evidence that suggested trans fat wasn't as bad as the CSPI claimed. Other companies, those that had already accepted that they would have to change their formulas again, favored the FDA's original sentiments about combining the labeling of two fats with different health effects. A few of them suggested that the FDA should not rush in to pass the proposal until they could establish standards for defining healthy trans fat intake through things like "low trans fat" health claims and a recommended daily value (Schleifer 2010).

Establishing a Daily Value for Trans Fat

After considering the available data, the FDA agreed to hold off on finalizing its proposal until it could devise a daily-value scale for measuring trans fat (US Food and Drug Administration 2003). As mentioned earlier, the FDA had already established the daily value for safe saturated fat intake in 1993 at about twenty grams, and had allowed products to declare themselves "reduced" in saturated fat at certain levels (McClellan 2003). Since none of the trans fat research suggested guidelines for exactly how much trans fat was safe to consume, the FDA decided to wait for recommendations from the health publications that had been involved in establishing the daily value for saturated fat. The three main reports that were to be taken into consideration were the "Dietary Guidelines for Americans" for 2000, the new guidelines by the National Cholesterol Education Program for 2001, and the Institute of Medicine and the National Academy of Sciences' "Dietary Reference Intakes for Energy, Carbohydrate, Fiber, Fat, Fatty Acids, Cholesterol, Protein, and Amino Acids" for 2002. All three sets of guidelines confirmed that trans fat was responsible for increasing bad cholesterol levels and should be avoided. They also said that consumers should eat products with as little trans fat as possible, and since there were no known health benefits for trans fat, none of the reports established a recommended safe daily intake (US Department of Agriculture 2000; US Food and Drug Administration 2003; Institute of Medicine 2005). The apparent lack of a daily value for trans fat added a new justification for defining it independently from saturated fat; new proposals would have to better acknowledge the differences in health effects between trans fat and saturated fat.

Changes in the Political Arena
and Insider Claimsmaking

Without any significant support from the public to put pressure on lawmakers, the anti–trans fat campaign depended on the slow insider policymaking that was taking place between the CSPI, lobbyists, and the FDA. The time spent debating the relative health effects of trans fat and saturated fat, coupled with the wait involved for establishing guideline recommendations, served to slow the momentum for making a final ruling. Trans fat labeling hit another bump in January 2001 when the commissioner of the FDA at the time, Jane Henney, quit her post and was not replaced until November 2002 (Rubin 2005). The lull in the anti–trans fat campaign's insider policymaking during the early 2000s meant that the cause needed new life if claims favoring trans fat labeling were to succeed.

Outside of the FDA and CSPI, a new political player arrived who hoped to hurry things along. In 2001, John Graham was appointed as the administrator of the Office of Information and Regulatory Affairs under the Office of Management and Budget. Previous to serving in that post, Graham had spent seventeen years working at the Harvard School of Public Health, where he had come in contact with Walter Willett and become familiar with research about trans fat (Graham 2003). In September 2001, Graham sent a letter to the secretary of health and human services, Tommy Thompson, that expressed his interest in resolving the trans fat issue. In the letter, Graham used some of the FDA's own statistics to reiterate and emphasize the cost effectiveness involved with solving the problem quickly: "10 years after the effective date, the rule would prevent 7,600 to 17,100 cases of [coronary heart disease] and avert 2,500 to 5,600 deaths per year. Over a 20-year period, FDA estimated the benefits of the proposed rule would range from $25 to $59 billion, while the costs were only $400 million to $850 million" (Graham 2001). Graham's repackaging of trans fat labeling as a financially beneficial endeavor, coupled with the political pressure he placed on policymakers, helped to reinvigorate the campaign's energy.

In November 2002, Mark McClellan was appointed as the new commissioner for the FDA (Rubin 2005). During the same month, the FDA amended its original 1999 proposal and reopened the comment period between November and December of 2002. By this time, the FDA had firmly decided that trans fat content should be listed on a line separately from saturated fat content, and embraced the idea that since no safe amount of trans fat could be established, the line should not be accompanied by a daily value. They requested comments, however, concerning the use of a bottom-of-label footnote, in place of a daily value, that would say "intake of trans fat should be as low as possible." The goal of the footnote, in the absence of a daily value, was to give consumers an idea about how much trans fat was too much (US Food and Drug Administration 2003).

Comments came in from groups that either supported or opposed parts, or the entirety, of the new proposal. Some of the major opponents were food manufacturers that were concerned about the impact the footnote might have on their business. The National Association of Margarine Manufacturers, the National Food Processors Association, and the Grocery Manufacturers of America all strongly opposed the footnote and used the findings from the Dietary Guidelines 2000 report and Institute of Health's 2002 report to support their stance. Their main argument was that the footnote would make consumers feel compelled to choose products that were completely devoid of trans fats at the cost of maintaining an overall balanced diet (Cristol 2002; Kretser 2003; National Food Processors Association 2000).

Consumer Attitudes and the Media

While concern about saturated fat has continued to the present day, public attitudes toward it, starting in the 1990s, were slowly changing. Some of this change was due to a shift in media coverage that began to express doubt about the hullabaloo created over saturated fat in the late 1980s, and suggested that people should reconsider which fats are considered "bad fats." While information about trans fat may not have been a constant feature in the health section of popular newspapers, there were a number of articles in the *New York Times* that emphasized how the Dutch and Harvard research could influence perceptions of margarine being a healthful alternative to butter (*New York Times* 1994; Webb 1990). One 1997 article from the *New York Times* suggested that consumers should put less emphasis on reducing fat intake because of new scientific findings suggesting that diets that were higher in fats while lower in carbohydrates were healthier (Brody 1997). A 1999 article in *Time* magazine reflected similar sentiments by warning readers that dietary ideas about what was considered good or bad had changed. The article said that stick margarine was just as bad as butter and that cholesterol-heavy foods, such as eggs, were okay in moderation (Lemonick and Park 1999). These underlying opinions provided a cultural arena wherein trans fat could be better recognized as bad by a public that had already begun to accept that the well-established ideas of which fats were bad were being challenged.

Public Recognition of Trans Fat, Missed Opportunity, and Success

The issue involving trans fat content in foods was finally thrust into the public eye in May 2003, when a new nonprofit group, BanTransFats.com, sued Kraft Foods for selling Oreos with trans fat to children. Unfortunately, this attention came too late, since the FDA comment period had ended in December of the previous year. BanTransFat.com did, however, send a petition to the FDA on May 22, 2003, that included comments from the general public supporting the use of the proposed trans fate footnote labeling (Joseph 2003).

On July 11, 2003, the FDA issued a final ruling from the 2002 amended proposal that took into consideration all the comments from the public during the comment period. Reflecting some of the standards set for saturated fat, it required that any amount of trans fat content over half a gram per serving must be labeled on a line listed below that for saturated fat content. However, since no daily value for trans fat was to be indicated next to the new line, a product could not claim itself to be "reduced" in trans fat. Instead, a product could declare itself to contain "zero grams of trans fat" even if it actually contained less than half a gram per serving. The FDA also decided against use of the proposed footnote that would warn consumers to limit their daily intake of trans fat to as little as possible. The ruling was slated to become effective January 1, 2006, in order to "minimize the need for multiple labeling changes and to provide additional time for compliance by small businesses to allow them to use current label inventories and phase in label changes" (US Food and Drug Administration 2003).

Conclusion

As issues that were competing for attention, the anti–saturated and trans fat campaigns received different amounts of media attention that were not directly dependent on the relative dangers that these fats posed to heart health, but rather on the relative success of the claims made by scientists and advocates in the public and political arenas.

While trans fat is now considered to be more dangerous, it was saturated fat that first became considered a problem by the general public. The esteemed Ancel Keys was able to bring public attention to saturated fat early on, and activists such as the CSPI and Philip Sokolof brought the resources and dedication necessary to gain legislation for that cause. The campaign to address trans fat, on the other hand, struggled to gather research that would reach the general public, and the CSPI, on its own, lacked the focused resources and dynamic leadership that were necessary to compete for the public's attention. The dominance of saturated fat as a problem in the minds of advocates, policymakers, and the general public created an environment where early claims against trans fat were marginalized and even attacked because they ran contrary to the well-established solution of replacing saturated fat with partially hydrogenated fat. These factors helped to tip the balance in saturated fat's favor, allowing it to gain a majority of the spotlight and become labeled much earlier than did trans fat.

After anti–saturated fat advocates declared victory in 1990 and public concern with saturated fat lessened, the claims for trans fat labeling still had to compete with the popular framework that had helped the anti–saturated fat campaign succeed. The CSPI assumed that the policy regarding trans fat would be a simple extension of the policy applied to saturated fat labeling, and asked the FDA to just add the two fat contents together on the same labeling line. The dangers of trans fat, however, could not be equated to those of saturated fat, and as more scientific evidence confirmed this, policymakers spent considerable time sorting out how trans fat should be labeled differently from saturated fat.

Confusion and skepticism surrounding the scientific evidence available to support the claims made about trans fat's health effects, combined with the ignorance of the general public concerning the issue, threatened to stall the forward momentum of legislation. Ultimately, it was a new insider claimsmaker, John Graham, who was able to motivate the policymakers by repackaging the claims to emphasize the fiscal benefits of passing the bill quickly. His connections to the scientific research community and his authority among the members of the polity provided enough pressure and influence to push through legislation for trans fat labeling. It took decades, however, for the cultural, scientific, and political arenas to change sufficiently to allow for a dynamic platform whereby trans fat labeling could succeed.

Note

I acknowledge Victor Perez for his contributions; his patience and considerable advice, guidance, and editing were instrumental in the construction of this chapter. Thanks also to Bill Fasano, Emma Jean Joseph, and the friends who provided comments.

14

Casinos and Smoke-Free Legislation: Claimsmaking About Policy Outcomes

Jenine K. Harris

People use many strategies in making and supporting claims. They may make claims without any evidence, they may "look and see" for themselves through casual observations, or they may conduct a scientific study. It is not uncommon to hear conflicting claims about an issue even when commentators have access to the same information. Even scientists' claims may conflict: researchers may use different data or take different approaches, with arguments published in academic journals about which statistics are better for understanding a situation. This chapter examines claimsmaking after the implementation of a controversial health policy, the Smoke-Free Illinois Act. As a tobacco researcher, I have followed the debate closely and participated in it as well.

Cigarette smoking is widely known to be a cause of numerous chronic diseases, including lung cancer, stroke, coronary heart disease, and others. It is estimated that more than 440,000 deaths each year in the United States, one of every five, are due to smoking. Social policies, including graphic warning labels on cigarette packaging, restrictions on tobacco advertising near schools, age limits on purchasing tobacco, and federal, state, and local taxes on tobacco have been shown to be among the most effective, and cost-effective, ways of reducing smoking.

One tobacco policy that has gained significant ground recently across the United States is the passage and implementation of smoke-free workplace laws. These laws approach the problem of smoking indirectly, focusing on protecting workers and patrons from exposure to secondhand smoke. Secondhand smoke is a combination of cigarette sidestream smoke, which comes directly from a lit cigarette, and mainstream smoke, which is exhaled during smoking. Secondhand smoke contains at least 250 toxic chemicals, including more than 50 that have been associated with cancer. Over forty years of research into the health effects of secondhand smoke has concluded that exposure increases the risk of developing serious health problems such as lung cancer and cardiovascular disease.

In response to the health risks, some states and communities across the United States have begun to adopt smoke-free workplace policies that limit smoking in public places. However, not all communities and states provide the same level of protection for workers and patrons. Typically, statewide smoke-free workplace policies are applied to one or more of three venues: workplaces, restaurants, and bars. As of April 2012, twenty-three states had 100 percent smoke-free policies in all workplaces, restaurants, and bars. An additional thirteen states had 100 percent smoke-free policies in one or two of these venues, and fourteen states had no statewide smoke-free policies (Americans for Nonsmokers' Rights 2012).

There are often exemptions to statewide smoke-free policies for specific locations such as small bars or gambling floors in casinos. Even in states with strong smoke-free workplace laws, casinos are typically exempted and allow smoking. As a result, casino workers have higher exposure to secondhand smoke compared to the general US population and other workers in the service industry.

In 2002, Delaware was the first state in the United States to implement a statewide smoke-free workplace policy (the Delaware Clean Indoor Air Act) that also covered racinos (combination racetrack and gambling venues) and other hospitality venues that were frequently exempted. Six years later, on January 1, 2008, Illinois became the first state to implement a statewide smoke-free law that prohibited smoking in stand-alone commercial casinos. Although some may have thought that the Smoke-Free Illinois Act would end the secondhand smoke problem for gamblers and casino employees across the state, the debate over smoke-free casinos was far from over.

Casinos in the Midwest

As of January 1, 2008, there were fifty casinos across Illinois and neighboring Iowa, Indiana, and Missouri. Iowa had the most, with sixteen casinos, Indiana had thirteen, Missouri had twelve, and Illinois had nine. Casinos vary by size and age, which affects their ability to compete for customers. Missouri's casinos were the largest, averaging 64,100 square feet, while Indiana's casinos averaged 51,700 square feet, Iowa's casinos 34,400 square feet, and Illinois's casinos 33,000 square feet. Illinois's casinos all opened between 1991 and 1994, while the three other states opened new casinos in 2007 and 2008. Between 25 and 33 percent of casinos in each state were within ten miles of the Illinois border. The map in Figure 14.1 shows casino locations across the four states. The closest casino for many residents of the Chicago area is across the border in Indiana.

Casinos are big business. In the four-state region, casinos admitted an average of 117,000 (Iowa), 144,000 (Illinois), 200,000 (Indiana), and 366,000 (Missouri) patrons per month between January 2007 and December 2008. Visits to casinos are taxed in two ways: casinos pay taxes on admissions and on wagering. In 2007, Iowa casinos paid $314.8 million in taxes, while Missouri casinos paid $417.3 million, Illinois casinos paid $833.9 million, and Indiana casinos paid $842.0 million. In addition to paying state taxes on admissions and revenues, casinos provide employment. In 2007 and 2008, Illinois casinos employed close to 8,000 people, Iowa casinos nearly 10,000, Missouri casinos approximately 12,000, and Indiana casinos about 16,000.

These figures clearly demonstrate that casinos are important players in the economies of all four states. What happens to all of this economic activity when one of these states changes the rules about smoking in its casinos? If the new policy threatens jobs and taxes, the perceived problem of secondhand smoke may seem less pressing, and policies intended to deal with that problem come under criticism.

When Illinois implemented its statewide smoke-free legislation, it became the only one of the four neighboring states to have smoke-free casinos. In the year following the implementation of the Smoke-Free Illinois Act, patron spending in Illinois casinos declined by over $400 million. The loss in patron spending meant a loss of approximately $200 million in tax revenue in the state. In addition, Illinois lost about 7.5 percent of its casino jobs in 2008. The timing of decreased patron

Figure 14.1 Casino Locations in Illinois and Neighboring States

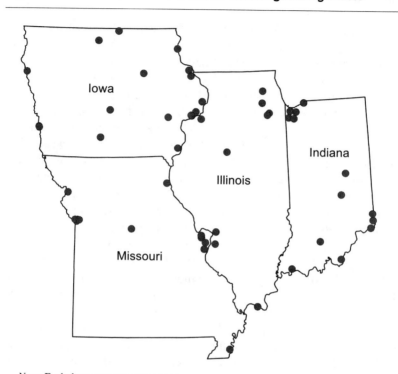

Note: Each dot represents one casino.

spending and the loss of jobs seemed to implicate the Smoke-Free Illinois Act as a threat to businesses and the overall economic health of Illinois. To some people, this sequence of events seemed to provide a "slam-dunk" argument to repeal the act and to vote against any similar measures. But things were more complicated than they appeared. There turned out to be different ways to construct the effects of this smoking policy and the causes of the casinos' economic problems.

Claimsmaking About the Smoke-Free Illinois Act

During the period from the implementation of the Smoke-Free Illinois Act in January 2008 through summer 2011, various claims-makers—residents, casino lobbyists, business owners, researchers, and legislators—tried to argue that the act ought to stay or go. While some claims were made in response to others, the debate was much messier than a simple back-and-forth conversation between supporters and opponents. Policy debates occur in diverse arenas: in political speeches, newspaper articles, online blogs, academic journals, and so on. Not everyone hears what others are saying. Claimsmaking can occur simultaneously or sequentially, with or without acknowledgment of the prior claims that have been put forth. For the sake of clarity, I have organized this section into a discussion of five issues, each with distinct claims. Readers should not assume that these points emerged in this chronological order. Instead, the list is simply my best attempt to clearly summarize the main arguments for and against the Smoke-Free Illinois Act over a two-and-a-half-year period.

Issue 1: Are Smoking and Gambling Linked?

Claim: Smoking and gambling go together. According to casino lobbyists and owners, casino patrons are more likely to be smokers compared to the general population. A pair of researchers from the University of Southern Mississippi agree: "In general . . . gamblers have a higher propensity to smoke than non-gamblers" (Bradley and Becker 2011). This claim has also made it into the general population; the blogger Arch City Madman, after listing several studies showing a relationship between smoking and gambling, stated: "Seems logical to me. More Smoking + More Gambling = More revenue to the state" (Arch City Madman 2011).

Claim: No, smoking and gambling don't go together. Despite smoky casino floors, most researchers and advocates disagree with the claim that casino patrons tend to be smokers. One study of Las Vegas casinos found that smoking rates among gamblers were lower than, or similar to, the smoking rates in the general population (Pritsos, Pritsos, and Spears 2008).

What about the Mississippi researchers who claimed that gamblers "have a higher propensity to smoke" and the studies reported by the Arch City Madman? The Mississippi researchers were interpreting the results of two prior research studies (Petry and Oncken 2002; McGrath and Barrett 2009). Both studies showed that *problem gamblers* were more likely to smoke, but problem gambling affects a very small proportion of those who go to casinos. Problem gamblers are

those gamblers who continue to gamble despite negative consequences and the urge to stop. The studies cited by the Arch City
Madman also reported on the relationship between problem gambling
and smoking. In other words, the link between smoking and gambling
is not as clear as it might first seem, applying primarily to the very
small number of problem gamblers.

Issue 2: Was the Downturn Due to the Economy?

Claim: Yes, it was the economy. So why was there a big decline in
patron spending when the Smoke-Free Illinois Act was implemented?
Even if it were true that gamblers are more likely to be smokers,
something other than the Smoke-Free Illinois Act might be responsible for changes in admissions and revenues in Illinois casinos. Casino
revenues may have declined after the smoking ban, but did other
important conditions change at the time of the law's passing, in
2008? Most readers will likely recall that the US economy took a
sharp turn for the worse around that time. Unemployment increased,
the housing market crashed, and many businesses went into decline.
Thus, we might expect that the casino business, too, would decline,
whether or not there was a new smoking policy.

The Springfield, Illinois, *State-Journal Register* addressed this
possible cause in an editorial in late 2008, arguing that the Smoke-
Free Illinois Act was casino operators' "favorite scapegoat." People
commented on the editorial by agreeing:

> Gas prices skyrocketed. The economy is in a tail spin. Home fore-
> closures are everywhere you look. Unemployment is high and
> going for outer space. But it is the smoking ban that is the only rea-
> son for casinos failing income. . . . No, I'm not buying into this
> farce. The only thing that the smoking ban can be blamed for is bad
> timing. It came into being when economic failures were looming
> anyway. (Seriously 2008)

Similarly, a study released in 2011—which I coauthored—examined
casino admissions across the four states in light of the economy (Harris
et al. 2011). Using complex statistical modeling, we found that all four
states experienced an economic downturn in 2008 that accounted for
changes in admissions across the states. While Illinois may have lost the
most admissions, it also had the worst economic climate. Most economists believe that the 2007–2009 recession was caused by a fall in the

housing market, and Illinois experienced the biggest housing-market decline across the four states. Given the worse economic climate in Illinois, it seems logical that Illinois casino admissions and revenues would drop the most.

Claim: No, it wasn't the economy. Not surprisingly, some people disagree that the economy was responsible for loss of revenues and admissions in Illinois casinos. In 2009, economists from the St. Louis Federal Reserve in Missouri used data on revenues and admissions reported by the Illinois state gaming commission from 1997 to 2008 as well as complex statistical techniques to examine whether the Smoke-Free Illinois Act was responsible for the $400 million decline (Garrett and Pakko 2009). These statistical models included variables to account for the implementation of the Smoke-Free Illinois Act *and* the economy, along with other factors such as additional gambling policy changes, the weather, and trends over time (i.e., seasonal differences in casino admissions and revenues). Their results indicated that the Smoke-Free Illinois Act was responsible for the drop in revenues in Illinois.

Claim: Yes, it really was the economy. In their 2009 analysis, Thomas Garrett and Michael Pakko claimed that the economy fared "roughly the same" across the four states and used this assumption in choosing their statistical strategy. However, measures of the economy show distinct differences between the states. In addition, Garrett and Pakko did not include a measure of the housing market in their statistical models. It is nearly impossible to measure or account for everything that influences an outcome in a statistical model, and making decisions about which variables to include is difficult. However, the lack of a measure of housing in the Garrett and Pakko study is, I would argue, a glaring omission given its importance as an indicator of the economy in the midst of a recession brought on by a housing-market collapse.

Issue 3: Did the Act Cause Smokers to Leave Illinois to Gamble in Neighboring States?

Claim: Yes, smokers left because of the act. In making the case for restoring smoking in Illinois casinos, one of the common claims set forth was that neighboring states had an unfair advantage because they allowed smoking in their casinos. Garrett and Pakko found that, while patron spending decreased in Illinois casinos, neighboring states did not suffer the same decline. In fact, compared to 2007 patron spending, Indiana, Iowa, and Missouri had small increases in patron spending in 2008. Indiana casinos even added jobs in 2008.

A 2009 *State Journal-Register* article argued that "casinos hit hardest were near state borders where gamblers had nearby smoking-allowed options." The article also quoted Illinois state representative Raymond Poe, who was asked what he thought of the Garrett and Pakko study: "It's pretty hard to argue with the statistics they have, particularly with casinos right across the river. . . . I think it makes it a lot easier for them [casinos] to make their case that it [the smoking ban] is affecting revenue" (Rushton 2009). In addition, an Illinois resident wrote a letter to the editor about people going across borders to gamble: "Missouri casinos . . . have one thing they can offer that Illinois casinos cannot. They can accommodate smoking customers. These casinos are not dumb; they freely advertise this. I have seen this in Quincy [Illinois], where the La Grange, Mo., casino has billboards . . . that clearly state that smokers are welcome there" (Palmer 2010).

Also in 2010, casino lobbyists organized a field trip for Illinois legislators to "see for themselves" the difference in foot traffic between a smoke-free Illinois casino and a nearby smoking-allowed Missouri casino. The legislators were driven to the Casino Queen in East St. Louis, Illinois, and then across the river to the Lumière casino in St. Louis, Missouri. "Among the witnesses was a Casino Queen lobbyist who argued, as other proponents do, that Illinois has lost some $500 million in two years to competition from neighboring states where smoking in the casinos is allowed. They revealed that about 20 state lawmakers toured the Queen and Lumière in St. Louis on Monday to see for themselves the difference in foot traffic" (McDermott 2011). The field trip may have worked; a 2011 news article quoted Illinois state representative Daniel Burke: "We have to provide these legitimate business enterprises a competitive playing field" (McKinney 2011).

Claim: No, smokers did not leave because of the act. Although the field trip for state legislators may have indeed shown that the Lumière casino was crowded and the Casino Queen was not, these two businesses were arguably not very comparable. The Casino Queen is located in economically depressed East St. Louis, an area that is home to fewer than 30,000 residents. In the year preceding the implementation of the Smoke-Free Illinois Act, East St. Louis was ranked among America's most dangerous cities for its extremely high rates of murder, rape, robbery, assault, burglary, and car theft. The Lumière is a brand-new, state-of-the-art casino sitting among restaurants and shops and within a short walking distance of the St. Louis Arch on the riverfront in downtown St. Louis, which is home to about 320,000 residents in the city limits and another million people in adjacent St. Louis County. Differences in foot traffic between these two casinos should be considered in light of all of these factors, not just as a result of smoking policy.

Casino customers may cross state borders for other reasons as well. Some residents in the region cross the border *into* Illinois to escape the smoke-filled Missouri casinos. Consider the opinion of this Missouri resident: "All I know is that the only casino in the St. Louis area that has gotten my money has been the Casino Queen, *due* to the smoking ban. . . . I will not set foot in the smoke infested Lumière or Rivercity casinoes" (*St. Louis Post-Dispatch* 2011). Others leave Illinois for the lower table limits and (apparently) delicious buffets in Indiana casinos:

> My husband and I made a list of all the reasons why we very seldom visit Illinois casinos anymore. In our opinion, it has little to do with the smoking ban. He enjoys playing craps and blackjack, and likes Indiana casinos because of the lower table stakes. The buffets and restaurants at the Indiana casinos are great. The comps we receive in the mail are higher from Indiana than Illinois, and we always play the same dollar amounts regardless of the state we play in. (Brokopp 2009)

In the case of the Illinois residents going to Indiana, state policies unrelated to smoking may be at fault. For example, Indiana has a "friendlier" regulatory climate for casinos; it has no restrictions on the number of slot machines and table games, whereas Illinois limits each casino to 1,200 slot machines and table games. This difference allows Indiana casinos to have more table games, which in turn allows for some tables to have lower table limits. Also, Indiana's Horseshoe Hammond casino is located closer to Chicago than are the four closest Illinois casinos and is a newer, $500 million establishment that is "in a class by itself in this market" (Brokopp 2009).

Issue 4: Do Smoke-Free Policies Affect Business?

Claim: Smoke-free policies improve business. Other claims applied to casinos stem from research on smoking policies in nongambling hospitality venues (restaurants, bars, hotels, etc.). Many of these studies have shown that smoke-free policies, such as the Smoke-Free Illinois Act, do not negatively affect—and may even increase—restaurant, bar, and hotel business (Glantz and Smith 1997; Sciacca and Ratliff 1998; Bartosch and Pope 2002; Glantz and Wilson-Loots 2003).

Using all of the claims about the loss of business in Illinois casinos as a foundation, a legislative amendment was introduced in 2010 to exempt casinos from the act. Soon after beginning discussion on this amendment, however, the Illinois legislature passed a major gaming expansion bill that permitted the building of five new smoke-free casinos in Illinois. These would be the first new casinos in Illinois since the early 1990s, and they are being built several years after the Smoke-Free Illinois Act was implemented. Some advocates for smoke-free casinos believe that this is an indicator that such casinos are good for the economy: "I just heard from [name] that a major gaming expansion bill just passed the IL legislature. It is on its way to the Governor's Desk and includes five new *smokefree* casinos plus adds slots to racetracks and more. Adding fuel to our message that states with smokefree laws build *more* smokefree casinos, rather than close them down" (Tegen 2011).

A test of this belief occurred in 2011 when the Rock Island casino in Illinois closed its old facility and opened a new (smoke-free) facility complete with hotel, restaurants, and shopping. After the opening, and overcrowding, of the new Rock Island casino, the president of the American Lung Association in Greater Chicago wrote the following letter, published in the *Chicago Tribune:*

> Opponents of the Smoke-Free Illinois Act (signed into law four years ago last Saturday) argued that gambling and smoking went hand-in-hand and they predicted empty casinos and catastrophic losses if the ban was enacted.
>
> Perhaps hindsight is 20/20, or perhaps we were right all along, but the smoke-free Des Plaines casino opening should show that casino patrons care less about being able to smoke and more about being able to entertain themselves with the chance to win big. Eighty-two percent of Illinoisans don't smoke and a recent, state-wide poll shows that 84% of voters still support the Smoke-Free Illinois Act.

New and shiny casinos draw crowds, not old and smoky ones.
(Wimmer 2011)

A follow-up e-mail from Kathy Drea, director of Public Policy
for the American Lung Association of Illinois, included the casino
revenue data comparing the new Rock Island facility that opened
(smoke-free) in December 2008 to its closest casino neighbor in
Davenport, Iowa (Drea 2011). The data showed the Rock Island casino consistently earning lower revenues than the Davenport casino
before and after passage of the Smoke-Free Illinois Act. However, as
soon as the new facility opened, revenues in the Rock Island casino
increased substantially and stayed consistently far above revenues in
the Davenport casino. It seems that "new and shiny casinos" may
indeed draw crowds, or at least revenue.

Claim: Smoke-free policies do not improve business. Other
parties disagree that smoke-free venues are good for business.
Studies demonstrating that business is improved in smoke-free hospitality venues are in conflict with the claims of many opponents to the
Smoke-Free Illinois Act, including Garrett and Pakko. When asked
about the conflict between the findings of their report and the scientific studies that show better business in smoke-free venues, Garrett
claimed that the prior studies were weak and unconvincing:

> There are some studies . . . that show a positive impact of smoking
> bans on bars and restaurants, however their statistical methodolo-
> gies are not very rigorous and the results are less than convincing.
> Most of the results out there that have some statistical weight actu-
> ally either find that there is a negative effect of smoking bans on
> bars and restaurants or no effect. (Soutar 2010)

Issue 5: Do Smoke-Free Policies Improve Health?

Claim: Yes, which is also good for the economy. One claim that
has gone largely unanswered by opponents of the Smoke-Free Illinois
Act is that of improved health for workers and patrons in smoke-free
casinos, and the economic benefits associated with improved health.
Policies mandating clean indoor air have been associated with reduc-
tions in disease, and with reducing indoor pollution levels in casinos
from worse than a highway at rush hour, to a tiny fraction of that
(Repace 2004). Better health leads to fewer health care costs. When

an amendment to the Smoke-Free Illinois Act was drafted in the Illinois legislature that proposed to allow Illinois casinos to permit smoking on the gambling floor until neighboring states implemented smoke-free casino policies, several large public health organizations spoke out against the exemption:

> Speaking against the measure was the American Heart Association, the American Cancer Society and the Illinois Department of Public Health, which argued that it's not clear the smoking ban is responsible for the revenue loss—and that, in any case, it's peanuts next to the $4 billion-plus in health care costs to Illinois from smoking.
>
> I didn't hear any debate about what kind of increased costs in terms of hospitals and health care costs as a result of going back to what we did before. I hear the argument on one side about this about the money, but we'll spend more if we allow this practice [smoking in casinos]. (McDermott 2010)

Some Illinois constituents agree in their letters to the editor, urging their fellow state residents to encourage their policymakers to think about health when it comes to smoke-free casinos:

> All casino workers and patrons deserve to breathe smoke-free air and we must fight to continue that protection. The casinos are claiming that the Smoke-Free Illinois Act—not the economic challenges of the past year—is responsible for a decline in their revenue. And despite polling that shows 84 percent of Illinois voters support Smoke-Free Illinois, lawmakers are considering putting the health of our citizens in jeopardy. (Wheet 2010)

Conclusion

Even after a law has been passed, policymakers continue to face pressures from constituents, activists, lobbyists, business owners, scientists, and others. These groups often hold competing perspectives on whether a law is beneficial or detrimental to a community and whether a law is too weak or overreaching. In the case of smoke-free casinos, common claims brought by lobbyists and business owners conclude that forcing casinos to be smoke-free will harm the industry by reducing the number of patrons who come to casinos, therefore reducing the tax receipts that support state and local governments in states with smoke-free casino policies. Public health advocates, on the other hand, often argue that the economic impact of laws mandating smoke-free casinos is not as dire as it is often portrayed, and that the health of a state's citizens should come first. Researchers contribute to the debate with analyses that are meant to be objective, but their studies can contradict each other and draw criticism.

Whether you find yourself agreeing more with the claims in favor of smoke-free casinos or with those against, two things are clear: the issue is complex, and the passage of a law is not the end of the debate. Although competing claims like those in Illinois have been made in states and communities across the country for years, the United States has had the tendency to adopt more and stronger smoke-free policies over time. Recently, however, opponents to smoke-free workplace policies have begun to see some success. Bills to weaken statewide smoke-free workplace laws were on the ballot in a record sixteen states in 2011. Three of these bills passed, weakening smoke-free workplace laws in Kansas, Nevada, and Oregon. In 2012, smoke-free workplace advocates expect to see new statewide smoke-free policies on the ballot in Kentucky, Oklahoma, Alabama, Indiana, Louisiana, and Mississippi along with more challenges to existing smoke-free laws in other states (Americans for Nonsmokers' Rights 2011). The debate will continue.

15

Global Policy Outcomes: Comparing Reactions to Post-Tsunami Aid

Lynn Letukas

Many studies of the construction of social problems involve case studies of claimsmaking in a bounded public arena—that is, one located in a fixed place and time (Hilgartner and Bosk 1988; Spector and Kitsuse 1973). While this can help sensitize researchers to how social problems develop in one arena, this approach ignores the construction of social problems across multiple arenas. Without comparative analyses of social problems, researchers are left to wonder how successful certain claims are beyond the particular arena in which they emerge.

A partial solution to this problem is to compare one troubling condition during the same period of time *within* different arenas, such as nations. For example, Abigail Saguy, Kjerstin Gruya, and Shanna Gong (2010) examine how obesity came to be seen as a social problem in France and the United States; their analysis suggests that the different constructions in the two nations reflect the distinctive social structure and culture within each country. However, some troubling conditions span the context of one particular culture or arena. These global social problems, such as HIV/AIDS, simultaneously affect more than one nation or public arena.

We need to better understand how the construction of social problems occurs across diverse public arenas and how these constructions inform, contend with, and influence policy implementation and policy outcomes. In particular, policy outcomes, or public reactions to social policies, have been neglected by sociologists of social problems. There are four general policy outcome constructions that can result from the creation of a new social policy: these argue that policies are effective, insufficient, excessive, or misguided (Best 2008). Since there are diverse interests in contemporary society, mass consensus that a social policy is *effective* tends to be rare. Consequently, greater scholarly attention has been directed toward the three possible public reactions that attempt to challenge a new social policy. First, a policy may be deemed *insufficient* when critics argue that the policy does not go far enough to address the original problem. Second, a policy may be deemed *excessive* when critics, who likely did not support the initial policy, try to convince the public and policymakers that its passage went too far and that reform is necessary. Finally, a policy may be deemed *misguided* when critics argue that policymakers incorrectly interpreted the troubling condition and suggest that the policy should be examined from a different approach.

Drawing upon constructionist theorizing, this chapter examines cross-national media accounts of responses to the 2004 Indian Ocean tsunami in an attempt to better understand the construction of global social problems and the dynamic interplay between claimsmaking activities and policy outcomes across four culturally diverse public arenas. Findings from this research suggest that there can be multiple, competing, and even conflicting constructions of social problems and that these can vary from place to place. For example, within the global social problem of the Indian Ocean tsunami, different nations constructed "glocalized" policy outcomes that ranged from effective in the United States, to excessive in India, to insufficient in Indonesia, and misguided in Thailand. Since global social problems occur within a context of globalization, a more detailed analysis of the forces under which globalization develops is necessary.

Globalization and Global Social Problems

Recent sociological research on globalization—or "the rapidly developing process of complex interconnections between societies, cultures, institutions and individuals world-wide"—can help us understand the construction of global social problems (Tomlinson 1999, p. 165). The notion that some troubling conditions are systemic enough to affect regions beyond one nation is an emerging area of inquiry

(Alasuutari 2008). Recent scholarship on globalization views the world as interconnected and increasingly interlinked (Sassen 2007). Reactions to the 2004 Indian Ocean tsunami are an example of the influence of globalization and how a catastrophe in one region of the world can elicit a global response, such as material and financial assistance, from other areas around the world. According to Maria Hellman and Kristina Riegert, the Indian Ocean tsunami represented a global catastrophe because it involved "large-scale loss of human life, affecting citizens far away from their home locations and generating significant pressure for intervention to alleviate the situation" (2009, p. 127). Previous research has discussed how the Indian Ocean tsunami affected nations in Europe (Hellman and Riegert 2009; Letukas, Oloffson, and Barnshaw 2009; Pantti 2009), but for the purposes of this analysis, I focus on how one donor nation (the United States) and three recipient nations (India, Indonesia, and Thailand) constructed relief efforts.

The realization that some social problems span national boundaries is often hidden by analyses of media content, because nearly all news coverage has a local, regional, or national context (Clausen 2004). For example, while cable news channels (such as CNN) may reach an international audience, their messages are largely tailored toward a national audience (Ritzer 2008). Thus, rather than a global media system that homogenizes information from developed to developing nations, press reports on global issues vary so as to reflect the interests and viewpoints of the nations where they are produced (Clausen 2004). This process of global forces blending with local preferences is known as *glocalization,* or "the interpenetration of the global and the local, resulting in unique outcomes in different geographic areas" (Ritzer 2003, p. 193). Glocalization moves beyond the concept of globalization and depicts a greater balance between global trends and local cultures that leads to the construction of new traditions, culture, and identities (Robertson 1992).

Glocalization may offer an important link for understanding how global social problems can be subject to multiple, competing, and even contradictory constructions of policies and policy outcomes. Drawing upon a glocalized approach, this chapter explores diverse policy assessments of material and financial assistance following the 2004 Indian Ocean tsunami. However, before exploring different policy outcome claims about tsunami relief, more detailed background on the tsunami itself is necessary.

The Indian Ocean Tsunami

On December 26, 2004, an earthquake measuring 9.0 on the Richter scale ripped open the ocean floor 150 miles off the coast of Sumatra, Indonesia, resulting in a release of energy equivalent to 23,000 Hiroshima atomic bombs (US Geological Survey 2004). This earthquake triggered one of the largest and most destructive tsunamis in recorded history, resulting in an estimated quarter-million fatalities, the loss of a million jobs, and the displacement of over one and a half million people in at least twelve countries (Inderfurth, Fabrycky, and Cohen 2005). These catastrophic conditions generated intensive mass media coverage of the affected South Asian nations, including the thousands of Western tourists who had been in those countries. This global media coverage, particularly in Western countries, led to individuals, organizations, and governments sending unprecedented amounts of financial and material assistance to the affected region (Clark 2006). Thus claimsmakers, especially the mass media, played an integral part in the construction of relief efforts in donor and recipient nations.

Data and Methods

Utilizing a qualitative content analysis, this chapter examines media constructions of relief efforts across one donor and three recipient nations following the 2004 Indian Ocean tsunami. While this study does not examine newspapers from all twelve nations affected by the tsunami, the sample includes articles that reference humanitarian efforts in three of the four hardest-hit nations. First, two major print media sources were selected for three nations (the *Washington Post* and *New York Times* for the United States; the *Statesman* and the *Hindustan Times* for India; the *Bangkok Post* and the *Nation*), and one newspaper and one newswire (the *Jakarta Post* and *Antara*) were selected for Indonesia. The South Asian newspapers and newswire were chosen based upon their considerable coverage of the 2004 tsunami and their availability in English, which provided consistency for comparison across each country. The time period of study, one year following the initial impact (December 26, 2004, to December 26, 2005), allowed for detailed analyses of relief efforts during both the short- and intermediate-term response and recovery periods, and during the beginning of the long-term recovery, as well as coverage marking the tsunami's one-year anniversary. Lexis-Nexis Academic was used to conduct a full-text database search using what a preliminary examination of news articles in each country found were the three most frequently used search terms to describe the tsunami relief efforts: "tsunami and relief," "tsunami and aid," and "tsunami and donation(s)." The search yielded a total of 6,168 newspaper articles. Following the removal of duplicate articles and articles with content not related to the 2004 tsunami, such as those detailing other disasters, a combined total of 2,005 articles remained. A subsample of every second article was selected, resulting in 303 US, 273 Indian, 238 Indonesian, and 188 Thai articles (for a total of 1,002 news articles).

Inductive coding procedures were utilized to allow for optimal flexibility in comparing emergent themes across donor and recipient nations (Strauss and Corbin 1990). After identifying major themes within each article, a coding guide was constructed that grouped major themes into general categories. In some cases, general themes were consistent across nations; however, separate coding guides were utilized to examine the emergent perceptions of assistance in each nation.

Analysis

Following the tsunami, the United States sent unprecedented amounts of financial and material assistance to all three of the affected nations in a concerted effort to resolve the humanitarian challenges brought about by the catastrophe. While these contributions were acknowledged in the recipient nations (India, Indonesia, and Thailand), each constructed the assistance as problematic for different reasons.

The Donor Perspective:
Media Constructions in the United States

The United States emerged from World War II as the most powerful economic and military force in the world (Craig et al. 2000). This unique position emboldened the United States to extend its economic, military, and political influence globally through a variety of diplomatic initiatives (Letukas and Barnshaw 2008). A major success in international diplomacy was the Marshall Plan (1947–1951), which provided a tremendous amount of humanitarian assistance to the allied nations of Europe following World War II (Price 1955). Following the Indian Ocean catastrophe, claimsmakers (such as President George W. Bush) discussed the implementation of a "new Marshall Plan" that would "commit billions of dollars for long-term programs" to save lives, stimulate economic development, and improve the political reputation of the United States in South Asia and globally (Usborne 2005). These efforts particularly targeted the predominantly Muslim nation of Indonesia and were constructed as critical for maintaining support for the US "war on terror":

> Polling has indicated that the U.S. tsunami effort has paid dividends to the United States' image in Indonesia. A survey of 1,200 Indonesians one month after the tsunami found that, for the first time, more Indonesians (40 percent) supported the U.S. terrorism fight than opposed it (36 percent). Sixty-five percent of those surveyed had a more favorable impression of the United States. (Kessler and Wright 2005)

Through the invocation of the collective memory of the once successful Marshall Plan, the mass media and political leaders constructed a favorable message to potential US donors and provided an image of the United States being seen as playing a unique role in foreign affairs, which would help boost US favorability internationally. This ideology prompted an image of the United States as a world power, part of a "core group of nations" that would lead a global relief effort in South Asia. News articles claimed that there was a great need for US aid and presented the unprecedented collective response of financial and material assistance pledged by organizations, the US government, and individual donors as a way to alleviate the South Asian relief problem. As Secretary of State Colin Powell put it: "The United States, the wealthiest nation in the world, is doing a phenomenal job in this unprecedented challenge, not only with a very large cash donation but also bringing in military and civil defense assets. . . . [C]learly the United States will be a major contributor to this international effort" (Hodge 2005). Self-congratulation was noted in several stories of "selfless Americans" who organized trendy "relief parties," rather than traditional cocktail parties, or who planned "aid vacations" to affected areas in Thailand (Boustany 2005; Levere 2005). As Table 15.1 indicates, the US news stories focused on the generosity of American donations (59.2 percent of stories featured this theme) and downplayed the affected nations' ability to handle the crisis (only 2.2 percent of stories portrayed the South Asian nations as self-sufficient). The US coverage depicted the

Table 15.1 Reactions to Post-Tsunami Aid: Emergent Themes in US Print Media

Theme	Presence in News Articles (percentage)
Generosity of US donations and favorable role of donors and US government	59.2
Social solidarity among Americans generated through donations	11.9
Relief requests from impacted South Asian nations (e.g., types of needed supplies)	10.4
Western vacationers impacted by the tsunami (e.g., wealthy tourists in Thailand)	8.9
Critique of US donor response	7.4
Self-sufficiency of impacted South Asian nations (e.g., Thai government helping Thai people)	2.2

Note: Percentages may not sum to 100 due to rounding.

tsunami as a problem in need of a solution, and the United States as having the best answer through the delivery of unprecedented amounts of assistance. US media coverage also glocalized the problem by showing how US citizens traveling abroad were affected, thus localizing the global problem for their audience.

Ultimately, claimsmaking activities emphasized the role of US donors in relief initiatives rather than relief requests from affected nations. Moreover, claimsmaking activities were overwhelmingly uncritical of international relief policies and portrayed US assistance as favorable. Thus the favorable construction of the new Marshall Plan is illustrative of a rare example of popular consensus toward the creation and implementation of an *effective* policy outcome. In contrast, claimsmakers in the Indian, Indonesian, and Thai public arenas were widely divergent in their constructions and evaluations of international donor relief.

The Recipient Perspective: Media Constructions in India, Indonesia, and Thailand

India. Since the 1950s, India has made a concerted effort to transform itself from a developing country into a world leader, through an emphasis on domestic security and stability and efforts to reduce the impact of

Table 15.2 Reactions to Post-Tsunami Aid: Emergent Themes in Indian Print Media

Theme	Presence in News Articles (percentage)
Generosity of Indian response to relief and recovery needs in India	57.6
Challenges that hinder relief and recovery efforts in India (e.g., volunteer convergence)	18.0
India's self-sufficiency and ability to recover from the tsunami without Western support	7.8
Social solidarity among Indians in response to relief efforts	6.6
Critique of Western relief efforts (e.g., inappropriate donations)	5.7
India's assistance to other impacted South Asian nations (e.g., supplies and support to Indonesia)	4.8

Note: Percentages may not sum to 100 due to rounding.

high population growth and unemployment (Muni and Mohan 2005). Following the tsunami, the social, political, and economic agenda in India was evident in the coverage of Indian relief and recovery efforts in the *Hindustan Times* and the *Statesman*. Although India suffered the third highest number of fatalities (over 16,000) and an immense amount of damage (an estimated $1.244 billion), much of the Indian media coverage focused on domestic relief efforts, notably in remote areas and coastal provinces, as detailed in Table 15.2 (Cosgrave 2007).

Indian mass media claimed that their government and local organizations were immediately involved in relief efforts and discussed how these groups were helping to lessen the impact of the tsunami: "Round the Clock Rescue, Relief Operations Mounted in Areas Hit by Tsunami Waves" (*Hindustan Times* 2004). The media also framed local government relief efforts as more acceptable than Western relief policies, as evinced by many stories that discussed inappropriate and culturally insensitive donations:

> A mountain-like pile of [dirty] garments almost resembling a heap of garbage in the middle of the yard. The shock at the sight of this man-made mountain was no less than that of the news of the tsunami itself. The victims were rejecting offers of old clothes, any self-

respecting human being would do so. With the entire thing reflecting an utter lack of sensitivity towards our unfortunate compatriots.
(*Statesman* 2005)

The Indian media construction of the ability of Indians to recover without international assistance was a prevalent theme (7.8 percent of stories), along with a critique of international involvement in relief and
recovery efforts (5.7 percent). These constructions sharply contrasted
with constructions by US media that framed recipients' response to
relief as favorable. Indian media claimed that US media criticized
India's decision to reject outside aid, and that sources such as Colin
Powell and George W. Bush framed India as weak and vulnerable
(*Hindustan Times* 2005b). However, Indian media not only justified the
decision of their government, but also used the public arena to reaffirm
India's emergence as a dominant power. Moreover, the effective
response of India was portrayed as extending beyond internal affairs, as
the Indian media also reported that India played a strong role in relief
assistance in other South Asian nations:

> The world is scratching its head after India [said] "Thanks, but no
> thanks" to international aid. The irony is that [because of] Western
> media [dominance]—and, therefore, opinion—many Indians too are
> perplexed by New Delhi foregoing aid. The Prime Minister [said]
> "We declined the offer because we didn't need it." India [also sent
> relief to] Sri Lanka within hours of the debacle and at least a week
> before the US marines reached there. (*Hindustan Times* 2005a)

These differing constructions of assistance by claimsmakers in
the United States and India illustrate how interpretations of global
social problems may diverge and how policy outcomes may be
viewed as *excessive*. In this instance, claimsmakers in the United
States viewed destruction brought about by the tsunami as a problem
to be solved with financial and material assistance, a view that led to
an unprecedented amount of relief being sent to affected nations such
as India. However, there appears to have been very little concerted
effort by claimsmakers in the United States to discuss what was needed by those in India. Consequently, the Indian press constructed US
aid as excessive, as evidenced by massive amounts of resources that
went unused. This, in turn, did not create a favorable view of foreign
assistance within the public arena of India. Rather, articles in the
Indian press promoted policies that emphasized India's governmental

response and self-reliance, and portrayed international involvement as excessive (*Hindustan Times* 2005a, 2005b).

While the Indian mass media did report on supply chain and convergence problems in remote regions, and while policy initiatives were created by the government to overcome these issues, these policies were not created to provide the international community with better access to remote regions, but rather to block future international material and financial assistance efforts. Such reporting of claims is consistent with glocalization, whereby India's status as an emerging economic power enabled elite claimsmakers, such as Prime Minister Manmohan Singh, to reject foreign assistance and emphasize the self-sufficiency of India, while helping other nation-states in need. As we shall see, this construction of, and reaction to, relief efforts sharply contrast with Indonesia and Thailand.

Indonesia. Indonesia is one of the most corrupt countries in the world. Long-term conflict in the country has caused an increase in government corruption and media censorship, and consequently a decrease in economic development related to the difficulty in attracting Western capital (Bhargava and Bolongaita 2004). In addition, the livelihood of many Indonesians is constantly threatened due to the lack of government commitment to eradicating poverty and the pervasiveness of corruption. This is illustrated by a recent survey showing that more Indonesians (over 70 percent) viewed corruption as a greater social problem than the state of the economy or unemployment (Bhargava and Bolongaita 2004). Preliminary work had begun to overcome some of the corruption problems with the "Aceh Social Reconstruction Agenda," an initiative of the government and civil society in the Aceh province; however, the onset of the Indian Ocean tsunami caused the project to cease in late 2004 (Bennett et al. 2006).

As the country located closest to the epicenter of the earthquake, Indonesia suffered more fatalities (more than 129,000) and had more displaced people (over 566,000) than any other nation (Bennett et al. 2006). The impact on Indonesia included the relocation of entire fishing communities and a 30 percent unemployment rate in the affected area, a rate comparable to that during the Great Depression in the United States (Kennedy 1999). To compound this catastrophe, Indonesia suffered another earthquake on March 28, 2005, in Nias, resulting in nearly 900 deaths and additional structural damage (Scheper, Patel, and Parakrama 2006).

The catastrophe, combined with a weakened government, resulted in a response largely without national coordination, placing much of the responsibility for relief efforts in the hands of the international community (Cosgrave 2007). This lack of confidence in Indonesia's ability to effectively respond was frequently reported in the Indonesian press: "Understandably the government was unprepared. . . . [I]t had no time to properly think through directions and effectively organize efforts, since a huge number of immediate and urgent problems had to be tackled" (*Jakarta Post* 2005b).

Frequent stories depicted themes of Indonesian vulnerability and emphasized the importance of donor relief in an effort to encourage support and solidarity among the international community, rather than the sort of national solidarity highlighted in the Indian media coverage:

> We are elated at the [international] response to this global disaster. UN Emergency Relief Coordinator Jan Egeland said, "The world is really coming together here in a way that we have probably never seen before." Politics and ideology now have to be put aside so that the international community can mount [one of the] biggest relief operation[s] since World War II. (*Jakarta Post* 2005a)

In sharp contrast to India, Indonesia was so reliant upon international assistance that claimsmakers often noted that any aid was acceptable (Scheper, Patel, and Parakrama 2006). Few articles criticized foreign efforts, with the majority of stories claiming that the international community was helpful, particularly within the first months following the catastrophe, as evidenced by Table 15.3, which shows that the most salient theme was appreciation for foreign assistance (42.4 percent).

In March 2005, when the US government made a tentative decision to withdraw support, the Indonesian government requested that international involvement in the region be extended, and the public began calling into question the initial favorability of international assistance:

> "We still need foreigners' assistance," [said] Ramlah, an Acehnese man, [because] "displaced people lack a reliable clean water supply and enough doctors, [and] the foreigners treat us better than the government." Many survivors are not convinced of the government's capabilities in assisting Aceh. Many Acehnese are more willing to trust foreigners. "We like the foreign volunteers." (*Jakarta Post* 2005c)

Table 15.3 Reactions to Post-Tsunami Aid: Emergent Themes in Indonesian Print Media

Theme	Presence in News Articles (percentage)
Favorable role of Western relief efforts in Indonesia	42.4
Relief requests (e.g., supplies, financial assistance) by Indonesians to Western nations	31.9
Challenges to relief and recovery efforts in Indonesia (e.g., corruption)	16.4
Dependency of Indonesia on support of Western nations in recovery efforts	7.8
Critique of Western nations' involvement in relief and recovery efforts in Indonesia	1.6

Note: Percentages may not sum to 100 due to rounding.

Popular sentiment for the continuation of international relief efforts was so strong that the *Jakarta Post* printed threatening claims projected toward the United States and its new Marshall Plan agenda:

> If the U.S. and international community fail to support long-term recovery efforts, and militant groups step into the breach, then positive feelings generated in the tsunami's immediate aftermath will fade. This might lend credence to conspiracy theories in the Islamic world that the tsunami was punishment for Indonesian impiety and assistance to U.S. counterterrorism efforts. (Jasparro 2005)

Thus the Indonesian media constructed policies within their public arena, such as the new Marshall Plan that retracted assistance within a three-month period, as *insufficient*—stating that they did not go far enough to resolve relief problems. However, when US policymakers decided that assistance would continue in Indonesia, claims concerning international relief were once again constructed favorably. Thus the resulting policy outcomes in Indonesia were in strong contrast to India's focus on self-reliance. These differences in the construction of the global social problem are embedded within a glocalized context, whereby Indonesia's weaker political system and the lower level of economic development made it more susceptible to the globalizing interests of the United States, compared to India.

Thailand. Thailand has a culture and identity rooted in its independence and avoidance of European imperialism during the eighteenth and nineteenth centuries. Unlike its neighboring countries, Siam (later Thailand) avoided colonization through a series of revolts and trade agreements and the development of a strong military within the Southeast Asian region (Letukas and Barnshaw 2008). Since the 1950s, Thailand has maintained an overall positive growth trend through a focus on physical and technological development and on tourism, the largest sector of the Thai economy, catering primarily to Western Europeans and Americans (Baker and Phongpaichit 2005).

Prior to the tsunami, Thailand was the most popular tourist destination in South Asia, with more than 10 million visitors annually (Baker and Phongpaichit 2005). Consequently, the tsunami resulted in Thailand having the highest estimated number of foreign tourist fatalities (more than 3,330), which generated substantial media coverage of dead or trapped tourists. Despite Thailand being the fourth most heavily affected nation in terms of mortality (4,600) and the second most economically affected, Thai English-language media initially focused on coastal tourist areas and reports of foreign tourists heroically surviving (Cosgrave 2007; Lewis 2006). In addition to survival accounts, Thai media also focused on the generous and hospitable treatment of foreigners:

> [News coverage] was positive about the ways the Thai government and people were helping foreign survivors. [On CNN] an American couple thank[ed] the Thai people [for] their kindness and assistance: "We were walking barefoot into a hospital and a nurse took off her shoes and gave them to my wife," said the husband. "We were overwhelmed by their kindness." (*Bangkok Post* 2005b)

In contrast to Indonesia, media in Thailand claimed that the immediate response of the Thai government was sufficient due to its emphasis on provisions for health services and the needs of fishing communities. These reports were followed by claims that an immediate emphasis would be placed on rebuilding hotels for the upcoming tourist season due to Thailand's dependence on income from foreign tourists to sustain its economy.

It is important to note that a significant percentage of readership of the *Nation* and the *Bangkok Post* consist of wealthy English-speaking Thai and international readers (Lewis 2006). Thus it is perhaps not surprising that claimsmakers in the Thai press discussed efforts to rebuild Thai resorts and the favorable treatment of foreign tourists, while simultaneously downplaying the devastation in coastal regions. However, despite this positive treatment toward Western tourists, critical claims were directed toward relief initiatives by international governments due to their failure to abide by the "no relief" requests by the Thai government: "The government made clear from the start that it did not want aid from other governments" (*Bangkok Post* 2005c). Requests for international assistance were largely limited to calls for more tourists, the lifeblood of the Thai economy, which was crucial for maintaining the nation's economic stability: "Foreigners wanting to assist tsunami victims could do best by maintaining their travel plans to the area" (*Bangkok Post* 2005a). Although open critique of international assistance made up a small proportion (3.4 percent) of the overall themes of post-catastrophe aid in the Thai public arena (see Table 15.4), when combined with relief requests (23.0 percent) and methods for economic recovery (12.1 percent), these interlocking themes paint a more comprehensive picture of how a small but vocal critique of inappropriate aid was constructed as problematic and contributed to a systemic problem of unfulfilled needs, which slowed the potential for economic recovery in Thailand.

Taken together, this critical construction of international relief contrasted with claims in the US public arena that all South Asian

Table 15.4 Reactions to Post-Tsunami Aid: Emergent Themes in Thai Print Media

Theme	Presence in News Articles (percentage)
Western relief and recovery efforts in Thailand	29.9
Impact of tsunami on tourism and Western tourists	23.6
Relief requests (e.g., tourists) by Thai government and people to Western nations	23.0
Impact of tsunami on Thai economy and Thai recovery methods (e.g., rebuild hotels, encourage travel)	12.1
Role of Thai government and local organizations in relief efforts	8.0
Critique of Western relief efforts in Thailand (e.g., Western nations not sending requested relief)	3.4

Note: Percentages may not sum to 100 due to rounding.

nations benefited from the new Marshall Plan. Rather, the Thai media constructed international donations as inappropriate and *misguided*. Although there was some evidence from the US media to conclude that the message of "aid vacations" to Thailand was one of the top priorities to rebuild the Thai economy, this was hardly viewed by the Thai media as Americans engaging in a "selfless" act. Rather, the Thai media constructed this response as serving the Americans' "own national interests" (Boustany 2005; Levere 2005). From the Thai perspective, US claimsmakers were not accurate in their construction of the most appropriate types of relief that would help stimulate the economy. According to Joel Best (2008), when actors have the wrong view of a troubling condition and consequently create policies around these views, the resulting public reactions toward the policy are critical and new claims emerge that suggest that the policy needs to be examined from a different approach. In this respect, findings from the Thai media suggest that the implementation of a misguided policy, or the wrong interpretation of a troubling condition, can make things worse for all parties involved.

The construction of the need for tourists is also illustrative of glocalization within the Thai public arena. When the United States attempted to provide general assistance in an effort to boost favorability and influence in Thailand, these activities were viewed largely as a misguided and unwarranted globalizing encroachment upon the specific needs of the Thai political system and its people. Since Thai claimsmakers could not universally reject foreign assistance, because they needed tourists and specific supplies, they took a decidedly glocal approach and constructed assistance that they viewed as essential for their local economic development as acceptable, while rejecting the rest.

Conclusion

The tremendous outpouring of financial and material assistance provided by Western citizens and governments generated multiple constructions of, and reactions to, relief efforts in donor and recipient nations following the 2004 Indian Ocean tsunami. This chapter has sought to develop and refine the concept of a *global social problem,* which is a troubling condition that spans multiple public arenas wherein social and political actors attempt to resolve troubling conditions. A global social problem need not inspire a single, global construction; similarly, a social policy may inspire different policy outcomes. Rather, there can be multiple, competing, and even conflicting constructions, and these can vary from place to place. For example, within the global social problem of the Indian Ocean tsunami, each nation constructed differing interpretations of policy outcomes. Media in the United States argued that the new Marshall Plan policy was favorable in South Asia, resulting in the construction of an *effective* policy outcome. In contrast, Western relief was constructed as *excessive* in India, because massive amounts of unusable aid hindered, rather than helped, the recovery process. In Indonesia, Western relief teams initially planned to leave the affected area after three months, resulting in the construction of an *insufficient* policy outcome. Finally, Thai media argued that Western relief was *misguided,* because requests for specific aid, such as tourists, were ignored (see Table 15.5).

This research is important to the development of constructionist theory because most constructionist research involves case studies of a single public arena. When researchers have studied multiple arenas, they have largely examined differences *within* each arena (Benson and Saguy 2005; Boyle, Songora, and Foss 2001; Saguy, Gruys, and Gong 2010). This chapter is among the first studies to highlight the important interplay of constructions *across* public arenas while still taking into account some of the important cultural aspects within each public arena. At present, the lack of a coherent global public arena wherein global social problems are constructed and contested has made exploring such problems challenging. However, by focusing on how globalization influences local actors in public arenas through a process of glocalization, this research offers some advan-

Table 15.5 Reactions to Post-Tsunami Aid: Policy Outcomes in Donor and Recipient Nations

Nation	Social Problem	Policy Outcome
United States	South Asian nations in need of relief; creation of new Marshall Plan	Effective
India	Culturally inappropriate donations	Excessive
Indonesia	No long-term recovery plan by Western nations	Insufficient
Thailand	Need Western tourists to help stimulate economy	Misguided

tages over previous comparative approaches. Specifically, focusing on the interplay of policy implementation and outcomes across arenas allows for observations about how powerful claimsmakers in one arena have the capacity to influence policy in another, and conversely, how other claimsmakers are able to resist, rearticulate, or accommodate such policies.

Scholars debate whether globalization will lead to a homogenization of cultures, but this research lends support to the notion that local culture can resist even some of the broadest and most powerful interests of globalization (Guillen 2001; Robertson 1992). Future constructionist research should develop a systematic framework for studying the *glocalization* of social problems construction. Such work has rich theoretical as well as policy implications. For example, if US policymakers had better taken into account the interests of local regions in providing assistance, the response might have produced more favorable post-tsunami reactions. Thus, by focusing on the forces that shape the glocalization of global social problems, constructionists can begin to examine how constructions of social problems vary across diverse nations and can better understand how these constructions create diverse policy outcomes. While there is still much work to be done, this chapter serves as a bridge to new directions in constructing global social problems theory and policy outcomes.

Note

I thank John Barnshaw for his helpful comments and suggestions on prior drafts.

Part 6

Afterword

16

Three Questions for Constructionism

Scott R. Harris and Joel Best

What are social problems? This book has approached them as social constructions rather than as objective conditions. There is no denying that human suffering and societal breakdowns do occur, but any given problem can be interpreted in many different ways. When things go wrong, understandings of what is happening—and what to do about it—are matters of perspective and even heated debate.

Constructionism has shaped many studies of social problems over the past three decades, but most social problems textbooks still adopt a fact-based, objectivist approach. In contrast, the chapters in this volume highlight the subjective aspect of the social problems process: how claimsmakers bring attention to problems, how the media cover these concerns, the reaction of the public, and how policymakers deal with the issues. In every stage of the social problems process, people try to convince others to believe and act upon their interpretations of the issue at hand.

Constructionism focuses on what all social problems have in common—interpretive claimsmaking. The constructionist approach offers a single, coherent perspective for making sense of the bewildering array of problems that demand our attention. This is one of the main reasons that many scholars (and students alike) have found constructionism to be very appealing.

Although constructionism has its followers, it also has its critics. Not everyone is comfortable with the premises and findings of constructionist studies. Moreover, constructionist scholars themselves do not always agree on how this perspective should be defined and used. This chapter outlines some of the criticisms and debates that surround constructionism (more detailed treatments of these complex theoretical issues can be found in Harris 2010; Holstein and Gubrium 2008; Holstein and Miller 2003; Loseke 2003).

In teaching constructionism, we have found that many students are intrigued but perplexed by this perspective. Students enjoy debating the pros and cons of adopting a constructionist mind-set. For that reason, this concluding chapter is structured around three discussion questions. We hope that this format invites students to participate in ongoing scholarly debates, rather than adopting the pose of passive spectators.

Is Constructionism Dangerous?

Some scholars—and students—find constructionism disorienting. Focusing on claimsmaking (rather than objective conditions) can be frustrating or annoying. Some even argue that constructionism itself is a social problem—that it is hazardous to the health of individuals and to society as a whole. Why might some people have these negative reactions?

The constructionist framework rests on a controversial foundation: the notion that nothing is inherently or automatically problematic. Any condition "X" can be interpreted as problem "Y" or "Z" or as not a problem at all. This deceptively simple premise has profound implications. It can undercut our commonsense belief that there is a real world with real problems. Constructionism fosters doubt.

The better we understand the constructionist framework, the more radically it can influence our everyday experiences of problems small and large. Suppose you were to watch a television commercial for a new medication that treats "social anxiety disorder." A constructionist mind-set would encourage you to consider whether the "symptoms" of this disorder—nervousness, avoidance of parties—could be portrayed as "natural" and "normal" rather than "problematic." You might imagine or investigate whether the problem could be reframed by focusing on social rather than chemical factors. (Could anxiety be caused by unnecessarily high expectations, or by a lack of collective effort to integrate all participants into social events, or by other factors?) A constructionist perspective may help you ask critical questions about the exact definition of "social anxiety disorder" (as opposed to, say, mere "shyness"), or about how one might count the number of people claimed to be affected by the disorder. When thinking like a constructionist, you might be more inclined to ask whether some interest groups (such as drug manufacturers) might benefit from particular claimsmaking about this problem, and who their audiences and opponents might be.

So far, so good. The dilemma is that the same sort of critical thinking can be applied to everything—from potentially minor issues like incivility to potentially serious issues like murder, rape, slavery, and genocide. For a constructionist, nothing is simple. Even "obviously" abhorrent practices can be and have been the source of rival claims. For example, slavery has been treated as a normal part of life, a moral imperative sanctioned by God, an effective business solution to labor costs, a just consequence of losing a war, and so on. Human beings can always produce divergent interpretations of any situation—even those that seem "self-evidently" morally reprehensible. From a constructionist point of view, there is no single truth about social problems, only competing truths. Yes, constructionists occasionally do (like other types of critical thinkers) choose to weigh the evidence and argue that some interpretations seem more trustworthy or workable than others. But their main focus tends to be studying claimsmaking, rather than engaging in or evaluating claimsmaking.

This can be disturbing for some people. Constructionism can seem amoral, even immoral. Many scholars and students want to know: What is *really* going on? Why is it happening? Who or what is to blame? What should be done about it? Constructionism does not provide easy answers to any these questions. Instead, it treats all answers to these questions as claims to be critically examined.

By itself, the constructionist framework does not seem to take an explicit stand for or against much of anything—except for, perhaps, the importance of thinking critically and carefully. This is unlike other important perspectives, such as feminism or Marxism, which begin with the premises that exploitation exists and is detrimental to individuals and groups. Similarly, some people with strong religious convictions can be offended by constructionism, since this perspective challenges the notion that certain behaviors are inherently sinful. By relentlessly gathering and scrutinizing competing claims, constructionism has the potential to weaken (or make less "obvious") any of the truths and ideals that people hold dear.

Consequently, there are scholars and students who react negatively to constructionist theory and research. They wonder why anyone would want to teach or learn such "toxic" material. Constructionism itself can be portrayed as a social problem, a manifestation of the "creeping relativism" that weakens important values and traditions in society.

When asked to defend their own perspective, constructionists can of course make a number of counterclaims. There are many reasons why a constructionist mind-set can be understood as "beneficial" rather than "detrimental." We'll discuss three, but perhaps you can think of others as well.

One way to counter the claim that "constructionism is dangerous" is to argue that constructionism makes you "smarter" and that being smarter is "good." As the chapters in this book have demonstrated, constructionism can provide a useful framework for making sense of how the world works. Thinking like a constructionist, and reading constructionist research, can yield valuable insights into the birth and death of social problems in our private lives and in society at large. Isn't it better to be informed than ignorant? Constructionism may not tell you *what* to think about the reality or morality of any particular problem, but it can help you understand *why* a problem appeared on society's radar screen and *how* its meaning is shaped by its claimsmakers and by its cultural and interactional contexts.

A second justification may appeal to students who feel shy or hesitant to voice their opinions. Here the argument is that constructionism—instead of encouraging people to be amoral—actually empowers students to explore and express their moral convictions. An awareness of the interpretive nature of claimsmaking can be emboldening because it gives you the confidence to question rather than submit to seemingly authoritative truths. People may tell you that you are too fat or thin, too loud or quiet, too rich or poor, too isolated or social. They may tell you that your neighborhood, school, town, country, or planet is endangered by a new or growing threat. A constructionist mind-set can help you ask, defiantly: Says who? How do they know? Are there other ways of portraying this (supposed) problem? Are there other "solutions" that are being neglected? Constructionism can encourage us to investigate or formulate alternative understandings to the seemingly authoritative claims we are exposed to on a daily basis.

Of course, defiance and outspokenness can be taken too far. It is certainly possible to be overly confident in our own opinions or too dismissive of the viewpoints of others. Arguably, a third benefit of constructionism minimizes this risk. One can reasonably argue that constructionism fosters a healthy attitude of humility in its adherents. If you are acutely aware that any situation can be portrayed in a number of ways, then you are much more likely to recognize the limitations of your own claims. You become a tentative questioner rather than a dismissive know-it-all. The constructionist mind-set fosters tolerance for and curiosity about diverse viewpoints, not cocky disrespectfulness. A constructionist cannot simply retreat into cynicism—insisting that "no one knows anything" or that "there is no point in trying to improve the world"—because those too are claims that must be examined critically. Constructionism can encourage you to require modesty from yourself just as you insist on modesty from others.

In short, some may argue that the constructionist perspective is dangerous to individuals and to society, since it undermines people's commonsense notions of truth and goodness. However, proponents of constructionism can argue that the perspective is enlightening, empowering, and humbling. Constructionism may not tell us what to believe or what to value, but it can help us make more careful decisions in both regards.

Is Constructionism Trivial and Impractical?

While the charge of dangerousness portrays constructionism as a threat to the health of individuals and to civilization itself, the charge of triviality and impracticality portrays constructionism as irrelevant.

Some react negatively to constructionism because they believe the perspective focuses on the "soft" realm of meanings instead of the "hard" world of facts. There are many scholars and students who prefer an objectivist mind-set, since it seems to deal more straightforwardly with the genuine suffering and injustice in the world. Every day, millions of human beings experience unnecessary pain, animals are abused, the environment is degraded, and crises are postponed for which future generations will be on the hook. There are real problems that need real solutions. Some believe that constructionism offers no help—or worse, that it may distract people or undermine their efforts to make positive changes in the world.

While constructionists do not deny the value of research that studies social conditions, they counter that the subjective dimensions of social problems are at least as important—if not more important—

than their objective dimensions. Remember that the objective properties of social problems do not necessarily determine whether a harmful condition will be noticed. People have selective attention, and can blithely ignore or favorably interpret situations that, to another individual or group, would be terribly disturbing. The objective properties of social problems also do not automatically tell us the best way to frame an issue: what kind of problem exists, what its causes and effects are, and whether a policy will work (or has worked) to reduce the problem. Far from trivial, subjective processes are at the heart of social problems. Some constructionists go so far as to claim that, in many important ways, "knowledge of the objective make-up of social problems is essentially useless" in comparison to knowledge of interpretive processes (Blumer 1971, pp. 305–306).[1]

For those who wish to advocate and enact social change in the world, constructionism is an extremely valuable tool. What could be more practical to an activist than an in-depth understanding of the claimsmaking processes that have occurred throughout the history of a social problem? Constructionist research on social problems provides guidelines for how to grab people's attention, convince them of your claims, and motivate them to pursue new policies or practices. Claimsmaking occurs at different levels: within a family, at the meeting of a local school board, in the halls of city, state, and federal governments, and so on. Virtually all of us take part, whether willingly or knowingly, in constructing social problems. Constructionist research illuminates the factors that determine whether claimsmakers succeed or fail in their efforts to persuade others and make changes. It's in your interest to read constructionist research, if you want to advance (or resist) a particular social agenda in your nation, state, community, or personal life.

Does Constructionism Really Offer a Distinct Approach to Social Problems?

Like the first two questions we have discussed—regarding the perceived dangerousness and triviality of constructionism—a third question also makes a potentially serious charge against this perspective. Some scholars and students wonder whether constructionism actually offers a distinct and coherent framework for the analysis of social problems. Even constructionists themselves have debated whether constructionist analyses are, in practice, really all that different from objectivist analyses. What are some of the reasons for these concerns?

Recall the basic distinction between objectivism—which conceptualizes problems as harmful conditions—and constructionism—which treats problems as claims or interpretations. This stark distinction is sometimes not as clear-cut as it seems. There are at least three areas of overlap that complicate the distinction between objectivism and subjectivism.

First, objectivists do pay (some) attention to subjective matters. It is not uncommon for objectivists to cite opinion polls, for example, in their discussions of what the public (or subsections thereof) thinks about an issue. They may collect data on how many Americans consider abortion to be a serious social problem, or what percentages of Democrats versus Republicans are in favor of legalizing marijuana. Objectivists' use of social surveys certainly does reveal *some* interest in what people think about social issues, even if those thoughts are narrowly restricted—as many survey respondents are forced to choose between options such as "yes" or "no" or "on a scale of 1 to 5." Moreover, objectivists engage in debunking: they seek to replace public misconceptions with accurate information. This is a laudable goal and a partial overlap with constructionism, insofar as objectivists focus on people's interpretations of social issues. However, a partial overlap does not make the two perspectives identical.

As long as objectivists' main focus is to find out the truth about social problems, then any attention they give to subjective matters will tend to be secondary. Constructionists think that objectivist scholars almost always give short shrift to claimsmaking. To remedy this neglect, constructionists spend more time studying, and in greater detail, the diverse range of claims that are made about problems, the individuals and groups who are producing and consuming those claims, the factors that influence which claims are made and whether they are accepted, and other subjective dimensions of social problems. Moreover, constructionists tend to be far more skeptical of expert knowledge, including the research produced by objectivist scholars. Objectivist research is often treated as a form of claimsmaking in constructionist analyses.

A second overlap is that constructionists do pay (some) attention to objective matters. Constructionists focus primarily on interpretive matters, but they do make assumptions and arguments about objective reality. For example, constructionists want to treat social contexts—such as cultural beliefs, economic interests, and the presence of different audiences—as real, in that they can shape whether a problem is noticed and what types of claims are made about it. Or, at the very least, "acts of claimsmaking" are treated by constructionists as real events in an observable world.

One subcamp of constructionist scholars, sometimes called "strict constructionists," attempts to minimize or eradicate any mention of objective reality in their work. Another subcamp, sometimes called "contextual constructionists," feels more comfortable incorporating objectivist concerns into their analyses. Both subcamps make claimsmaking their primary focus, which separates them from objectivists. However, both subcamps also reference objective reality—even strict constructionists can't help but do so on occasion. As a result, here too is a complicating overlap that will likely always remain between the objectivist and constructionist approaches to social problems, no matter how "strictly interpretive" a scholar attempts to be.

A third threat to the distinctiveness of constructionism concerns terminology. Constructionists can be difficult to distinguish from objectivists because both kinds of scholars use the exact same concepts to make very different arguments. Some constructionists like to think that they "own" the term *construction*," but sadly it just isn't so. The term was popularized by interpretive scholars, but they can't control how others use it. Anyone—including an objectivist—can say that he or she is studying "the social construction of reality," or that they are investigating how reality is created, produced, maintained, changed, and so on. All of these concepts can be given a relatively objective or interpretive spin; their meaning is flexible.[2]

For example, objectivists might use constructionist-sounding terms to analyze the problem of divorce. The rate of marital dissolution in a society, they might argue, is "socially constructed" because it is contingent upon or shaped by a number of social factors, such as the laws that make it difficult (or easy) to obtain a divorce, the stigma (or lack thereof) that is attached to divorce, and the employment opportunities that women have (or not) to support themselves on their own. The divorce rate in a society is contingent on a number of social factors. Thus this objective social problem could be described as something that is "not automatic" since it is "created" or "constructed" as people make choices in response to the opportunities and constraints they face.

This is not what interpretive scholars mean by "constructionism." Nor is it the meaning we have given the term in this book. When interpretive scholars say that social problems are constructed, they are focused on the creation of meaning rather than on the creation of objective conditions. Their main focus is on the construction of versions or understandings of problems, not of the objective reality of the problems themselves. The problem of divorce, then, would be handled differently by interpretive scholars. A constructionist scholar would focus on claimsmaking about divorce. In order for divorce to exist as a (subjective) problem in society, some person or group has to notice it, interpret it as bothersome, tell others about it, and so on. Not everyone agrees that the divorce rate is a problem—it could be portrayed as beneficial in many respects (e.g., people aren't stuck in bad marriages). Among those who agree that divorce is a problem, interpretations will vary with respect to its causes (e.g., "selfishness," "lack of faith in God," "gender inequality"), the rate at which it is happening (e.g., disagreements over measurement strategies), what to do about it (e.g., mandatory premarital counseling, providing greater financial supports to low-income families, convincing husbands to do more housework), and other aspects of the problem. A constructionist's first priority would be to investigate the full range of claims that are made about the problem of divorce, and to study who is making them, the kinds of rhetorical strategies claimsmakers use, how their audiences react to the claims, and so on. For a constructionist, the problem of divorce is created when people talk it into being. Objective and interpretive scholars may at times use an overlapping terminology, but their work differs greatly.

Thus there are at least three reasons that people may doubt that constructionism provides a distinct framework for the analysis of social problems: objectivist scholars pay (some) attention to subjective matters, constructionist scholars pay (some) attention to objective matters, and both sets of scholars use the same terminology to make different kinds of arguments. Despite these overlaps, we have argued that constructionism still offers a distinct and alternative framework. Its differences with objectivism may at times be merely a matter of degree, but the degrees are large and can have important consequences for how we think about and study social problems.

Final Thoughts

All perspectives are imperfect. Every point of view has its blind spots and biases, and constructionism is no different. A constructionist orientation emphasizes meanings over facts, and for that reason (among

others) it is not universally loved or adopted. Nevertheless, a constructionist perspective has much to offer—as the diverse chapters of
this book have demonstrated. Anyone who wants to learn to think
carefully and deeply about social problems should explore the main
tenets, concepts, and findings of constructionist research.

Given the large number of social problems claims that we are
continuously exposed to, it is tempting to act gullibly (and simply
believe what we hear) or cynically (and disbelieve or ignore what we
hear). When possible, a more sensible option is to chart a middle
path: to think *critically* about social problems. We believe that constructionism provides some very helpful tools for intelligently analyzing the claimsmaking that pervades our private lives and public
discourse. We hope you'll agree.

Notes

1. At the same time, Herbert Blumer (1971, p. 305) does encourage
objectivist scholars to continue to attempt to collect objective facts about
social problems, correct misinformation, and guide policy discussions.

2. It may be frustrating to realize that social scientists do not agree on
how to define and use their basic terminology. Scholars are human beings,
and as such they make creative use of words. Every reader of this book does
the same thing. Consider a brief example. You probably have used the word
"ball" (or "balls") to refer to a soccerball, a football, a baseball, a baseball
that is pitched outside the strike zone (as in "the count is three balls and two
strikes"), a formal dance, sexual intercourse, testicles, courage ("he's got
balls"), or intelligence ("she's on the ball"), among other options. If you can
give so many different meanings to a single word, so too can scholars. As
speakers and listeners, and as writers and readers, our task is to try to be
clear about what particular meaning is being assigned to a term, in the current context of its use. We would argue that, compared to laypersons, scholars spend more time and effort trying to clearly define their terms.

References

About Nantucket." 2011. Town and County of Nantucket. Retrieved August 6, 2011. http://nantucket-ma.gov/Pages/NantucketMA_WebDocs/about.

Ackerman, Lisa. 2011. "Our Story." Irvine, CA: Talk About Curing Autism. Retrieved November 5, 2011. http://www.tacanow.org/about-taca/our-story.

Alaska Bridge Veterinary Services. 2011. "Products." Retrieved September 27, 2011. http://bridgevet.com

Alasuutari, Paul. 2008. "Constructionist Research and Globalization." Pp. 767–783 in *Handbook of Constructionist Research,* edited by James Holstein and Jaber Gubrium. New York: Guilford.

Alexander, Bruce K. 2008. *The Globalization of Addiction: A Study in the Poverty of Spirit.* New York: Oxford University Press.

Alexander, Steve. 2001. "Arguing over the Phone; Look, No Hands." *Star Tribune,* July 16.

Alpert, Elaine J. 2001. "Have We Overlooked the Most Common Cause of Maternal Mortality in the United States?" *Journal of Midwifery and Women's Health* 46:3.

Altheide, David L. 1992. "Gonzo Justice." *Symbolic Interaction* 15:69–86.

———. 1996. *Qualitative Media Analysis.* Thousand Oaks, CA: Sage.

Altheide, David L., and Robert P. Snow. 1979. *Media Logic.* Beverly Hills: Sage.

American Heart Association. 2010. "A History of Trans Fat." Retrieved March 22, 2011. http://www.heart.org/HEARTORG/GettingHealthy/FatsAndOils/Fats101/A-History-of-Trans-Fat_UCM_301463_Article.jsp.

American Psychiatric Association. 2010. "APA Announces Draft Diagnostic Criteria for DSM-5." February 10. Retrieved September 30, 2011. http://www.dsm5.org/Newsroom/Documents/Diag%20%20Criteria%20 General%20FINAL%202.05.pdf.

Americans for Nonsmokers' Rights. 2011. "Smokefree Legislative Recap and Vision for 2012." *ANR Update,* 30(4), Winter. Retrieved June 6, 2012. http://www.no-smoke.org.

———. 2012. "Overview List—How Many Smokefree Laws?" Retrieved June 6, 2012. http://www.no-smoke.org.

Amnesty International. 2010. "Deadly Delivery: The Maternal Health Care Crisis in the USA." Retrieved September 1, 2011. http://www .amnestyusa.org/dignity/pdf/DeadlyDelivery.pdf.

Andrews, Edmund. 2007. "Fed Shrugged As Subprime Crisis Spread." *New York Times,* December 18.

Angel Ashes. 2011. Homepage. Retrieved September 10, 2011. http://www .angelashes.com.

Anonymous. 1723. *Onania, or the Heinous Sin of Self-Pollution and All of Its Frightful Consequences, in Both Sexes Considered, with Spiritual and Physical Advice to Those Who Have Already Injured Themselves with This Abominable Practice.* 9th ed. London: Elizabeth Rumball for Thomas Crouch, Bookseller.

Anthony Eddy's Wildlife Studio. 2011. Homepage. Retrieved September 10, 2011. http://www.pet-animalpreservation.com.

Appleyard, Bryan. 2008. "Nassim Nicholas Taleb: The Prophet of Doom and Boom." *Times of London,* June 1.

Arch City Madman. 2011. "Illinois Encourages People to Smoke!" *The Great Illuminator,* March 30. Retrieved June 10, 2011. http://www .thegreatilluminator.com.

ARI (Autism Research Institute). 2009a. "The Autism Collaboration's 'Parents as Partners' Research Initiative." San Diego, CA: Autism Research Institute. Retrieved December 23, 2009. http://www.autism .org/guidingprincipals.htm.

———. 2009b. "The Autism Explosion." San Diego, CA: Autism Research Institute. Retrieved November 17, 2009. http://www.autism.com/ari /editorials/ed_explosion.htm.

———. 2009c. "Our Partners." San Diego, CA: Autism Research Institute. Retrieved November 17, 2009. http://www.autism.com/ari/partners.htm.

Atrash, Hani K., Herschel W. Lawson, Tedd V. Ellerbrock, Diane L. Rowley, and Lisa M. Koonin. N.d. (circa 1995). "Pregnancy-Related Mortality." Pp. 141–154 in *From Data to Action: CDC's Public Health Surveillance for Women, Infants, and Children,* edited by Lynne S. Wilcox and James S. Marks. Washington, DC: US Department of Health and Human Services, Public Health Service, Centers for Disease Control and Prevention.

Badkhen, Anna. 2008. "Three Teen Suicides Shake Nantucket." *Boston Globe,* January 16.

Baker, Chris, and Pasuk Phongpaichit. 2005. *A History of Thailand.* New York: Cambridge University Press.

Baker, Jeffrey P. 2008. "Mercury, Vaccines, and Autism: One Controversy, Three Histories." *American Journal of Public Health* 98:244–253.

Bangkok Post. 2005a. "SOS to the World: Please Visit." January 17.

———. 2005b. "A Heart-Warming Response." January 23.

———. 2005c. "Big Spender May Grow Small." October 4.

Barker, Kristin K. 2008. "Electronic Support Groups, Patient-Consumers, and Medicalization: The Case of Contested Illness." *Journal of Health and Social Behavior* 49:20–36.

Bartosch, William J., and Gregory C. Pope. 2002. "Economic Effect of Restaurant Smoking Restrictions on Restaurant Business in Massachusetts, 1992 to 1998." *Tobacco Control* 11(suppl. 2):ii38–42.

Bass, Sharon L. 1988. "The Growth of Car Phones Is Busy, Busy." *New York Times,* December 11.

Bauman, Zygmunt. 1987. *Legislators and Interpreters: On Modernity, Post-Modernity, and Intellectuals.* Cambridge: Polity.

Baxter, Christopher. 2008. "June Grad Was 4th in Less Than 2 Years." *Boston Globe,* August 11.

Bean, Allison. 2006. "Medical Experts Hope to Have Internet Addiction Recognized More Often." *Washington Square News,* April 11.

Becker, Howard S. 1963. *Outsiders: Studies in the Sociology of Deviance.* New York: Free Press.

Begley, Sharon. 2009. "The Vaccine-Autism Scare." *Newsweek,* March 2.

Bell, Alan, and Martin S. Weinberg. 1979. *Homosexualities: A Study of Diversity Among Men and Women.* New York: Simon and Schuster.

Beloved Pet Cremation Service. 2011. Homepage. Retrieved September 10, 2011. http://www.belovedpetcremation.com.

Bennett, Jon, William Bertrand, Clare Harkin, Stanley Samarasinghe, and Hemantha Wickramatillake. 2006. *Coordination of International Humanitarian Assistance in Tsunami-Affected Countries.* London: Tsunami Evaluation Coalition.

Benson, Rodney, and Abigail C. Saguy. 2005. "Constructing Social Problems in an Age of Globalization: A French-American Comparison." *American Sociological Review* 70:233–259.

Bernanke, Ben. 2006. "Outlook of the U.S. Economy." Statement before the Joint Economic Committee, US Congress, April 27. Retrieved October 15, 2011. http://www.federalreserve.gov/newsevents/testimony/bernanke 20060427a.htm.

Bernard, S., A. Enayati, L. Redwood, H. Roger, and T. Binstock. 2001. "Autism: A Novel Form of Mercury Poisoning." *Medical Hypotheses* 56:462–471.

Berns, Nancy. 2011. *Closure: The Rush to End Grief and What It Costs Us.* Philadelphia: Temple University Press.

Best, Joel. 1987. "Rhetoric in Claims-Making: Constructing the Missing Children Problem." *Social Problems* 34:101–121.

———. 1989. *Images of Issues: Typifying Contemporary Social Problems.* New York: Aldine de Gruyter.

———. 1990. *Threatened Children: Rhetoric and Concern About Child-Victims.* Chicago: University of Chicago Press.

——— (ed.). 1995. *Images of Issues: Typifying Contemporary Social Problems.* 2nd ed. New York: Aldine de Gruyter.

———. 1997. "Victimization and the Victim Industry." *Society* 34 (May–June):9–17.

———. 1999. *Random Violence: How We Talk About New Crimes and New Victims.* Berkeley: University of California Press.

———. 2001. *Damned Lies and Statistics: Untangling Numbers for the Media, Politicians, and Activists.* Berkeley: University of California Press.

———. 2004. *More Damned Lies and Statistics: How Numbers Confuse Public Issues.* Berkeley: University of California Press.

———. 2008. *Social Problems.* New York: Norton.

Best, Joel, and Gerald Horiuchi. 1985. "The Razor Blade in the Apple: The Social Construction of Urban Legends." *Social Problems* 32:488–499.

Best Friends of Mississippi. 2011. Homepage. Retrieved September 27, 2011. http://www.bestfrnds.com.

Bhargava, Vanity, and Wmil Bolongaita. 2004. *Challenging Corruption in Asia.* Washington, DC: World Bank.

Blaxill, Mark F. 2004. "What's Going On: The Question of Time Trends in Autism." *Public Health Reports* 119:536–551.

Blaxill, Mark F., L. Redwood, and S. Bernard. 2004. "Thimerosal and Autism: A Plausible Hypothesis That Should Not Be Dismissed." *Medical Hypotheses* 62:788–794.

Bloch, Jon. P. 1998. *New Spirituality, Self, and Belonging: How New Agers and Neo-Pagans Talk About Themselves.* Westport: Praeger.

Blume, Elaine. 1988. "The Truth About Trans: Hydrogenated Oils Aren't Guilty As Charged." *Nutrition Action Healthletter* 15:8–10.

Blumer, Herbert. 1971. "Social Problems as Collective Behavior." *Social Problems* 18:298–306.

Bogard, Cynthia J. 2003. *Seasons Such as These: How Homelessness Took Shape in America.* Hawthorne, NY: Aldine de Gruyter.

"Boston Education Level Profile and Enrollment Statistics." 2011. CLRSearch. Retrieved September 19, 2011. http://www.clrsearch.com/Boston _Demographics/MA/Education-Level-and-Enrollment-Statistics.

Bourdieu, Pierre. 1984. *Distinction: A Social Critique of the Judgement of Taste.* London: Routledge and Kegan Paul.

Boustany, Nora. 2005. "A Swede's New Challenge." *Washington Post,* June 22.

Boyce, Patricia Simino. 1998. "The Social Construction of Bereavement: An Application to Pet Loss." Unpublished PhD dissertation, City University of New York.

Boyle, Elizabeth, Fortunata Songora, and Gail Foss. 2001. "International Discourse and Local Politics: Anti-Female-Genital-Cutting Laws in Egypt, Tanzania, and the United States." *Social Problems* 48:524–544.

Bradley, Gregory, and Cherylynn Becker. 2011. "An Assessment of the Impact of a Voluntary Smoking Ban on Casino Visitation." *Proceedings of the Academy for Studies in Business* 3(1):1–6.

Bragg, Mary Ann. 2008. "Nantucket Teen's Death an Apparent Suicide." *Cape Cod Times.* August 10.

Brainard, Curtis. 2010. "Maternal Mortality Mix-Up/Press Turns Out Disjointed Coverage of Politics, Data." *Columbia Journalism Review: The Observatory.* Retrieved April 17, 2010. http://www.cjr.org/the _observatory/maternal_mortality_mixup.php.

Brandt, Eric J. 2011. "Deception of Trans Fats on Food and Drug Administration Food Labels: A Proposed Revision to the Presentation of Trans Fats on Food Labels." *American Journal of Health Promotion* 25:157–158.

Brody, Jane E. 1997. "Making Sense of Latest Twist on Fat in the Diet." *New York Times,* November 25.

Brokopp, John. 2009. "Smoking Ban May Not Be All That Ails Illinois Casinos." *Casino City Times,* May 20. Retrieved July 23, 2011. http://brokopp.casinocitytimes.com.

Brown, Angela K. 2005. "Man Accused of Killing Pregnant Ex-girlfriend, Her Son." *Denton Record-Chronicle,* February 23.

Brown, Curt. 1996. "Cabbie Sues Motorist Who Rear-Ended Him, Blaming Cellular Phone." *Star Tribune,* June 22.

———. 2007. "Eyes Are Everywhere but on the Road." *Star Tribune,* January 27.

Brown, Phil. 1992. "Popular Epidemiology and Toxic Waste Contamination: Lay and Professional Ways of Knowing." *Journal of Health and Social Behavior* 33:267–281.

———. 1995. "Naming and Framing: The Social Construction of Diagnosis and Illness." *Journal of Health and Social Behavior* 35(extra issue):34–52.

———. 1997. "Popular Epidemiology Revisited." *Current Sociology* 45:137–156.

Buekens, Piere. 2001. "Editorial: Is Estimating Maternal Mortality Useful?" *Bulletin of the World Health Organization* 79(3):179.

Bullough, Vern L. 1977. "Challenges to Societal Attitudes Toward Homosexuality in the Late Nineteenth and Early Twentieth Centuries." *Social Science Quarterly* 58:29–44.

Burris, Val, Emery Smith, and Ann Strahm. 2000. "White Supremacist Networks on the Internet." *Sociological Focus* 33:215–235.

Carnes, Patrick. 1983. *The Sexual Addiction.* Minneapolis: Compcare.

———. 1992. *Don't Call It Love: Recovery from Sexual Addiction.* New York: Bantam.

———. 1997. "Sex Addiction Q&A." Retrieved on May 29, 2007. http://www .sexhelp.com/sa_q_and_a.cfm.

———. 2001. *Out of the Shadows: Understanding Sexual Addiction.* 3rd ed. City Center, MN: Hazelden.

Case, Karl, and Robert Shiller. 2003. "Is There a Bubble in the Housing Market?" *Brookings Papers on Economic Activity* 2:299–362.

———. 2006. "Full House." *Wall Street Journal,* August 30.

Cassidy, John. 2009. *How Markets Fail: The Logic of Economic Calamities.* New York: Farrar, Straus, and Giroux.

CDC (Centers for Disease Control). 1998. "Maternal Mortality: United States, 1982–1996." *MMWR [Morbidity and Mortality Weekly Report]* 47:705–707.

———. 1999. "Achievement in Public Health, 1900–1999: Healthier Mothers and Babies." *MMWR [Morbidity and Mortality Weekly Report]* 48:849–858.

———. 2010. "How Many Children Have Autism?" Retrieved September 19, 2011. http://www.cdc.gov/ncbddd/features/counting-autism.html.

CEMD (Confidential Enquires in Maternal Deaths). 2001. *Why Mothers Die, 1997–1999: The Fifth Report of the Confidential Enquires in Maternal Deaths in the United Kingdom.* London: Royal College of Obstetrics and Gynaecologists Press.

Cha, Ariana Eunjung. 2007. "In China, Stern Treatment for Young Internet 'Addicts.'" *Washington Post,* February 22.

Chang, Jeani, Laurie D. Elam-Evans, Cynthia J. Berg, Joy Henderson, Lisa Flowers, Kristi A. Seed, and Carla J. Syverson. 2003. "Pregnancy-Related Mortality Surveillance: United States, 1991–1999. *Surveillance Summaries, MMWR [Morbidity and Mortality Weekly Report]* 52(SS-2):1–8.

Chang, Jeani, Cynthia J. Saltzman, and Linda E. Herndon. 2005. "Homicide: A Leading Cause of Injury Deaths Among Pregnant and Postpartum Women in the United States, 1991–1999." *American Journal of Public Health* 95:471–477.

Cheng, Maria. 2010. "Lancet: Sharp Drop in Maternal Deaths Worldwide." Associated Press. Retrieved April 15, 2010. http://www.google .com/hostednews/ap/article/ALeqM5j-phKb8xCQcxd8xanFFF7f1IN3o AD9F2UIVO0.

Chermak, Steven M. 1994. "Crime in the News Media: A Refined Understanding of How Crime Becomes News." Pp. 95–130 in *Media,*

Process, and the Social Construction of Crime: Studies in Newsmaking Criminology, edited by Gregg Barak. New York: Garland.

Christiansen, Lydia R. 2006. "Pregnancy-Associated Deaths: A 15-Year Retrospective Study and Overall Review of Maternal Pathophysiology." *American Journal of Forensic Medicine and Pathology* 27:11–19.

Clare, Linda, Julia M. Rowlands, and Rebecca Quin. 2008. "Collective Strength: The Impact of Developing a Shared Social Identity in Early-Stage Dementia." *Dementia* 7:9–30.

Clark, Candace. 1997. *Misery and Company: Sympathy in Everyday Life.* Chicago: University of Chicago Press.

Clark, Nigel. 2006. "Disaster and Generosity." *Geographical Journal* 171:384–386.

Clausen, Lisbeth. 2004. "Localizing the Global: 'Domestication' Processes in International News Production." *Media, Culture, Society* 26:25–44.

Coates, Heather. 2009. "Autism Spectrum Disorders: Wading Through the Controversies on the Web." *Medical Reference Services Quarterly* 28:259–267.

Cohen, Paula H. 2006. "Trans Fats: The Story Behind the Label." *Harvard Public Health Review,* Spring. Retrieved April 3, 2011. http://www .hsph.harvard.edu/review/rvw_spring06/txt_spring06_transfats.html?__ utma=1.113061817.1333501102.1333501102.1333501102.1.

Connelly, Marjorie. 2009. "Many in U.S. Want Texting at the Wheel to be Illegal." *New York Times,* November 1.

Conner, Ken. 2007. "A Selfless Pro-Life Choice: Adoption as an Alternative to Abortion." Lifenews.com, May 14. Retrieved September 25, 2011. http://www.lifenews.com/2007/05/14/nat-3118.

Conrad, Peter. 2007. *The Medicalization of Society: On the Transformation of Human Conditions into Treatable Disorders.* Baltimore: Johns Hopkins University Press.

Consumer News and Business Channel. 2009. "The Investors." *House of Cards,* February 12. Retrieved October 15, 2011. http://www .cnbc.com/id/15840232?video=1029066462&play=1.

Cook, Gretchen. 2004. "Laci Peterson's Murder Dramatizes Common Danger." Women's E-News. Retrieved January 1, 2006. http://www .womensenews.org.article.cfm/dyn/aid/2069/context/archive.

Cornog, Martha. 2003. *The Big Book of Masturbation: From Angst to Zeal.* San Francisco: Down There Press.

Cosgrave, John. 2007. *Synthesis Report: Expanded Summary—Joint Evaluation of the International Response to the Indian Ocean Tsunami.* London: Tsunami Evaluation Coalition.

Craig, Albert, William Graham, Donald Kagan, Steven Ozment, and Frank Turner. 2000. *The Heritage of World Civilizations.* Vol. 2. Upper Saddle River, NJ: Prentice Hall.

Cristol, Richard E. 2002. *Re: Docket No. 94P-0036; Food Labeling: Trans Fatty Acids in Nutrition Labeling, Nutrient Content Claims, and Health Claims; Reopening of the Comment Period.* Washington, D.C. National Association of Margarine Manufacturers. Retrieved June 14, 2012. http://www.fda.gov/ohrms/dockets/dailys/02/Dec02/121602/94p-0036 -c002283-vol67.pdf.

CSPI (Center for Science in the Public Interest). 2011a. "About CSPI." Retrieved September 28, 2011. http://www.cspinet.org/about/index.html.

———. 2011b. "Highlights from 40 Years of Accomplishments." Center for Science in the Public Interest. Retrieved May 10, 2011. http://www .cspinet.org/about/accomplishments.html.

CTIA (Cellular Telecommunications Industry Association). 2011. "The Wireless Industry Overview." Retrieved September 17, 2011. http://www .ctia.org/advocacy/policy_topics/topic.cfm/TID/17/CTID/3#3.

Dannenberg, A. L., M. D. Carter, H. W. Lawson, D. M. Ashton, S. F. Dorfman, and E. H. Graham. 1995. "Homicide and Other Injuries as Causes of Maternal Death in New York City, 1987 Through 1991." *American Journal of Obstetrics and Gynecology* 172:1557–1564.

Darby, Robert. 2003. "The Masturbation Taboo and the Rise of Routine Male Circumcision: A Review of the Historiography." *Journal of Social History* 36:738–757.

Davies, P., S. Chapman, and J. Leask. 2002. "Antivaccination Activists on the World Wide Web." *Archives of Disease in Childhood* 87(1):22–25.

Davis, Joseph E. 2005. *Accounts of Innocence: Sexual Abuse, Trauma, and the Self.* Chicago: University of Chicago Press.

DCMS (Department of Culture, Media, and Sport). 2003a. *Report of the Working Group on Human Remains.* London.

———. 2003b. *Scoping Survey of Historic Human Remains in English Museums Undertaken on Behalf of the Ministerial Working Group on Human Remains.* London.

De Moraes, Lisa. 2011. "By Holding Court in Caylee Case, 'Nancy Grace' Reigns Supreme." *Washington Post,* July 7.

deFiebre, Conrad. 2005. "'Hang Up and Drive' Is Law on Sunday." *Star Tribune,* December 30.

DeJohn Pet Services. 2011. Homepage. Retrieved September 26, 2011. http://www.dejohnpetservices.com.

D'Emilio, John. 1997. "Capitalism and Gay Identity." Pp. 169–178 in *The Gender Sexuality Reader: Culture, History, Political Economy,* edited by Roger N. Lancaster and Micaela di Leonardo. New York: Routledge.

Dietz, Patricia M., and Roger W. Rochat. 1998. "Differences in the Risk of Homicide and Other Fatal Injuries Between Postpartum Women and Other Women of Childbearing Age: Implications for Prevention." *American Journal of Public Health* 88:641–643.

Dignified Pet Services. 2011. Homepage. Retrieved September 20, 2011. http://dignifiedpetservices.com.

DiMaggio, Paul, Eszter Hargittai, W. Russell Neuman, and John P. Robinson. 2001. "Social Implications of the Internet." *Annual Review of Sociology* 27:307–336.

Donn, Jeff. 1999. "Study Finds 6% of Internet Users Have Addiction to It." *Herald-Sun,* August 23.

Drea, Kathy. 2011. "Revenue Comparison – Rock Island IL Casino (Smokefree) vs Davenport IA Casino (Allows Smoking)." Smokefreecasinos-talk Google Group, August 5. Retrieved June 6, 2012. http://groups.google .com/group/smokefreecasinos-talk/.

Dream Land Pet Memorial Center. 2011. Homepage. Retrieved September 15, 2011. http://dreamlandpetcremation.com.

Drezner, Daniel W., and Henry Farrell. 2004. "Web of Influence." *Foreign Policy* 145:32–40.

Dumenco, Simon. 2008. "Are Always-Connected Consumers Really Virtual Crackheads?" AdAge Mediaworks, March 31. Retrieved April 3, 2012. http://adage.com/article/the-media-guy/connected-consumers-virtual -crackheads/125987.

Dunn, Jennifer L. 2010. *Judging Victims: Why We Stigmatize Survivors and How They Reclaim Respect.* Boulder: Lynne Rienner.

Earl, Jennifer, and Alan Schussman. 2003. "The New Site of Activism: On-Line Organizations, Movement Entrepreneurs, and the Changing Location of Movement Decision Making." *Research in Social Movements, Conflicts, and Change* 24:155–187.

Ellis, Havelock. 1900. *Studies in the Psychology of Sex: The Evolution of Modesty, The Phenomena of Sexual Periodicity, Auto-Eroticism.* Philadelphia: F. A. Davis.

Ertelt, Steven. 2006. "Abortions Cause Severe Depression for Women, New Study Shows." Lifenews.com, January 2. Retrieved September 25, 2011. http://www.lifenews.com/2006/01/02/nat-1941.

———. 2009a. "Kansas Okays Abortion Ultrasound Bill: Governor Kathleen Sebelius Pressured to Sign." Lifenews.com, March 18. Retrieved September 25, 2011. http://www.lifenews.com/2009/03/18 /state-3954.

———. 2009b. "Post-Abortion Counselor Confirms Abortions Cause Women Mental Health Issues." Lifenews.com, January 14. Retrieved September 25, 2011. http://www.lifenews.com/2009/01/14/nat-4741.

———. 2009c. "Women Who Regret Their Abortions Will Speak Out at Upcoming March for Life." Lifenews.com, January 21. Retrieved September 25, 2011. http://www.lifenews.com/2009/01/21/nat-4766.

Faber, David. 2009. *And Then the Roof Caved In: How Wall Street's Greed and Stupidity Brought Capitalism to Its Knees.* Hoboken, NJ: Wiley.

Fackler, Martin. 2007. "In Korea, a Boot Camp Cure for Web Obsession." *New York Times,* November 18.

Fairwinds Pet Loss and Memorial Services. 2011. Homepage. Retrieved September 10, 2011. http://www.fairwinds-forever.com.

"Family Planning Response." 2010. Nantucket Suicide Prevention Coalition, June. Retrieved May 8, 2011. http://www.nantucket-ma.gov/Pages /NantucketMA_HS/Questionaire%20responses.pdf.

Family Violence Prevention Fund. 2006. "Domestic Violence Is a Serious, Widespread Social Problem in America: The Facts." Retrieved April 15, 2006. http://www.endabuse.org/resources/facts.

FBI (Federal Bureau of Investigation). 2000. *Uniform Crime Reports.* Retrieved April 15, 2006. http://www.fbi.gov/ucr/ucr.htm.

Federwisch, Anne. 1997. "Internet Addiction?" *Nursing Week,* August 8. Retrieved September 30, 2010. http://www.nurseweek.com/features/97-8 /iadct.html.

Fessler, A. 2006. *The Girls Who Went Away: The Hidden History of Women Who Surrendered Children for Adoption in the Decades Before* Roe v. Wade. New York: Penguin.

Fforde, Cressida. 2001. "Submission to the Working Group on Human Remains." *Report of the Working Group on Human Remains.* London: Department of Culture, Media, and Sport.

Fforde, Cressida, and Jane Hubert. 2002. "Introduction: The Reburial Issue in the Twenty-First Century." Pp. 1–16 in *The Dead and Their Possessions,* edited by C. Fforde, J. Hubert, and P. Turnbull. London: Routledge.

Fildes, J., L. Reed, N. Jones, M. Martin, and J. Barrett. 1992. "Trauma: The Leading Cause of Maternal Death." *Journal of Trauma* 32:643–645.

Filipponio, Frank. 2007. "*Redline* Plays Fast and Furious with Exotics." *Autoblog,* January 6. Retrieved May 1, 2010. http://www.autoblog .com/2007/01/06/redline-plays-fast-and-furious-with-exotics.

Fishman, Mark, and Gray Cavender (eds.). 1998. *Entertaining Crime: Television Reality Programs.* Hawthorne, NY: Aldine de Gruyter.

Fitzpatrick, Michael. 2004. *MMR and Autism: What Parents Need to Know.* New York: Routledge.

———. 2009. *Defeating Autism: A Damaging Delusion.* New York: Routledge.

Fluke's Aftercare. 2011. Homepage. Retrieved September 15, 2011. http://www .flukesaftercare.com.

Fontaine, J., and A. M. Parmley. 2007. "The Furor over Maternal Homicide: Are We Losing Sight of the Primary Issue?" *Criminal Justice Policy Review* 18:153–167.

Forever Pets. 2011. Homepage. Retrieved September 27, 2011. http://www .foreverpets.com.

Forum on Child and Family Statistics. 2005. "America's Children: Key National Indicators of Well-Being, 2005—Adolescent Mortality." Retrieved March 15, 2008. http://childstats.ed.gov/americaschildren/hea8.asp.

Foster, Hal (ed.). 1985. *Postmodern Culture*. London: Pluto.

Foti, Jim. 2010. "Keep Your Eyes on the Road: Federal Transportation Officials Are on a Mission to Ban Cell-Phone Use While Driving; Is That Overkill?" *Star Tribune,* January 13.

Foucault, Michel. 1988 [1986]. *The History of Sexuality: The Care of the Self*. Vol. 3. New York: Vintage.

———. 1990 [1978]. *The History of Sexuality: An Introduction*. Vol. 1. New York: Vintage.

Fox, Nick, Katie Ward, and Alan O'Rourke. 2005. "Pro-Anorexia, Weight-Loss Drugs, and the Internet: An 'Anti-Recovery' Explanatory Model of Anorexia." *Sociology of Health & Illness* 27:944–971.

Fox, Richard L., Robert W. Van Sickel, and Thomas L. Steiger. 2007. *Tabloid Justice: Criminal Justice in an Age of Media Frenzy*. Boulder: Lynne Rienner.

Freudenberg, Nicholas, Sarah P. Bradley, and Monica Serrano. 2009. "Public Health Campaigns to Change Industry Practices That Damage Health: An Analysis of 12 Case Studies." *Health Education and Behavior* 36:230–249.

Freudenberg, Nicholas, and Sandro Galea. 2008. "The Impact of Corporate Practices on Health: Implications for Health Policy." *Journal of Public Health Policy* 29:86–104.

Frye, V. 2001. "Examining Homicide's Contribution to Pregnancy-Related Deaths." *Journal of the American Medical Association* 285(11):21.

Fuld, Richard. 2008. "Testimony of Richard S. Fuld, Jr." US House of Representatives, Committee on Oversight and Government Reform, October 6.

Furedi, Frank. 2004. *Where Have All the Intellectuals Gone? Confronting 21st Century Philistinism*. London: Continuum.

———. 2006. "The End of Professional Dominance." *Society* 43 (November–December):14–18.

Garrett, Thomas A. and Michael R. Pakko. 2009. "The Illinois Smoking Ban and Casino Revenues." Federal Reserve Bank of St. Louis, Working Paper no. 2009-027A.

Gatrell, Anthony C., and Susan J. Elliott. 2009. *Geographies of Health: An Introduction*. 2nd ed. Malden, MA: Wiley-Blackwell.

Generation Rescue. 2009a. "Are We Poisoning Our Kids in the Name of Protecting Their Health?" Retrieved August 1, 2009. http://www.generationrescue.org.

———. 2009b. "Cal-Oregon Vaccinated vs. Unvaccinated Survey." Retrieved December 11, 2009. http://www.generationrescue.org/survey.html.

———. 2009c. "More Vaccines—More Autism." Retrieved October 4, 2009. http://www.generationrescue.org.

Gerber, Jeffrey S., and Paul A. Offit. 2009. "Vaccines and Autism: A Tale of Shifting Hypotheses." *Clinical Infectious Diseases* 48:456–461.

Gibson, Margaret. 1997. "Clitoral Corruption: Body Metaphors and American Doctors' Constructions of Female Homosexuality, 1870–1900." Pp. 108–132 in *Science and Homosexualities,* edited by Vernon A. Rosario. New York: Routledge.

Gillett, James. 2003. "Media Activism and Internet Use by People with HIV/AIDS." *Sociology of Health & Illness* 25:608–624.

Gittelsohn, John, and Ronald Campbell. 2007. "High Roller of Home Loans." *Orange County Register,* May 20. Retrieved May 1, 2010. http://www.ocregister.com/articles/loan-35300-quick-says.html.

Glantz, Stan A., and Lisa R. A. Smith. 1997. "The Effect of Ordinances Requiring Smoke-Free Restaurants and Bars on Revenues: A Follow-Up." *American Journal of Public Health* 87:1687–1693.

Glantz, Stan A., and Rebecca Wilson-Loots. 2003. "No Association of Smoke-Free Ordinances with Profits from Bingo and Charitable Games in Massachusetts." *Tobacco Control* 12:411–413.

Glassner, Barry. 1999. *The Culture of Fear: Why Americans Are Afraid of the Wrong Things.* New York: Basic.

Goldberg, Ivan. 1995. "Internet Addiction Disorder (IAD): Diagnostic Criteria." PsyCom.net, March 16. Retrieved September 30, 2010. http://web.urz.uni-heidelberg.de/Netzdienste/anleitung/wwwtips/8/addict.html.

Good Morning America. 2007. "Murder Is One of Top Causes of Death for Pregnant Women." June 26. Retrieved June 10, 2012. http://abcnews.go.com/GMA/story?id=3316485&page=1#.T9ehjBevKSo.

Good Shepherd Pet Services. 2011. Homepage. Retrieved September 20, 2011. http://www.goodshepherdpet.com/index.php.

Goodwin, Jeff, James M. Jasper, and Francesca Polletta (eds.). 2001. *Passionate Politics: Emotions and Social Movements.* Chicago: University of Chicago Press.

Governors Highway Safety Association. June 2011. "Cell Phone and Texting Laws." Retrieved June 24, 2011. http://www.ghsa.org/html/stateinfo/laws/cellphone_laws.html.

Graham, John D. 2001. "Prompt Letter." Retrieved May 11, 2011. http://www.reginfo.gov/public/prompt/hhs_prompt_letter.html.

———. 2003. "Statement of John D. Graham." Retrieved May 10, 2011. http://georgewbushwhitehouse.archives.gov/omb/legislative/testimony/graham/030930_graham.pdf.

Granja, A. C., E. Zacarias, and S. Bergstrom. 2002. "Violent Deaths: The Hidden Face of Maternal Mortality." *British Journal of Obstetrics and Gynecology* 187:1213–1216.

Greenfield, Jeanette. 2007. *The Return of Cultural Treasures.* 3rd ed. Cambridge: Cambridge University Press.

Grinker, Roy Richard. 2007. *Unstrange Minds: Remapping the World of Autism.* New York: Basic.

Grohol, John. 2008. "Teen Suicide on an Isolated Island." PsychCentral.com, January 16. Retrieved March 16, 2011. http://psychcentral.com/blog /archives/2008/01/16/teen-suicide-on-an-isolated-island/.

Guillen, Mauro E. 2001. "Is Globalization Civilizing, Destructive or Feeble? A Critique of Five Key Debates in the Social Science Literature." *Annual Review of Sociology* 27:235–260.

Gurak, Laura J., and John Logie. 2003. "Internet Protests, from Text to Web." Pp. 25–46 in *Cyberactivism: Online Activism in Theory and Practice*, edited by M. McCaughey and M. D. Ayers. New York: Routledge.

HAD (Honouring the Ancient Dead). N.d. (circa 2007). "HAD Feedback on the DCMS Guidance for the Care of Human Remains in Museums." Retrieved June 15, 2012. http://www.honour.org.uk/node/40.

Hardey, Michael. 1999. "Doctor in the House: The Internet as a Source of Lay Health Knowledge and the Challenge to Expertise." *Sociology of Health & Illness* 21:820–835.

———. 2001. "'E-Health': The Internet and the Transformation of Patients into Consumers and Producers of Health Knowledge." *Information, Communication & Society* 4:388–405.

Hardman, Charlotte, and Graham. Harvey (eds.). 2000. *Pagan Pathways: A Complete Guide to the Ancient Earth Traditions*. London: Thorsons.

Harris, Gardiner, and Anahad O'Connor. 2005. "On Autism's Cause, It's Parents vs. Research." *New York Times,* June 25.

Harris, Jenine K., Bobbi J. Carothers, Douglas A. Luke, Hiie Silmere, Timothy D. McBride, and Martin Pion. 2012. "Exempting Casinos from the Smoke-Free Illinois Act Will Not Bring Patrons Back: They Never Left." *Tobacco Control* 21(3):373–376.

Harris, Scott R. 2010. *What Is Constructionism? Navigating Its Use in Sociology.* Boulder: Lynne Rienner.

Harvey, Graham, and Charlotte Hardman (eds.). 1995. *Paganism Today: Wiccans, Druids, the Goddess, and Ancient Earth Traditions for the Twenty-First Century.* London: Thorsons.

Heaven's Pets. 2011. Homepage. Retrieved September 20, 2011. http://www .heavenspets.com.

Heavenly Paws Pet Cremations. 2011. Homepage. Retrieved September 18, 2011. http://www.heavenlypaws.com.

Hellman, Maria, and Kristina Riegert. 2009. "Transnational News and Crisis Reporting: The Indian Ocean Tsunami on CNN and Swedish TV4." Pp. 127–148 in *After the Tsunami: Crisis Communication in Finland and Sweden,* edited by Ullamaija Kivikuru and Lars Nord. Goteborg, Sweden: Nordicom.

Henderson, Diedtra. 1996. "Oh, What a Tangled Web Lonely Computer Addicts Weave." *Austin American-Statesman,* March 19.

Hendrick, Bill. 1997. "Web Is a Catalyst for Cupid, Compulsivity." *Times Union,* October 1.

Hilgartner, Stephen, and Charles Bosk. 1988. "The Rise and Fall of Social Problems: A Public Arenas Model." *American Journal of Sociology* 94:53–78.

Hilton, Jodi. 2007. "Less Homework, More Yoga, from a Principal Who Hates Stress." *New York Times,* October 27.

Hindustan Times. 2004. "Round the Clock Rescue, Relief Operations Mounted in Areas Hit by Tsunami Waves." December 27.

———. 2005a. "Thanks, but No Thanks." January 5.

———. 2005b. "Tsunami All Over TV." January 8.

Ho, Elanor M., JoAnne Brown, William Graves, and Michael K. Lindsay. 2002. "Maternal Death at an Inner-City Hospital, 1949–2000." Paper presented at the annual meeting of the Society for Maternal-Fetal Medicine, New Orleans.

Hochschild, Arlie Russell. 1979. "Emotion Work, Feeling Rules, and Social Structure." *American Journal of Sociology* 85:551–575.

———. 1983. *The Managed Heart: The Commercialization of Human Feeling.* Berkeley: University of California Press.

Hodge, Warren. 2005. "With $2 Billion Donated, U.N. Now Needs Help to Deliver Aid." *New York Times,* January 2.

Holstein, James A., and Jaber F. Gubrium (eds.). 2008. *Handbook of Constructionist Research.* New York: Guilford.

Holstein, James A., and Gale Miller (eds.). 2003. *Challenges and Choices: Constructionist Perspectives on Social Problems.* Hawthorne, NY: Aldine de Gruyter.

Hooker, Evelyn. 1957. "The Adjustment of the Male Overt Homosexual." *Journal of Projective Techniques* 21:18–31.

Horon, Isabelle L. 2005. "Underreporting of Maternal Deaths on Death Certificates and the Magnitude of the Problem of Maternal Mortality." *American Journal of Public Health* 95:478–482.

Horon, Isabelle L., and Diana Cheng. 2001. "Enhanced Surveillance for Pregnancy-Associated Mortality: Maryland, 1993–1998." *Journal of the American Medical Association* 285:1455–1459.

IITAP (International Institute for Trauma and Addiction Professionals). 2001. "What Is Sexual Addiction." Retrieved June 12, 2007. http://www.iitap.com/general_definitions.cfm.

Inderfurth, Karl, David Fabrycky, and Stephen Cohen. 2005. "The 2004 Indian Ocean Tsunami: Six Month Report." Washington, DC: Sigur Center for Asian Studies.

Institute of Medicine. 2005. "Dietary Reference Intakes for Energy, Carbohydrate, Fiber, Fat, Fatty Acids, Cholesterol, Protein, and Amino Acids." National Academies Press. Retrieved June 14, 2012. http://www.nap.edu/catalog/10490.html.

———. 2011. *Adverse Effects of Vaccines: Evidence and Causality.* Washington, DC: National Academy of Sciences.

IoI (Institute of Ideas). 2003. "Objects to Bury or Ancestors to Study?" Debate transcript. London.

Irvine, Janice M. 2005 [1991]. *Disorders of Desire: Sexuality and Gender in Modern American Sexology.* Philadelphia: Temple University Press.

Jackson, Brian. 1997. "Hooked on Net? Join the Crowd." *Chicago Sun-Times,* August 16.

Jakarta Post. 2005a. "Global Relief." January 4.

———. 2005b. "Role of Donors in Reconstruction." January 18.

———. 2005c. "Acehnese Want Foreign Volunteers to Stay." March 26.

Jaroff, Leon. 1991. "A Crusader from the Heartland: Philip Sokolof." *Time,* March 25.

Jasparro, Christopher. 2005. "Opportunities in Tsunami's Wake." *Jakarta Post,* March 30.

Jasti, Sunitha, and Szilvia Kovacs. 2010. "Use of Trans Fat Information on Food Labels and Its Determinants in a Multiethnic College Student Population." *Journal of Nutrition Education and Behavior* 42:307–314.

Jenkins, Philip. 1998. *Moral Panic: Changing Concept of the Child Molester in Modern America.* New Haven: Yale University Press.

Jenkins, Tiffany 2010. *Contesting Human Remains in Museum Collections: The Crisis of Cultural Authority.* New York: Routledge.

Johnson, John M. 1995. "Horror Stories and the Construction of Child Abuse." Pp. 17–32 in *Images of Issues: Typifying Contemporary Social Problems,* 2nd ed., edited by Joel Best. Hawthorne, NY: Aldine de Gruyter.

Johnson, Keith R. 2006. "Biostatistician or Women's Advocate? Adaptation in the Maternal Mortality Profession." Paper presented at the annual meeting of the American Sociological Association, Montreal.

Johnson, Nicola F. 2009. *The Multiplicities of Internet Addiction: The Misrecognition of Leisure and Learning.* Burlington, VT: Ashgate.

Johnson, Peter. 2006. "When It Comes to True Crime, Nancy Grace Is on the Case." *USA Today,* February 19.

Jones, Jeffrey M. 2010. "Americans Still Perceive Crime As On the Rise." Gallup Poll. Retrieved September 26, 2011. http://www.gallup.com /poll/144827/Americans-Perceive-Crime-Rise.as.

Jorion, Philippe. 1997. *Value at Risk: The New Benchmark for Controlling Market Risk.* New York: McGraw-Hill.

Joseph, Stephen L. 2003. "Citizen Petition Regarding Trans Fat Labeling." Bantransfats.com. Retrieved May 10, 2011. http://www.fda.gov/ohrms /dockets/dailys/03/Jun03/060303/94p-0036-cp00002–01-vol1.pdf.

Kahn, Richard, and Douglas Kellner. 2004. "New Media and Internet Activism: From the 'Battle of Seattle' to Blogging." *New Media Society* 6:87–95.

Kardiner, Abram. 1964. "The Flight from Masculinity." Pp. 17–39 in *The Problem of Homosexuality in Modern Society,* edited by Hendrik M. Ruitenbeek. New York: E. P. Dutton.

Katz, Jonathan Ned. 1995. *The Invention of Heterosexuality.* New York: Dutton.

Keck, Margaret E., and Kathryn Sikkink. 1998. *Activists Beyond Borders: Advocacy Networks in International Politics.* Ithaca: Cornell University Press.

Kellogg, Cecily. 2009. "Juno, or Why Adoption Isn't Cute." *Uppercase Woman,* January 22. Retrieved October 18, 2011. http://uppercase-woman.com/2008/01/22/juno-or-why-ado.

Kennedy, David. 1999. *Freedom from Fear: The American People in Depression and War, 1929–1945.* New York: Oxford University Press.

Kennedy, Hubert. 1997. "Karl Heinrich Ulrichs, First Theorist of Homosexuality." Pp. 26–45 in *Science and Homosexualities,* edited by Vernon A. Rosario. New York: Routledge.

Kerr, Margaret Anna. 2009. "The Autism Spectrum Disorders/Vaccine Link Debate: A Health Social Movement." Unpublished PhD dissertation, University of Pittsburgh.

Kessler, Glenn, and Robin Wright. 2005. "Earthquake Aid in Pakistan Might Help U.S. Image." *Washington Post,* October 13.

Killingbeck, Donna. 2001. "The Role of Television News in the Construction of School Violence as a 'Moral Panic.'" *Journal of Criminal Justice and Popular Culture* 8:186–202.

King, Marissa, and Peter Bearman. 2009. "Diagnostic Change and the Increased Prevalence of Autism." *International Journal of Epidemiology* 38:1224–1234.

Kinsey, Alfred C., Wardell B. Pomeroy, and Clyde E. Martin. 1948. *Sexual Behavior in the Human Male.* Philadelphia: Saunders.

Kirby, David. 2005. *Evidence of Harm: Mercury in Vaccines and the Autism Epidemic—A Medical Controversy.* New York: St. Martin's.

Klapper, Joseph T. 1960. *The Effects of Mass Communication.* New York: Free Press.

Koch-Weser, Susan, Ylisabyth S. Bradshaw, Lisa Gualtieri, and Susan S. Gallagher. 2010. "The Internet as a Health Information Source: Findings from the 2007 Health Information National Trends Survey and Implications for Health Communication." *Journal of Health Communication* 15:279–293.

Kogan, Michael D., Stephen J. Blumberg, Laura A. Schieve, Coleen A. Boyle, James M. Perrin, Reem M. Ghandour, Gopal K. Singh, Bonnie B. Strickland, Edwin Trevathan, and Peter C. van Dyck. 2009. "Prevalence of Parent-Reported Diagnosis of Autism Spectrum Disorder Among Children in the US, 2007." *Pediatrics* 124(4):1–9.

Koltnow, Barry. 2007. "Fast and Furious." *Orange County Register,* April 11.

Koonin, Lisa M., Andrea P. MacKay, Cynthia J. Berg, Hani K. Atrash, and Jack C. Smith. 1997. "Pregnancy-Related Mortality Surveillance,

United States, 1987–1990." *Surveillance Summaries, MMWR [Morbidity and Mortality Weekly Report]* 46(SS-4):17–36.

Kozup, J., S. Burton, and E. H. Creyer. 2006. "The Provision of Trans Fat Information and Its Interaction with Consumer Knowledge." *Journal of Consumer Affairs* 40:163–176.

Krafft-Ebing, R. V. 1904. *Psychopathia Sexualis with Especial Reference to Antipathic Sexual Instinct: A Medico-Forensic Study.* 10th ed. Translated by F. J. Rebman. New York: Rebman.

Kretser, Alison. 2003. "Request for Extension of Comment Period." Grocery Manufacturers of America. Retrieved May 10, 2011. http://www.fda.gov/ohrms/dockets/dailys/03/Sept03/092903/03n-0076-ext0005-vol1.pdf.

Krulewitch, Cara J., Marie Lydie Pierre-Louis, Regina de Leon-Gomez, Richard Guy, and Richard Green. 2001. "Hidden from View: Violent Deaths Among Pregnant Women in the District of Columbia, 1988–1996." *Journal of Midwifery and Women's Health* 46:4–10.

Krulewitch, Cara J., Darryl W. Roberts, and Linda S. Thompson. 2003. "Adolescent Pregnancy and Homicide: Findings from the Maryland Office of the Chief Medical Examiner, 1994–1998." *Child Maltreatment* 8:122–128.

LaHood, Ray, and Jim Guest. 2011. "New CR Poll: Younger Drivers More Likely to Text and Drive, Less Likely to View as a Danger." US Department of Transportation. Retrieved March 9, 2011. http://www.distraction.gov/files/for-media/2011/2011-03-04-cr-dot-distracted-driving-initiative.pdf.

Laqueur, Thomas W. 2003. *Solitary Sex: A Cultural History of Masturbation.* Brooklyn: Zone.

Lawson, Terry. 2007. "Redline." *Detroit Free Press,* April 20. Retrieved May 1, 2010. http://www.rottentomatoes.com/m/redline.

Lee, Ellie. 2003. *Abortion, Motherhood, and Mental Health.* New York: Aldine de Gruyter.

Lee, John D., Kristie L. Young, and Michael A. Regan. 2009. "Defining Driver Distraction." Pp. 31–40 in *Driver Distraction: Theory Effects and Mitigation,* edited by Michael A. Regan, John D. Lee, and Kristie L. Young. Boca Raton, FL: CRC Press.

Legator, Marvin S., Barbara L. Harper, and Michael J. Scott (eds.). 1985. *The Health Detective's Handbook: A Guide to the Investigation of Environmental Health Hazards by Nonprofessionals.* Baltimore: Johns Hopkins University Press.

Lemonick, Michael, and Alice Park. 1999. "Eating Smart." *Time,* July 19.

Letukas, Lynn, and John Barnshaw. 2008. "A World System Approach to Post-Catastrophe International Relief." *Social Forces* 87:1063–1987.

Letukas, Lynn, Anna Olofsson, and John Barnshaw. 2009. "Solidarity Trumps Catastrophe? An Empirical and Theoretical Analysis of Post-

Tsunami Media in Two Western Nations." Pp. 107–125 in *After the Tsunami: Crisis Communication in Finland and Sweden,* edited by Ullamaija Kivikuru and Lars Nord. Goteborg, Sweden: Nordicom.

Levere, Jane. 2005. "Making the World Better, One Vacation at a Time." *New York Times,* November 20.

Levine, Jerome. 1998. *The Clinton Syndrome: The President and the Self-Destructive Nature of Sexual Addiction.* New York: Crown.

Levitt, S., and L. Hadland. 2006. "Museums and Human Remains." Paper presented to: *Respect for Ancient British Human Remains conference.* November 17.

Lewis, Glen. 2006. *Virtual Thailand: The Media and Cultural Politics in Thailand, Malaysia, and Singapore.* New York: Routledge.

Lewis, Michael. 2010. *The Big Short: Inside the Doomsday Machine.* New York: Norton.

Lin, Chung-Tung J., and Steven T. Yen. 2010. "Knowledge of Dietary Fats Among US Consumers." *Journal of the American Dietetic Association* 110:613–618.

Ling, Rich. 2008. *New Tech, New Ties.* Cambridge: Massachusetts Institute of Technology Press.

Lofland, John. 2003. *Demolishing a Historic Hotel: A Sociology of Preservation Failure in Davis, California.* Davis, CA: Davis Research.

Loseke, Donileen R. 1992. *The Battered Woman and Shelters: The Social Construction of Wife Abuse.* Albany: State University of New York Press.

———. 2000. "Ethos, Pathos, and Social Problems: Reflections on Formula Narratives." *Perspectives on Social Problems* 12:41–54.

———. 2001. "Lived Realities and Formula Stories of 'Battered Women.'" Pp. 107–126 in *Institutional Selves: Troubled Identities in the Postmodern World,* edited by Jaber F. Gubrium and James A. Holstein. New York: Oxford University Press.

———. 2003. *Thinking About Social Problems: An Introduction to Constructionist Perspectives.* 2nd ed. Hawtorne, NY: Aldine de Gruyter.

Lowney, Kathleen S. 1999. *Baring Our Souls: T.V. Talk Shows and the Recovery of Religion.* Hawthorne, NY: Aldine de Gruyter.

———. 2008. "Claimsmaking, Culture, and the Media in the Social Construction Process." Pp. 331–353 in *Handbook of Constructionist Research,* edited by James Holstein and Jabir Gubrium. New York: Guilford.

Lundman, Richard J. 2003. "The Newsworthiness and Selection Bias in News About Murder: Comparative and Relative Effects of Novelty and Race and Gender Typifications on Newspaper Coverage of Homicide." *Sociological Forum* 18:357–386.

Lupton, Deborah. 2003. *Medicine as Culture: Illness, Disease, and the Body in Western Societies.* 2nd ed. Thousand Oaks, CA: Sage.

Magliozzi, Tom, and Ray Magliozzi. 2000. "Driver Distracted by Cell Phone Hit Her Car, Killed Her Daughter." *Star Tribune,* January 29.

Maines, Rachel P. 1999. *The Technology of Orgasm: "Hysteria," the Vibrator, and Women's Sexual Satisfaction.* Baltimore: Johns Hopkins University Press.

Makari, George J. 1998. "Between Seduction and Libido: Sigmund Freud's Masturbation Hypotheses and the Realignment of His Etiological Thinking, 1897–1905." *Bulletin of the History of Medicine* 72:638–662.

Mann, Ruth M. 2000. *Who Owns Domestic Abuse? The Local Politics of a Social Problem.* Toronto: University of Toronto Press.

Maratea, R. J. 2009. "Virtual Claimsmaking: The Role of the Internet in Constructing Social Problems." Unpublished PhD dissertation, University of Delaware.

Marcotty, Josephine. 1987. "With Car Phones, Business Is Never on Hold." *Star Tribune,* November 9.

Marcum, Keith. 2009. "The Epidemic of Autism: One Professional View from a Parent." *Exceptional Parent* 39(4):34.

Marks, James S. 2002a. "Efforts to Improve Women's Health." Testimony before the Committee on Health, Education, Labor, and Pensions, US Senate, April 25. Retrieved April 12, 2008. http://www.cdc.gov/washington/testimony/wh042502.htm.

———. 2002b. "Safe Motherhood: Values, Purpose, and Possibility." *Maternal and Child Health Journal* 6:269–271.

Marmol, J. G., A. L. Scriggins, and R. F. Vollman. 1969. "History of the Maternal Study Committees in the United States." *Obstetrics and Gynecology* 34:123.

Masters, William H., and Virginia E. Johnson. 1966. *Human Sexual Response.* Boston: Little, Brown.

———. 1970. *Human Sexual Inadequacy.* Boston: Little, Brown.

Matson, Johnny L., and Noha F. Minshawi. 2006. *Early Intervention for Autism Spectrum Disorders: A Critical Analysis.* New York: Elsevier.

McCann, Kateri. 2006a. "The Myth of the Happy Birthmother." *Wet Feet,* August 15. Retrieved October 18, 2011. http://wetfeet.typepad.com/wet_feet/2006/08/trajectory.html.

———. 2006b. "What Did It Feel Like?" *Wet Feet,* December 11. Retrieved October 18, 2011. http://wetfeet.typepad.com/wet_feet/2006/12/what_did_it_fee.html.

———. 2008. "Juno and Beyond." *Wet Feet,* January 24. Retrieved October 19, 2011. http://wetfeet.typepad.com/wet_feet/2008/01/juno-and-beyond.html#comments.

———. 2009. "OK, Adoption." *Wet Feet,* March 19. Retrieved October 18, 2011. http://wetfeet.typepad.com/wet_feet/2009/03/index.html.

McCarthy, Jenny. 2008. *Mother Warriors: A Nation of Parents Healing Autism Against All Odds.* New York: Dutton.

McClellan, Mark B. 2003. Food and Drug Administration Docket no. 03N-00. Retrieved May 10, 2011. http://www.fda.gov/OHRMS/DOCKETS/98fr /03n-0076-nap0001.pdf.

McDermott, Kevin. 2010. "Illinois May Let in Smokers at Casinos." *St. Louis Post-Dispatch,* November 16.

McDonald, Lawrence, and Patrick Robinson. 2009. *A Colossal Failure of Common Sense: The Inside Story of the Collapse of Lehman Brothers.* New York: Crown Business.

McGrath, Daniel S., and Sean P. Barrett. 2009. "The Comorbidity of Tobacco Smoking and Gambling: A Review of the Literature." *Drug and Alcohol Review* 28:676–681.

McKinney, D. 2011. "Illinois House Votes to Lift Casino Smoking Ban." *The Herald-News: A Chicago Sun-Times Publication,* March 29. Retrieved June 6, 2012. http://heraldnews.suntimes.com.

McLeod, Mike. 1995. "For Some Users There's No Time for Dinner." *Augusta Chronicle,* November 26.

Meade, Lauren K. 2007. "Needham Confronts Teen Suicide." *Boston Globe,* February 12.

Memorials.com. 2011. Homepage. Retrieved September 15, 2011. http://www .memorials.com.

Mensink, R. P., and Martijn B Katan. 1990. "Effect Of Dietary Trans Fatty Acids on High-Density and Low-Density Lipoprotein Cholesterol in Healthy Subjects." *New England Journal of Medicine* 323:439–445.

Mickadeit, Frank. 2007. "I Smelled Trouble with the Car Wreck." *Orange County Register,* November 15. Retrieved May 1, 2010. http://www .ocregister.com/news/sadek-200396-million-porsche.html.

Mihm, Stephen. 2008. "Dr. Doom." *New York Times,* August 15.

Monahan, Brian A. 2010. *The Shock of the News: Media Coverage and the Making of 9/11.* New York: New York University Press.

Mooney, Chris. 2009. "Vaccination Nation." *Discover,* June.

Morris, Jane. 2002. "Bones of Contention." *The Guardian,* July 9.

Morrison, Kara. 1999. "Psychologist: Web Addiction Growing Problem." *Lincoln Journal Star,* October 29.

Mott, Maryann. 2007. "Pet Funeral Homes Comfort Grieving Owners." LiveScience.com, November 15. Retrieved August 22, 2008. http://www.livescience.com/animals/071115-pet-angel.html.

Muni, S. D., and Raja Mohan. 2005. "India's Options in a Changing Asia." Pp. 52–79 in *India and Emerging Asia,* edited by R. R. Sharma. New Delhi: Sage.

Nannini, Angela, Judith Weiss, Rebecca Goldstein, and Sally Fogerty. 2002. "Pregnancy-Associated Mortality at the End of the Twentieth Century: Massachusetts, 1990–1999." *Journal of the American Medical Women's Association* 57:140–143.

Nantucket Alliance for Substance Abuse Prevention. 2008. "Strategic Plan for Youth." February. Retrieved May 8, 2011. http://www.asapnantucket.org/assets/files/docs/ASAP_VIEW_StratPlan_Feb08.pdf.

"Nantucket Demographics Summary." 2011. CLRSearch. Retrieved September 19, 2011. http://www.clrsearch.com/Nantucket_Demographics/MA.

"National Food Processors Association. 2000. "Letter from National Food Processors Association to FDA on Proposed Trans Fat Labeling Rule." Food and Drug Administration Docket no. 94P-0046, Document no. C2139.

NCQA (National Committee for Quality Assurance). 2010. "The State of Healthcare Quality: Reform, the Quality Agenda, and Resource Use." Washington, DC.

Needham Coalition for Suicide Prevention. 2008. "A Report to the Community: From the Needham Coalition for Suicide Prevention." Town of Needham. Retrieved May 8, 2011. http://www.needhamma.gov/DocumentView.aspx?DID=2033.

"Needham Coalition for Suicide Prevention." 2011. Town of Needham. Retrieved May 8, 2011. http://www.needhamma.gov/index.aspx?NID=1329.

"Needham Demographics." 2011. Town of Needham. Retrieved September 19, 2011. http://www.needhamma.gov/index.aspx?NID=231.

"Needham, Massachusetts (MA) Profile." 2011. Retrieved September 19, 2011. http://www.city-data.com/city/Needham-Massachusetts.html.

Neuman, R. P. 1975. "Masturbation, Madness, and the Modern Concepts of Childhood and Adolescence." *Journal of Social History* 8(3):1–27.

Nevada Pet Cremation (Pet Urns). 2011. Homepage. Retrieved September 24, 2011. http://www.petcremationnevada.com/default.aspx.

New York Regency Forest Pet Memorial Park. 2011. Homepage. Retrieved September 15, 2011. http://www.regencyforest.com.

New York Times. 1994. "Fat in Margarine Is Tied to Heart Problems." *New York Times,* May 16.

———. 2000. "Cell Phones and Safety." *New York Times,* July 19.

———. 2009. "Timeline: The Selling of the Cell Phone and Warnings Unheeded." *New York Times,* December 7. Retrieved October 1, 2011. http://www.nytimes.com/interactive/2009/12/07/technology/07distracted-timeline.html?scp=5&sq=distracted%20driving&st=Search.

NHM (Natural History Museum). 2006. *Natural History Museum Human Remains Advisory Panel Advice to Trustees Meeting, 16th November 2006.* London.

NHTSA (National Highway Traffic Safety Administration). 2011. "Statistics and Facts About Distracted Driving." Retrieved October 15, 2011. http://www.distraction.gov/stats-and-facts.

Niederdeppe, Jeff, and Dominick L. Frosch. 2009. "News Coverage and Sales of Products with Trans Fat: Effects Before and After Changes in Federal Labeling Policy." *American Journal of Preventive Medicine* 36:395–340.

NIMH (National Institute of Mental Health). 2004. "Autism Spectrum Disorders: Pervasive Developmental Disorders." Washington, DC: US Department of Health and Human Services. Retrieved November 13, 2008. http://www.nimh.nih.gov/health/publications/autism/index.shtml.

Nip, Joyce Y. M. 2004. "The Queer Sisters and Its Electronic Bulletin Board: A Study of the Internet for Social Movement Mobilization." *Information, Communication & Society* 7:23–49.

Noonan, Erica. 2007. "Shared Resolve, Grief on Suicides; Schools Ramp Up Preventive Services." *Boston Globe,* March 29.

Novella, Steven. 2007. "The Anti-Vaccination Movement." *Skeptical Inquirer* 31(6): 25–31.

O'Brien, Keith. 2007. "Four Too Many." *Boston Globe Magazine,* February 25.

———. 2008. "Out From the Shadow of Teen Suicide." *Boston Globe,* January 17.

Offit, Paul A. 2008. *Autism's False Prophets: Bad Science, Risky Medicine, and the Search for a Cure.* New York: Columbia University Press.

Oosterhuis, Harry. 1997. "Richard von Krafft-Ebing's 'Step-Children of Nature': Psychiatry and the Making of Homosexual Identity." Pp. 67–88 in *Science and Homosexualities,* edited by Vernon A. Rosario. New York: Routledge.

———. 2000. *Stepchildren of Nature: Krafft-Ebing, Psychiatry, and the Making of Sexual Identity.* Chicago: University of Chicago.

Orcutt, James D., and J. Blake Turner. 1993. "Shocking Numbers and Graphic Accounts: Quantified Images of Drug Problems in the Print Media." *Social Problems* 40:190–206.

Oz, Mehmet. 2011. "The Oz Diet." *Time,* September 12.

PA State Pet Memorial & Cemetery. 2011. Homepage. Retrieved September 20, 2011. http://pastatepetmemorial.com

Painter, Kim. 1989. "Is There Long-Term Trauma for Women?" *USA Today,* January 26.

Pallin, Daniel J., Vandana Sundaram, Fabienne Laraque, Louise Berenson, and David R. Schomberg. 2002. "Active Surveillance of Maternal Mortality in New York City." *American Journal of Public Health* 92:1319–1322.

Palmer, John M., Jr. 2010. "Modify Law to OK Smoking in Casinos." *State Journal-Register,* November 19. Retrieved May 5, 2011. http://www.sj-r.com.

Panchal S., A. M. Arria, and S. A. Labhsetwar. 2001. "Maternal Mortality During Hospital Admission for Delivery: A Retrospective Analysis Using a State-maintained Database." *Anesthesia and Analgesia* 93:134–141.

Pantti, Mervi. 2009. "Wave of Compassion: Nationalist Sentiments and Cosmopolitan Sensibilities in the Finnish Press Coverage of the Tsunami Disaster." Pp. 83–105 in *After the Tsunami: Crisis Communication in Finland and Sweden,* edited by Ullamaija Kivikuru and Lars Nord. Goteborg, Sweden: Nordicom.

Park, Han Woo, Mike Thelwall, and Randolph Kluver. 2005. "Political Hyperlinking in South Korea: Technical Indicators of Ideology and Content." *Sociological Research Online* 10(3).

Pattinson, R. C., and M. Hall. 2003. "Near Misses: A Useful Adjunct to Maternal Death Enquiries." *British Medical Bulletin* 67:231–243.

Paulson, Henry. 2008. "Statement by Secretary Henry M. Paulson, Jr. on Treasury and Federal Housing Finance Agency Action to Protect Financial Markets and Taxpayers." US Department of Treasury press release, September 7. Retrieved May 1, 2010. http://www.treasury.gov /press-center/press-releases/Pages/hp1129.aspx.

Pawluch, Dorothy. 1983. "Transitions in Pediatrics: A Segmental Analysis." *Social Problems* 30:449–465.

Pawlich, Dorothy. 1996. *The New Pediatrics: A Profession in Transition.* Hawthorne, NY: Aldine de Gruyter.

Pearse, Warren H. 1977. "Maternal Mortality Studies—Time to Stop?" *American Journal of Public Health* 67:815.

Peippo, Kathleen. 2006. "Hazelden Foundation." *International Directory of Company Histories.* Gale Group.

Perez, Victor W. 2010. "The Rhetoric of Science and Statistics in Claims of an Autism Epidemic." *Advances in Medical Sociology* 11:203–221.

Perpetual Pet. 2011. Homepage. Retrieved September 15, 2011. http://www .perpetualpet.net.

Pet Angel Memorial Center. 2011. Homepage. Retrieved September 20, 2011. http://www.petangelmemorialcenter.com.

Pet Dignity Pet Funeral Services. 2011. Homepage. Retrieved September 27, 2011. http://www.freewebs.com/petdignity.

Pet Heaven Express. 2011. Homepage. Retrieved September 20, 2011. http://www.petheavenexpress.com.

Pet Owner Alert. 2011. Homepage. Retrieved September 20, 2011. http://www .petowneralert.org/introduction.html.

Pet Urns Unlimited. 2011. Homepage. Retrieved September 8, 2011. http://www.peturnsunlimited.com.

Petry, Nancy M., and Cheryl Oncken. 2002. "Cigarette Smoking Is Associated with Increased Severity of Gambling Problems in Treatment-Seeking Gamblers." *Addiction* 97:745–753.

Pfohl, Stephen. 1977. "The 'Discovery' of Child Abuse." *Social Problems* 24:310–323.

Pittman, Mark. 2007. "Bass Shorted 'God I Hope You're Wrong' Wall Street." *Bloomberg News,* December 19. Retrieved October 15, 2011.

http://www.bloomberg.com/apps/news?pid=newsarchive&sid=aC5bZp U8S6f4.

Pitts, Victoria. 2004. "Illness and Internet Empowerment: Writing and Reading Breast Cancer in Cyberspace." *Health: An Interdisciplinary Journal for the Social Study of Health, Illness, and Medicine* 8:33–59.

Plummer, Ken. 1995. *Telling Sexual Stories: Power, Change, and Social Worlds.* London: Routledge.

Poltorak, Mike, Melissa Leach, James Fairhead, and Jackie Cassell. 2005. "'MMR Talk' and Vaccination Choices: An Ethnographic Study in Brighton." *Social Science & Medicine* 61:709–719.

Popper, Karl. 2002 [1963]. *Conjectures and Refutations: The Growth of Scientific Knowledge.* London: Routledge.

Poulson, Stephen. 2009. "Autism, Through a Social Lens." *Contexts* 8(2):40–45.

Prevention Institute. 2002. "Nutrition Labeling Regulations." Retrieved September 28, 2011. http://thrive.preventioninstitute.org/CHI_labeling .html#two.

Price, Harry. 1955. *The Marshall Plan and Its Meaning.* Ithaca: Cornell University Press.

Prins, Nomi. 2009. *It Takes a Pillage: Behind the Bailouts, Bonuses, and Backroom Deals from Washington to Wall Street.* Hoboken, NJ: Wiley.

Pritsos, Chris A., Karen L. Pritsos, and Karen E. Spears. 2008. "Smoking Rates Among Gamblers at Nevada Casinos Mirror US Smoking Rate." *Tobacco Control* 17:82–85.

Radsch, Courtney C. 2005. "Driver-Cellphone Laws Exist, but Their Value Is Disputed." *New York Times,* January 18.

Ramirez, Eddy. 2009. "Schools Battle Student Stress with Creative Strategies." *U.S. News & World Report,* March 20. Retrieved April 4, 2012. http://www.usnews.com/education/articles/2009/03/20/schools-battle -student-stress-with-creative-strategies.

Ramsay, Sarah. 2001. "Study Uncovers 'Disturbing' Level of Pregnancy-Associated Homicide." *The Lancet* 357:1021.

Reeves, Kathleen. 2009. "Ultrasound Before Abortion: A Wasteful Bullying Tactic." RH Reality Check, February 11. Retrieved September 25, 2011. http://www.rhrealitycheck.org/blog/2009/02/11/ultrasound-before -abortion-a-wasteful-bully-tactic.

Repace, James. 2004. "Respirable Particles and Carcinogens in the Air of Delaware Hospitality Venues Before and After a Smoking Ban." *Journal of Occupational and Environmental Medicine* 46(9):887–905.

Restall Orr, E. 2004. "Honouring the Ancient Dead." *British Archaeology* 77, July.

Reuters. 1997. "Net 'Addiction' Cited in Neglect Case." *San Jose Mercury News,* June 17.

Richardson, Kay. 2005. *Internet Discourse and Health Debates.* New York: Palgrave Macmillan.

Richtel, Matt. 2009a. "Dismissing the Risks of a Deadly Habit." *New York Times,* July 19.

———. 2009b. "The New Study Found That When Truckers Texted, Their Collision Risk Was 23 Times Greater Than When Not Texting." *New York Times,* July 28.

Ritzer, George. 2003. "Rethinking Globalization: Glocalization/Grobalization and Something/Nothing." *Sociological Theory* 21:193–209.

———. 2008. *The McDonaldization of Society.* 5th ed. Thousand Oaks, CA: Pine Forge.

Robertson, Roland. 1992. *Globalization: Social Theory and Global Culture.* London: Sage.

Robinson, Bryan. 2005. "Why Pregnant Women Are Targeted." *ABC News,* February 24. Retrieved August 11, 2011. http://abcnews.go.com/US /LegalCenter/story?id=522184&page=1.

Robinson, Paul. 1989. *The Modernization of Sex: Havelock Ellis, Alfred Kinsey, William Masters, and Virginia Johnson.* Ithaca: Cornell University Press.

Rochat, R. W., L. M. Koonin, H. K. Atrash, and J. F. Jewett. 1988. "Maternal Mortality in the United States: Report from the Maternal Mortality Collaborative." *Obstetrics and Gynecology* 72: 91–97.

Rodman, Gilbert B. 2003. "The Net Effect: The Public's Fear and the Public Sphere." Pp. 11–48 in *Virtual Publics: Policy and Communication in an Electronic Age,* edited by B. E. Kolko. New York: Columbia University Press.

Rogers, Kara. 2011. "Trans Fat: History of Trans Fat." *Britannica Online Encyclopedia.* Retrieved May 10, 2011. http://www.britannica.com /EBchecked/topic/1085248/trans-fat/281338/History-of-trans-fat.

Rolling Acres Memorial Gardens. 2011. Homepage. Retrieved September 20, 2011. http://www.visitrollingacres.com.

Romer, Daniel, Kathleen Hall Jamieson, and Sean Aday. 2003. "Television News and the Cultivation of Fear of Crime." *Journal of Communication* 53:88–104.

Rosenman, Ellen Bayuk. 2003. "Body Doubles: The Spermatorrhea Panic." *Journal of the History of Sexuality* 12:365–399.

Rosenthal, Phil. 2011. "New Newspaper Circulation Figures Beyond Compare, Thanks to New Metrics." *Chicago Tribune,* May 3. Retrieved May 20, 2011. http://newsblogs.chicagotribune.com/towerticker /2011/05/new-newspaper-circulation-figures-beyond-compare-thanks -to-new-metrics.html.

Rowan, Edward L. 1989. "Masturbation According to the Boy Scout Handbook." *Journal of Sex Education & Therapy* 15(2):77–81.

Rubin, Rita. 2005 "FDA Commissioner's Post Could Be Difficult to Fill." *USA Today,* September 25. Retrieved May 10, 2011. http://www .usatoday.com/news/health/2005-09-25-fda-chief_x.htm.

Rushton, Bruce. 2009. "Casino Revenue Plummets; Gaming Lobbyists Blame Smoking Ban." *State Journal-Register,* August 14. Retrieved November 14, 2010. http://www.sj-r.com.

Russell, Ginny, and Susan Kelly. 2011. "Looking Beyond Risk: A Study of Lay Epidemiology of Childhood Disorders." *Health, Risk & Society* 13:129–145.

Ryan, Sara, and Katherine R. Cole. 2009. "From Advocate to Activist? Mapping the Experiences of Mothers of Children on the Autism Spectrum." *Journal of Applied Research in Intellectual Disabilities* 22:43–53.

Ryan, Steven. 2008. "Needham High School Principal Paul Richards to Step Down." *Needham Times,* November 7.

Sabo, Robin M., and Julie M. Lorenzen. 2008. "Consumer Health Web Sites for Parents of Children with Autism." *Journal of Consumer Health on the Internet* 12:37–49.

Saguy, Abigail C., and Kjerstin Gruys. 2010. "Morality and Health: News Media Constructions of Overweight and Eating Disorders." *Social Problems* 57: 231–250.

Saguy, Abigail, Kjerstin Gruys, and Shanna Gong. 2010. "Social Problem Construction and National Context: News Reporting on 'Overweight' and 'Obesity' in the U.S. and France." *Social Problems* 57:586–610.

Sang-Hun, Choe. 2010. "In South Korea, Parents' Internet Game-Playing Cost Baby's Life." *New York Times,* May 29.

SASH (Society for the Advancement of Sexual Health). 2012. Retrieved in June 2012. http://sash.net/.

Sassen, Saskia. 2007. *A Sociology of Globalization.* New York: Norton.

Schaffer, Rebecca, Kristine Kuczynski, and Debra Skinner. 2008. "Producing Genetic Knowledge and Citizenship Through the Internet: Mothers, Pediatric Genetics, and Cybermedicine." *Sociology of Health & Illness* 30:145–159.

Scheper Elizabeth, Smruti Patel, and Arjuna Parakrama. 2006. *The Impact of the Tsunami Response on Local and National Capacities.* London: Tsunami Evaluation Coalition.

Schleifer, David. 2010. "Reforming Food: How Trans Fats Entered and Exited the American Food System." Unpublished PhD dissertation, New York University.

Schneider, Jennifer P. 2004. "Editorial Sexual Addiction and Compulsivity: Twenty Years of the Field, Ten Years of the Journal." *Sexual Addiction and Compulsivity* 11(1–2):3–5.

Schoenberg, Nara. 2008. "The Trouble with 'Juno.'" *Chicago Tribune,* February 21.

Schoetz, David. 2011. "Teen Suicides Shatter Nantucket Serenity." *ABC News.* Retrieved March 16, 2011. http://abcnews.go.com///?id=4476181&page=1.

Schreibman, Laura. 2005. *The Science and Fiction of Autism.* Cambridge: Harvard University Press.

Schwalbe, Michael, Sandra Godwin, Daphne Holden, Douglas Schrock, Shealy Thompson, and Michael Wolkomir. 2000. "Generic Processes in the Reproduction of Inequality: An Interactionist Analysis." *Social Forces* 79:419–452.

Sciacca, John P., and Michael I. Ratliff. 1998. "Prohibiting Smoking in Restaurants: Effects on Restaurant Sales." *American Journal of Health Promotion* 12:176–184.

Seriously. 2008. "Comments: Our Opinion—Casinos Not Above State Smoking Ban." *The State Journal-Register,* October 2. Retrieved June 6, 2012. http://www.sj-r.com.

Shadigian, Elizabeth M., and Samuel T. Bauer. 2005. "Pregnancy-Associated Death: A Qualitative Systematic Review of Homicide and Suicide." *Obstetrical and Gynecological Survey* 60:183–190.

Shaker Anonymous. 2009. "Breaking the Silence: Living Pro-Lifers' Choice for Women." *Shakesville,* March 17. Retrieved October 18, 2011. http://shakespearessister.blogspot.com/2009/03/breaking-silence-on-living-pro-lifers.html.

Shiffman, Jeremy. 2000. "Can Poor Countries Surmount High Maternal Mortality?" *Studies in Family Planning* 31:274–289.

Shiller, Robert. 1981. "Do Stock Prices Move Too Much to Be Justified by Subsequent Changes in Dividends?" *American Economic Review* 71:421–436.

———. 1984. "Stock Prices and Social Dynamics." *Brookings Papers on Economic Activity* 2:457–510.

———. 2003. "From Efficient Markets Theory to Behavioral Finance." *Journal of Economic Perspectives* 17:83–104.

———. 2005. *Irrational Exuberance.* 2nd ed. New York: Doubleday.

———. 2008. *The Subprime Solution: How Today's Global Financial Crisis Happened, and What to Do About It.* Princeton: Princeton University Press.

Simpson, Moira. 1996. *Making Representations: Museums in the Post-Colonial Era.* London: Routledge.

Smith, Jack C., Joyce M. Hughes, Penelope S. Pekow, and Roger W. Rochat. 1984. "An Assessment of the Incidence of Maternal Mortality in the United States." *American Journal of Public Health* 74:780–783.

Snow, David, and Robert Benford. 1992. "Master Frame and Cycles of Protest." Pp. 133–155 in *Frontiers in Social Movement Theory,* edited by Aldon D. Morris and Carol McClurg Mueller. New Haven: Yale University Press.

Solinger, R. 2000. *Wake Up Little Susie: Single Pregnancy and Race Before Roe v. Wade.* New York: Routledge.

Sondik, Edward J. 1999. "Healthy People 2000: Maternal and Infant Health Progress Review." Transcript of live broadcast, May 5. Retrieved March 19, 2008. http://www.cdc.gov/nchs/about/otheract/hp2000/childhlt /childhlt.htm.

Soros, George. 2008. *The New Paradigm for Financial Markets: The Credit Crisis of 2008 and What It Means.* New York: PublicAffairs.

Soulliere, Danielle M. 2003. "Prime-Time Murder: Presentations of Murder on Popular Television Justice Programs." *Journal of Criminal Justice and Popular Culture* 10:12–38.

Soutar, Paul. 2010. "St. Louis Fed: No Ifs, Ands, or Butts, Smoking Ban Hurt Revenues." KansasWatchdog.org, July 23. Retrieved July 22, 2011. http://kansas.watchdog.org/4348/st-louis-fed-no-ifs-ands-or-butts -smoking-ban-hurt-revenues/.

Spector, Malcom, and John I. Kitsuse. 1973. "Social Problems: A Re-Formulation." *Social Problems* 21:145–159.

St. George, Donna. 2004a. "Many New or Expectant Mothers Die Violent Deaths." *Washington Post,* December 19.

———. 2004b. "Researchers Stunned by Scope of Slayings: Further Studies Needed, Most Agree." *Washington Post,* December 19.

St. Louis Post-Dispatch. 2011. "Discussion: Smoking Ban Didn't Hurt Illinois Casinos, Study Says." June 28. Retrieved July 15, 2011. http://www.stl-today.com/business/columns/david-nicklaus/article_9167c7d2-a143 -11e0-8f59-001a4bcf6878.html?mode=comments&page=2.

Stallings, Robert. 1995. *Promoting Risk: Constructing the Earthquake Threat.* Hawthorne, NY: Aldine de Gruyter.

Stanley, Doug. 1997. "Hooked on the Net." *Tampa Tribune,* November 10.

Star Tribune. 1997. "Talking on Cell Phone and Driving Don't Mix, Study Finds." February 13.

The Statesman. 2005. "Now & Again: Of Pride and Prejudice." February 9.

Steakley, James D. 1997. "*Per Scientiam ad Justitiam:* Magnus Hirschfeld and the Sexual Politics of Innate Homosexuality." Pp. 133–154 in *Science and Homosexualities,* edited by Vernon A. Rosario. New York: Routledge.

Steiman, Mandy, Rebecca Simon, Lisa Reisinger, and Eric Fombonne. 2010. "Trends in Autism Rates: Is There an Epidemic?" Pp. 163–193 in *Increasing Awareness of Child and Adolescent Mental Health,* edited by M. Elena Garralda and Jean-Philippe Raynaud. Lanham: Aronson.

Stekel, Wilhelm. 1950. *Auto-Eroticism: A Psychiatric Study of Onanism and Neurosis.* Translated by James S. Van Teslaar. New York: Liveright.

Stengers, Jean, and Anne Van Neck. 2001. *Masturbation: The History of a Great Terror.* Translated by Kathryn A. Hoffman. New York: Palgrave.

Stolberg, Michael. 2000. "Self-Pollution, Moral Reform, and the Venereal Trade: Notes on the Sources and Historical Context of *Onania* (1716)." *Journal of the History of Sexuality* 9(1–2):37–61.

Strauss, Anslem, and Juliet Corbin. 1990. *Basics of Qualitative Research: Grounded Theory Procedures and Techniques.* Newbury Park, CA: Sage.

Stuart, Emily. 2008. "Expert: Internet Addiction Should Be Deemed a Mental Disorder." *Daily Reveille,* April 10.

Stutts, Jane C., Donald W. Reinfurt, Loren Staplin, and Eric Rodgman. 2001. "The Role of Driver Distraction in Traffic Crashes." AAA Foundation for Traffic Safety. Retrieved August 9, 2010. http://www.aaafoundation.org/pdf/distraction.pdf.

Sundeen, Matt. 2007. "Cell Phones and Highway Safety." National Conference of State Legislatures, *2006 State Legislative Update.* Retrieved October 17, 2011. http://www.ncsl.org/print/transportation /2006cellphone.pdf.

TACA (Talk About Curing Autism). 2009a. "Autism Studies & Related Medical Conditions." Irvine, CA. Retrieved August 3, 2009. http://www.tacanow.org.

———. 2009b. "TACA Family Stories." Irvine, CA. Retrieved December 20, 2009. http://www.talkaboutcuringautism.org.

Taleb, Nassim. 1997a. "Against Value-at-Risk: Nassim Taleb Replies to Philippe Jorion." January 31. Retrieved May 1, 2010. http://www .fooledbyrandomness.com/jorion.html.

———. 1997b. *Dynamic Hedging: Managing Vanilla and Exotic Options.* New York: Wiley.

———. 2001. *Fooled by Randomness: The Hidden Role of Chance in the Markets and in Life.* New York: Texere.

———. 2007. *The Black Swan: The Impact of the Highly Improbable.* New York: Random.

———. 2009. "Foreword." Pp. xi–xvii in *Lecturing Birds on Flying: Can Mathematical Theories Destroy the Financial Markets?* edited by Pablo Triana. Hoboken, NJ: Wiley.

Tan, Andy S. L. 2009. "A Case Study of the New York Trans-Fat Story for International Application." *Journal of Public Health Policy* 30:3–16.

Tegen, Annie. 2011. "IL Casino Expansion Passes: More Smokefree Casinos in Illinois." May 31. Retrieved May 31, 2011. http://groups.google.com /group/smokefreecasinos-talk.

Teicholz, Nina. 2004. "Heart Breaker." *Gourmet,* June.

Terry, Jennifer. 1997. "The Seductive Power of Science in the Making of Deviant Subjectivity." Pp. 271–296 in *Science and Homosexualities,* edited by Vernon A. Rosario. New York: Routledge.

———. 1999. *An American Obsession: Science, Medicine, and Homosexuality in Modern Society.* Chicago: University of Chicago Press.

Time. 1961. "Medicine: The Fat of the Land." January 13.

Tissot, Samuel-Auguste. 1769. *L'Onanisme: Dissertation sur les Maladies Produites par la Masturbation.* Paris: Marc Chapuis.

Tomlinson, John. 1999. "Culture Globalisation: Placing and Displacing the West." Pp. 165–177 in *The Media Reader: Continuity and Transformation,* edited by Hugh MacKay and Tim O'Sullivan. London: Sage.

Treating Autism. 2010. "Parents' Stories." Retrieved June 6, 2010. http://www.treatingautism.co.uk/parents-stories.

Triana, Pablo. 2009a. *Lecturing Birds on Flying: Can Mathematical Theories Destroy the Financial Markets?* Hoboken, NJ: Wiley.

———. 2009b. "Nassim Taleb Got It Right." *Infectious Greed: Finance and the Money Culture,* July 15. Retrieved October 15, 2011. http://paul.kedrosky.com/archives/2009/07/guest_post_nass.html.

US Bureau of the Census. 2002. *Statistical Abstracts of the United States, 2001.* Washington, DC.

US Department of Agriculture. 2000. *Report of the Dietary Guidelines Advisory Committee on the Dietary Guidelines for Americans, 2000.* Retrieved May 4, 2011. http://www.cnpp.usda.gov/Publications/Dietary Guidelines/2000/2000DGCommitteeReport.pdf.

US Department of Health and Human Services. 2000. *Healthy People 2010.* Washington, DC.

US Food and Drug Administration. 1995. "Nutritional Labeling and Education Act (NLEA) Requirements (8/94–2/95)." Retrieved September 28, 2011. http://www.fda.gov/ICECI/Inspections/InspectionGuides/ucm074948.htm.

———. 2003. "Food Labeling; Trans Fatty Acids in Nutrition Labeling; Consumer Research to Consider Nutrient Content and Health Claims and Possible Footnote or Disclosure Statements; Final Rule and Proposed Rule." *Federal Register 68 FR 41433,* July 11. Retrieved May 11, 2011. http://www.fda.gov/Food/LabelingNutrition/LabelClaims/NutrientContentClaims/ucm110179.

US Geological Survey. 2004. "Earthquake in the News." Retrieved September 8, 2008. http://earthquake.usgs.gov/eqcenter/eqinthenews/2004/usslav/#summary.

"U.S. Maternal Mortality Greatly Underreported, Collaborative Study Finds." 1988. *Family Planning Perspectives* 20:243–244.

US Statistical Abstract. 2000. "Table no. 13. Resident Population by Sex and Age: 1999." Retrieved August 11, 2011. http://www.census.gov/prod/2001pubs/statab/sec01.pdf.

USA Today. 2009. "More States Considering Mandating Ultrasounds Before Abortions." *USA Today,* February 8.

Usborne, David. 2005. "America Urged to Devise Marshall Plan for Asia." *The Independent,* January 3.

Van Aelst, Peter, and Stefaan Walgrave. 2002. "New Media, New Movements? The Role of the Internet in Shaping the 'Anti-Globalization' Movement." *Information, Communication & Society* 5:465–493.

Vataj, Marina. 2005. "Not So Fantastic: Staffers Work on Their Football Rosters." *New York Post,* November 14.

Veldkamp, Elmer. 2009. "The Emergence of 'Pets as Family' and the Socio-Historical Development of Pet Funerals in Japan." *Anthrozoos* 22:333–346.

Wachtler, Scott. 2010. "Meet Your Needham Neighbor: Nick Galatis, Raising Awareness for Suicide Prevention." *Needham Times,* December 23.

Ward, Bill. 2010. "Drive-by Texting; Sending Messages While Behind the Wheel Is Hardly Just a Youthful Pursuit; Adults Are to Blame, Too, a New Study Says." *Star Tribune,* July 31.

Watson, Stephen T. 2007. "Caught in the Hypnotic Web of the Internet." *Buffalo News,* October 31.

Watts, Thomas G. 1997. "Internet Dependency Should Be Viewed Seriously, Study Says." *Dallas Morning News,* August 15.

Weber, Max 1946. *From Max Weber: Essays in Sociology,* edited by H. Gerth and C. Mills. New York: Free Press.

Webb, Denise. 1990. "Eating Well." *New York Times,* August 29.

Webster's New World Dictionary Online. 2009. "Word of the Year: Distracted Driving." Retrieved March 18, 2011. http://wordoftheyear.wordpress.com /2009/11/02/word-of-the-year-2009.

Weeks, Linton. 1997. "A Little Too Wired." *Washington Post,* July 10.

Weinberg, Martin, and Collin Williams. 1974. *Male Homosexuals: Their Problems and Adaptations.* Oxford: Oxford University Press.

Wheet, Ann. 2010. "Forum: Don't Support Smoking Ban Exemption for Casinos." *Journal-Star,* November 20. Retrieved February 5, 2011. http://www.pjstar.com.

WHO (World Health Organization). 1993. *Coverage of Maternity Care: A Tabulation of Available Information.* 3rd ed. Geneva.

———. 2002. *Maternal Mortality in 2000: Estimates Developed by WHO, UNICEF, UNFPA.* Geneva.

———. 2007. *Maternal Mortality in 2005: Estimates Developed by WHO, UNICEF, UNFPA, and the World Bank.* Geneva.

Willett, Walter C., and Albert Ascherio. 1994 "Trans Fatty Acids: Are the Effects Only Marginal?" *American Journal of Public Health* 84:722–724.

Williams, Mark. 2010. *Uncontrolled Risk: The Lessons of Lehman Brothers and How Systemic Risk Can Still Bring Down the World Financial System.* New York: McGraw-Hill.

Wimmer, Harold. 2011. "Casinos Don't Need Smoking." *Chicago Tribune,* August 1. Retrieved August 2, 2011. http://articles.chicagotribune.com.

Wise, David, and Paul R. Brewer. 2010. "Competing Frames for a Public Health Issue and Their Effects on Public Opinion." *Mass Communication and Society* 13:435–457.

Wochos, Sarah. 2007. "Cutting the Fat: States Look for a Way to Fight Obesity." *Council of State Governments,* June.

Wroughton, Lesley. 2009. "Global Write-Downs May Hit £2.8 Trillion." Reuters, April 21. Retrieved October 15, 2011. http://uk.reuters.com /article/idUKTRE53K3KX20090421.

Yeargan Pet Cremation Services. 2011. Homepage. Retrieved September 10, 2011. http://yearganpetburials.com.

Young, Kimberly B. 1998. *Caught in the Net.* New York: Wiley.

Zemach, Rita. 1984. "What the Vital Statistics System Can and Cannot Do." *American Journal of Public Health* 74:756–758.

The Contributors

Rachel J. Bacon is an undergraduate student studying sociology and geography at the University of Delaware.

John Barnshaw is a postdoctoral fellow in the Department of Sociology at the University of South Florida. His research explores risk in a variety of contexts ranging from epidemiology and public health, to disasters and crises, to economics and globalization. His most recent research focuses on the social construction of policymaking and policy outcomes following the recent economic crisis.

Nancy Berns is associate professor of sociology at Drake University. Her teaching and research interests are in the areas of grief, death, violence, media, and social constructionism. She is the author of *Closure: The Rush to End Grief and What It Costs Us* (2011) and *Framing the Victim: Domestic Violence, Media, and Social Problems* (2004).

Joel Best is professor of sociology and criminal justice at the University of Delaware. His most recent books are *Everyone's a Winner: Life in Our Congratulatory Culture* (2011), *The Stupidity Epidemic: Worrying About Students, Schools, and America's Future* (2011), and *Social Problems,* 2nd ed. (2013).

Jennifer L. Dunn is a professor and chair of the Department of Sociology, Anthropology, and Social Work at Texas Tech. She has published her research on the social construction of victimization in a variety of journals, including *Social Problems, Sociological Inquiry, Deviant Behavior,* and *Symbolic Interaction.* Her newest book is *Judging Victims: Why We Stigmatize Survivors and How They Reclaim Respect* (Lynne Rienner, 2011).

Liahna E. Gordon is associate professor of sociology at California State University, Chico, where she also runs the Sexual Diversity Studies program. Her research links individuals' sexual experiences with cultural constructions of sexuality within their political, historical, and economic contexts.

Jenine K. Harris is an assistant professor in the public health program at the George Warren Brown School of Social Work at Washington University in St. Louis. Her research examines clean indoor air and other tobacco policies, often from a systems or network perspective.

Scott R. Harris is professor of sociology at Saint Louis University. He is the author of *What Is Constructionism?* (Lynne Rienner, 2010)—which received the Cooley Award from the Society for the Study of Symbolic Interaction—as well as *The Meanings of Marital Equality* (2006).

Michelle Horstmeier is a graduate student at Iowa State University, and studied sociology as an undergraduate at the University of Missouri–Columbia. Her research interests include the social impacts of poverty reduction through the use of indigenous knowledge and underutilized plant species in developing nations.

Tiffany Jenkins is the arts and society director of the Institute of Ideas, and a visiting fellow at the London School of Economics. Her research explores controversies in the cultural sector and cultural property issues such as repatriation. She is the author of *Contesting Human Remains in Museum Collections: The Crisis of Cultural Authority* (2010).

Keith Roberts Johnson is adjunct professor of sociology at Oakton Community College in the Chicago area, where he remains active in teaching, writing, and research. His interests include social science methodology and applications, occupations and professions, and family dynamics.

Lynn Letukas is an assistant professor in the Department of Sociology and Archaeology at the University of Wisconsin–La Crosse. Her current research focuses broadly on the construction of social problems in areas of political discourse, public policy, globalization, and disaster.

R. J. Maratea is assistant professor of criminal justice at New Mexico State University. His research focuses on the sociological implications of mass communication, with a particular focus on new media technology, deviance, social control, and the construction of social problems.

Brian A. Monahan is assistant professor of sociology at Marywood University. He is the author of *The Shock of the News: Media Coverage and the Making of 9/11* (2010). His current research examines the role of mass media in the production of crime concerns.

Marguerite L. O'Leary is an undergraduate student at the University of Delaware pursuing a degree in sociology and business administration.

Peter F. Parilla is a professor in the Department of Sociology and Criminal Justice at the University of St. Thomas in St. Paul, Minnesota. He has taught criminology and criminal justice courses there since 1982. His research interests are in the areas of crime and delinquency and experiential education in criminal justice.

Victor W. Perez is an assistant professor in the Department of Sociology and Criminal Justice at the University of Delaware. His interests include the lay production of health knowledge and social movements that challenge scientific consensus.

David Schweingruber is associate professor of sociology at Iowa State University. His research, in the symbolic interactionist tradition, is concerned with the cultural and cognitive premises that guide social behavior in a variety of settings, including formal organizations, political demonstrations, and romantic events. He is currently researching Christian faculty at public universities.

Index

About the Book

Internet addiction. Cell phone–distracted drivers. Teen suicide. Economic recession. The health risks of trans fats. The carefully selected collection of case studies in *Making Sense of Social Problems* is designed to help students understand and critically evaluate a wide range of contemporary social issues.

The cases are organized to highlight a series of key elements:

- why "objective" claims deserve critical attention
- how advocates bring attention to issues
- why expert interpretations may change over time
- the role of the media in shaping or distorting concerns
- the consequences of public policy

Reflecting the promise of the constructionist approach, the result is a powerful set of tools for systematically investigating social problems. It can be used by itself or together with such texts as *Joel Best's Social Problems*.

Joel Best is professor of sociology and criminal justice at the University of Delaware. **Scott R. Harris** is professor of sociology at Saint Louis University.